PRISONERS OF LIBERATION

Four Years in a Chinese Communist Prison

ALLYN *and* ADELE
RICKETT

Prisoners of Liberation

Four Years in a Chinese Communist Prison

Anchor Books
ANCHOR PRESS/Doubleday
Garden City, New York.

PRISONERS OF LIBERATION
was originally published by Cameron Associates, Inc., in 1957.

Anchor Books edition: 1973
ISBN: 0-385-03490-3
Library of Congress Catalog Card Number 73–75158

To Our Parents

On arriving home in 1955 after spending some seven years in China, four of them in a Chinese Communist prison, we were besieged with questions concerning our experiences there. People especially expressed a deep interest in the obvious change in our viewpoints which had taken place during those years.

To answer these questions, we decided to write a book, thinking at the time that with our combined efforts, the project would take at the most a few months. However, no sooner had we begun than complications arose. Since our primary purpose was to depict the change which took place in the individual thinking of each of us, it was impossible to write collectively as "we did so and so" or "we felt so and so." Secondly it soon became evident that the experience of one of us alone would have been enough to fill two or three volumes.

If we wanted to write a book together then, we would have to condense our material and at the same time find a form which would permit the telling of both our stories as a continuous whole. It was only after much discussion, writing and rewriting that we finally devised what we felt to be a workable plan. Each of us concentrated on those experiences which he felt most significant to his own change and then alternately having our say, wove them together into what we hope is a unified presentation.

We also found ourselves confronted by the problem of names. Not wishing to embarrass any innocent persons, we decided to use fictitious names throughout except for the two Americans who were in prison with us.

Philadelphia, March 1957

INTRODUCTION

"Thought reform"—*ssu-hsiang kai-tsao*—is a most unfortunate term. It conjures up images of 1984, brainwashing, and various Oriental niceties and as a result diverts us from a serious consideration of the important issues underlying the thought reform process. Stripped of emotionalism and of Cold War and other ideological rhetoric, the fundamental question is: what must be done to get people to act in a particular manner—that is, to have people avoid certain "undesirable" actions and undertake certain other "desirable" ones? Implicit in this question is a series of others. In what manner and on what bases are norms of behavior determined for a society or a group? How are these norms communicated to the public? What means are used to get a group and its members to adhere to the norms? What happens when a person fails to adhere? And finally, what are the human and material costs in carrying out this course of action? Phrased in this manner, the thought reform process is of obvious interest to us, not only because it adds to our understanding of China, but no less importantly because it also concerns problems arising in our own society. Perhaps this entire area would be more understandable if we called it socialization rather than thought reform.

The Chinese subsume under the rubric of thought reform a very wide range of activities. On one end of the spectrum is the intense long-term process, such as the four-year prison experience with several "study sessions" each day described by the Ricketts. Next is a possibly more intense but much shorter-term variation. This often occurs, for example, during "rectification" and other kinds of campaigns when for a limited period of time specific persons are attacked or particular lines of action vigorously promoted. Toward the other end of the spectrum is the "regular" group study sessions that all persons engage in for ten or more hours a week. They study not only political matters, but also try to upgrade their cultural levels and professional skills. In addition, these groups carry out a variety of activities involving management of minor local affairs. Finally, we might also include a kind of self-cultivation whereby an individual studies on his own—again, the matters studied vary greatly—to improve himself.

This spectrum of activities can be described in a different manner. In some cases, a person has committed a serious anti-social act and his treatment is the primary order of business. Depending on the intensity of the effort and the amount of time spent, thought reform, if carried out properly, probably could produce a kind of spiritual catharsis and lead to basic changes in attitude and behavior. Even where this does not occur, the person has learned how it must conform his behavior to terminate his present "treatment" and to prevent future conflicts. In other cases, the principal object is not to "cure" a deviant, but rather to prevent deviation from occurring in the first place. This usually takes place during ordinary group or individual study, when people consider what is permissible and impermissible conduct for particular situations, on what bases these distinctions are made, and what are the consequences of non-compliance. This effort is relatively low-keyed and is continuous. Finally, it is important to note that thought reform is not merely a weapon with which to attack deviants nor a prophylaxis to guard against deviation—although the defining and criticizing of anti-social conduct necessarily entails a thorough discussion of what is proper conduct. There are many cases where thought reform also is used in a much more positive and constructive sense to increase political consciousness, to explain social policies, to teach specific techniques, or even to raise the cultural level of the public. Again, much of this takes place through ordinary group or individual study.

It is clear that the methods of thought reform differ greatly for these different tasks. For all the differences, however, there is a central core to these efforts which can be called "the thought reform process."

In the most general terms, each of the above-described situations begins with a set of people who do not feel the same way about a particular issue. This might be due to disagreements over facts or policy, to ignorance, to indifference, or to anti-social attitudes on the part of some. Each situation ends with everyone more or less in agreement, and with everyone acting in conformity to that agreement. As far as possible, agreement is reached through persuasion rather than coercion, since genuine understanding and acceptance of a policy lead to a higher level of compliance.

More importantly, the thought reform process rests on a fundamental premise that a person's "thoughts" are in fact "reformable." This is not as simple a statement as it might appear. Such a premise is intimately linked with one's philosophical view of the basic nature of man. Without getting too esoteric, the Chinese Communists appear to believe that man is educatable, and perhaps even that man's nature is basically good. (Fortunately, both the Confucian tradition and Marxist doctrine agree here.) Consequently, when a person behaves improperly, it is possible to show him the error of his ways and teach him proper behavior. In addition, this process of "reform" is not extremely difficult. A man is not evil by nature and can be educated; going further, if man is by nature good, then when good and evil are presented to him, he will "naturally" choose the former. Approaching the same question from a positive direction, where a group is in disagreement over a particular issue, careful and rational discussion by that group will result, even without outside guidance, in correct decisions almost all the time. This is the basis of the mass line.

I think the Chinese take the idea of the perfectability

of man very seriously and literally. I also think that while the West makes many pious statements about this concept, on the whole we do not believe in it. Thus, our society does virtually nothing to help criminals reform, seems to feel that externally established laws are necessary to control both individuals and officials, and in general believes that, absent such restraining influences, man's "base" nature will lead him to act in an undesirable and harmful manner—the very opposite of the Chinese mass line. This divergence in philosophical outlook accounts for many of the differences between the two societies and also helps to explain why many of the practices of each society appear so foreign and queer to the other.

A second major aspect of thought reform in China is that there is a great deal of it. Again, this is not as simple as it sounds. The Chinese devote a staggering amount of human and material resources to this effort. By now, each adult has engaged in perhaps ten thousand hours of regular study sessions. In addition, production sometimes is curtailed so that rectification or other campaigns can be implemented. Probably the best illustration of the willingness to spend resources is the Ricketts' description of the extraordinarily painstaking handling of their own cases. By way of contrast, our society devotes almost no resources to the prison system or to the problems of rehabilitation or post-release reintegration. Similarly, formal programs of socialization and education end after childhood, rather than continue throughout one's adult life.

It is not entirely clear to me why the Chinese place such great emphasis on thought reform work. Perhaps it is just a "given": the possession of Truth carries with it the evangelical zeal to convert all non-believers. A variation of this idea might be the traditional Chinese view that the "superior man" had a social duty to teach his less enlightened brethren. Another reason might be that the Chinese view a "just" society as one where each person is able to fulfill his potential. Hence, one's "good" nature should be promoted and one's "evil" tendencies eradicated; similarly, if a person deviates from correct conduct, the rest of society has a duty to help salvage him. On a less abstract level, the Chinese may favor the thought reform process because it is an effective and cheap mechanism for communicating orders from the center to the local levels, adapting central directives to local conditions, and ensuring that these orders are carried out.

The "central core" of the thought reform process also involves a common set of specific techniques. Initially, there often is some attempt to disorient a person. This might be done by outright attacks on one's positions or by posing for discussion ("some comrades say . . .") questions to which there are not clear answers. The ensuing uncertainty, confusion, and even despair renders a person ready to have his thoughts reoriented along "correct" lines.

The disorientation-reorientation effort makes careful and extensive use of positive incentives. Negative incentives and sanctions are present, of course, and are used when a person is especially recalcitrant. In general, however, coercion is downplayed. The goal of thought reform is to change one's way of thinking; and while one may be forced to act in a particular way, one cannot be forced to adopt a particular set of beliefs.

Thus, there usually is not total condemnation of a person. Each man is in part his own creation and in part a product of social conditions. When a person acts improperly, society must bear part of the blame. This approach has several good effects. First, since the fault is not totally one's own, a person is able to retain some measure of self-esteem—something very important to have if he is to be reintegrated into society. At the same time, society has a responsibility to change those conditions that contributed to the problem. It cannot, for example, abandon a criminal after his reform and release and merely return him to the same milieu from which he had originally come. It also must help to provide educational training, job training, suitable employment, and the like. Finally, a person is provided with a method for carrying out and for rationalizing his reform. He can admit that he had acted improperly in the past and analyze what aspects of his behavior were "caused" by social conditions and what aspects were his own doing. The former will be changed by society; the latter he must change himself. He will do so, of course, since having now seen the "truth," he "naturally" will choose to act properly. The above considerations were especially important in the years just after Liberation, when many ills could be blamed on the bad conditions in the old society and when the new regime could promise and carry out large and conspicuous changes.

Positive incentives are used more directly in other ways. In the case of a criminal, for example, there is constant stress that total reintegration is in fact possible. Since a person is not basically evil and is educatable, it is possible for him to see the error of his ways and to reform completely. Thereafter, no stigma need attach, and he is just like any other person. Going much further, the former criminal is offered a chance to help to build the New China and to be a part of an exciting and rewarding effort. The attractiveness of this offer cannot be underestimated, since it gives a person purpose and hope.

Part of the positive incentives come in the form of praise for a person's every improvement and advance. In addition, deeds supplement words and thereby give the words greater weight and reality. Thus, the Ricketts described the teaching of illiterates to read and the promotion to cell leader and the return to dignity of a former cringing, whimpering pickpocket.

The situation is similar in the non-criminal area. The formula of unity-criticism-unity ensures that one does not get condemned for disagreeing, so long as the second unity is reached after the debate. People whose thinking and actions are "progressive" receive much praise. And there also is a stress on being a part of the building of a better and greater New China. In addition, activities such as discussions, debates, and study of central policies involve a considerable amount of local decision making and autonomy. This heightens one's sense of participation and importance and produces considerable positive incentive to participate to an even larger extent.

Another important characteristic of the thought reform process is the use of "small groups." Everyone belongs to one or more such groups where he lives, works, or has other principal associations. These groups consist of twenty or so people. They meet frequently and handle a wide range of functions, including being the focal points where much information and policy from above are disseminated to the public. Thus, on any particular issue, the group members will study relevant materials and discuss the pros and cons. In the process, broad central directives are translated into local terms; this includes the clarification of ambiguities and the opportunity to introduce local initiatives and variations. The final result is that each person knows quite clearly "the rules of the game" for that issue. Presumably, he also has internalized the norms of behavior described by the central policy and refined by the concrete local discussion. The group's role does not end here. Thereafter, members continue to comment upon each other's conduct and to "help" whoever may be straying from the correct path. These really are quite desirable features since they enable people to take part in the formulation of the rules governing their own behavior and also let people "police" themselves.

Interaction within a group generally is lively. Nonparticipation in the work of the group is not a possibility, since that in itself is a sign of backwardness and recalcitrance. Beyond that, there appears to be a kind of "group dynamic" that impels people to take part, perhaps much like the dynamics of encounter groups and T-groups in this country.

While I am quite impressed by the potential usefulness of thought reform, I am by no means suggesting that it is a panacea for the problems facing China or any other society. Indeed, thought reform has many severe limitations. For example, this book clearly shows the importance of having an able group leader. If there are many millions of small groups in China, are there many millions of able group leaders? If there are many millions of such able people, are the small groups the place to concentrate them? The answers to both questions might well be yes; we do not know for sure.

Another problem might be that with the passage of time, group interaction becomes more mechanical and leadership more bureaucratic. This might occur because the strident enthusiasm required by the Communists simply cannot be kept up for a long period of time or even because some people are suffering a partial loss of faith as various political and economic policies meet setbacks. The passage of time also might render the thought reform process more difficult to carry out because immediately after Liberation, a person might claim that many of his anti-social tendencies were due to social conditions (from the old society). This is quite difficult to claim twenty-three years after Liberation and consequently most of the "fault" lies within the person himself. Again, we can raise these questions, but we do not know the answers.

This discussion should not be concluded without returning to one of the first points made: thought reform is not something unknown to this society. Can we analogize "regular study sessions" to advertising? Clearly, advertisers believe that advertising works and that people can be convinced to follow certain lines of conduct—i.e., buy certain products. There also is a great deal of advertising consuming large amounts of human and material resources. Positive incentives are stressed ("so many good things will happen to you if you use this product"), although some negative incentives are poised in the background ("embarrassed by dandruff or bad breath?"). Group pressure plays an important role ("is your neighbor's wash cleaner?"). There even is control of information ("laboratory tests show . . .").

Or else, can first-year law school be analogized to intense long-term thought reform? Again, there is a belief that "reform" can be accomplished and a willingness to devote large amounts of resources to it. In addition, considerable disorientation—whether or not intentionally caused by the faculty/group leaders—sets in at the beginning of this process, followed by varying degrees of confusion and despair. At the proper moment, hope is held out ("if you will only learn to think in a lawyer-like manner, everything will clear up"). There is no condemnation of the inner man ("it is not your fault that your liberal arts undergraduate background did not teach you to think clearly"). Positive incentives are used ("you can be a lawyer and do wonderful things"), although negative incentives also are present (embarrassment in front of one's class mates). And most of all, there is that overpowering group dynamics and peer pressure.

These clearly are not perfect analogies—but then they are not so imperfect either.

Finally. I must comment on the great differences in climate since the Ricketts' release and the first publication of this book more than fifteen years ago. At that time, there appears to have been questions about the Ricketts' loyalty, mental stability, and reliability. There certainly was considerable hostility. Even the publishers felt the necessity of including a kind of "apology" *cum* psychiatrists' certification in the Publishers' Introduction. Today that entire sequence looks so ugly and silly. Perhaps truly, the times they are a-changing.

Victor H. Li
Stanford University Law School
1972

1

Rick: October 26, 1950, was my twenty-ninth birthday. It also marked approximately the end of our first two years in Peking—two years spent studying Chinese at Tsinghua and Yenching Universities in preparation for a teaching career back in the United States. By way of celebration Dell had invited a small group of close friends, Chinese and American, to a party in the house of an American missionary on the Yenching campus. The affair should have been a jolly one as we warmed ourselves before the crackling blaze in the wide fireplace of Miss Brown's spacious home. But in spite of our efforts to appear gay an ominous tenseness pervaded the atmosphere.

This was brought into sharp focus when Dell suddenly turned to our Chinese-American friend, George Lee, and asked curiously, "Say, George, what was that movie in the auditorium last night?"

George's round face lost its usual cheerful beam and he shifted his weight uncomfortably, as if trying to find some measure of support in the big armchair in which he was sitting.

"Why, uh," he hesitated, and gazed unseeingly at the sparks which shot up as part of the burning log fell into the grate.

His uneasiness was spreading rapidly to the rest of us when the appearance of the cook bringing in the traditional birthday cake with its tiny candles aglow provided a welcome interruption. As if deliberately trying to throw off the unpleasantness of the past few minutes, everyone applauded enthusiastically and jokingly urged me to make a wish before blowing out the candles.

I paused for a moment, my mind wandering. There were many things to be asked for, but there was one which took precedence over all others—"I only hope we can get out of this country and back home without running into real trouble."

There was a certain grim desperation in my playing this childish game, for I knew the answer to Dell's question about the movie. It had been a propaganda film showing the results of American bombing in North Korea and the terrible destruction and brutality of the war. From what I had heard, the reactions of the audience had reflected the increasing bitterness of the Chinese toward the United States. What made the showing of the movie especially disturbing to me was the fact that it accompanied the first vague rumors I had heard just that day of Chinese forces operating in North Korea. If China had actually entered the war Dell and I were faced with a difficult situation.

It had all seemed so inconsequential that day in late August, 1948, when I had been called to the office of the 13th Naval District Headquarters Intelligence Section in Seattle. We had just been awarded our Fulbright grants for study in Peking and were eagerly waiting to board the freighter which was to take us to China. The call had been unexpected but understandable, since during the Second World War I had been a Naval Intelligence Japanese language officer in the Marine Corps and had kept my reserve status after release from active duty.

During the interview the Naval lieutenant in charge had been studiedly casual when he said that they had heard I was on my way to China and would appreciate it if I would keep my eyes open for them and report back when I returned. I had been elated by the flattering idea that Naval Intelligence considered me somewhat of an expert on China and, since their request fitted right in with my plans to study conditions there while preparing my Ph.D. dissertation, I had readily agreed. At the time I had thought little about the possible consequences. Even while I was regularly supplying information to the American Consulate in Peking after the Communists took control of the city I had had no really clear realization that my espionage activities would involve me in any serious danger.

With the outbreak of the Korean war on June 25, 1950, however, the situation had taken on a different light. One British official who had become my intelligence contact after the American Consulate had withdrawn that spring advised us to think of leaving, but Dell and I had finally decided that since the United States and China did not seem to have come to the point of out-and-out war it was worth trying to remain on as two of the few American observers left in the country. However, as the summer progressed I had begun to have certain doubts about our decision.

In September I heard several reports of troops being moved from South China to Manchuria in preparation for entering the Korean war if American forces were to approach the Chinese–Korean frontier. I had duly informed the British of what I had learned, but still it seemed too fantastic that the Chinese would actually dare go to war against all the power of the United States. Yet, as our troops neared the Yalu River, I listened intently to every Voice of America broadcast for any word of Chinese moves, and at the same time prayed nothing would happen.

Now, with the reports of Chinese troops crossing the Yalu, my worst fears seemed to have been confirmed. If the Chinese had entered the war in force Dell and I might be in for more than just ordinary internment. In wartime to be caught as a spy . . . Should we try to leave now? Perhaps it was not too late. But, on the other hand, would not matters be made even worse by our appearing to run away?

Repeating the wish uppermost in my mind, I put an end to my wandering thoughts and quickly blew out the candles. By the time the diversion created by the arrival of the cake had passed the conversation had already turned to lighter matters. It was not until after the party, as we were walking along the pitch-black path across the campus, that Dell brought up the subject of the movie again. She was silent when I told her what had happened.

For the next few days I procrastinated, in the hope that the rumors from North Korea would prove unfounded. But by November 3 there was no longer any doubt. Coming to a sudden decision, I cycled across the campus to the women's dormitory where Dell was living.

Dell: I heard Rick shouting my Chinese name, Li Yu-an, from the gate outside the dormitory and hurried out, wondering why he should be calling for me at this hour of the morning when he was usually studying in the library.

"I think it's time for us to go home," he said in an exaggeratedly calm voice. "Let's go in to the police station on the one o'clock bus and make application for our exit permits right away."

The words sounded sweet to my ears and I laughed excitedly, "We can't go fast enough to suit me!"

We went into town right after lunch and headed for the police station. When asked by the young, bespectacled clerk behind the counter why we were applying for exit permits at this time, Rick said seriously, "I just received a letter from my mother saying my father is very ill. I must return home at once."

"Well, do you have the letter with you?" queried the clerk politely.

"Ah, no-o-o, but I can bring it in the next time I come if you want to see it," Rick managed to answer.

I wondered how he was going to produce the nonexistent letter, but the clerk brushed the matter aside, and we proceeded to fill out the forms.

A friend of ours, Harriet Mills, a Fulbright student from Columbia University with whom we stayed whenever we went into the city, had also decided that the time had come to return home, so we agreed to join forces in preparations for leaving. Ship passage was tight at that point, but we were able to make reservations on a boat leaving Tientsin within ten days or so. Surely our exit permits would be in our hands by then and all the last-minute details taken care of.

On Friday, November 3, we moved into Harriet's everything we intended to take with us, and that night was devoted to writing up the packing lists. Every article which went into the trunks had to be listed in both Chinese and English for customs inspection. It was a terrible job. Two friends who were proficient in Chinese and another who was a good typist stayed with us all night to write out the lists. We had all studied the more dignified language of the Foreign Service and Chinese history, and anguished cries of, "What's the Chinese word for 'girdle'?" brought forth hoots from the others. By eight o'clock the next morning everything had been listed and the trunks were ready to be taken away by the shipping company.

The next few days were ones of anxious waiting. We seemed to live from one Voice of America broadcast to the next, hoping against hope that the Third World War had not broken upon us. Our lives seemed to hang on the outcome of events in the United Nations, where the Chinese delegation was answering charges of aggression in Korea.

"If they'll just keep talking," said Harriet one afternoon in a voice charged with nervous tension, "we've got a chance to make it, but once they stop—" she shook her head, "we're finished."

Either she or Rick made daily telephone calls or trips to the police station to check on our exit permits, but one day followed another without word.

It was impossible to think of doing any studying in this time of suspense. During the day we could run around attending to odds and ends of details, but by late afternoon we would return to the cold house and huddle around the fireplace in a room which seemed even more bleak in the absence of those little personal possessions which had already been packed. Speculation about our permits, rumors about the war, and wild imaginings about what life in a concentration camp would be like were our main topics of conversation.

Rick maintained an air of bravado. He seemed quite sure of himself, but his tenseness was sometimes revealed in sudden outbursts in arguments with Chinese friends, during which he all but openly cursed the People's Government. One night he and Harriet became involved in a violent discussion with a young graduate student at Peking University who was a member of the Communist Party. I was shocked that with such a person Rick should be so open in his condemnation of the Chinese role in Korea and what he called a reign of terror against all anti-Communist opposition in China. Afterwards he was remorseful for his hasty words, but, as he said, he just could not seem to contain himself any longer.

In contrast to Rick's explosiveness, I fell back on the old formula which had carried me through crises for years—I withdrew my emotions to a high hill where nothing could touch me and then said to myself, what comes will come. It was inconceivable to me that anything really adverse could happen to us. Unfortunate things happened to other people but we had always escaped any serious trouble before.

As the days slipped by without any word from the police station, we felt the possibility of detention growing stronger. When a German friend left in a group of displaced persons being returned to Germany, we gave her a code to send to our parents so that we could give them an indirect means of knowing our situation. As it happened, we never used the code, but the state of our minds at that time can be seen from the incident.

Finally, late in the afternoon of November 15, 1950, we received a call from the police station asking Rick and Harriet to come down the next morning. We were so sure that our permits had come through that in the morning, after the others went off, I closed the locks on all our suitcases and sat impatiently awaiting the hour to go to the train.

I had been looking forward to this day for a long time. Back in 1948, when we were applying for our Fulbright grants while studying at the University of Pennsylvania, the prospect of coming to China had been intensely exciting for both of us. Though I had developed an interest in the Far East only after I had met Rick at the Boulder, Colo., Naval Intelligence Japanese Language School in 1943, I had quickly become as enthusiastic as he about studying in China. When, in describing to me his interview with Naval Intelligence in Seattle, he mentioned that they had suggested that I help him collect information I had responded eagerly, flattered that they considered me capable of being useful in this respect.

All during our long trip across the Pacific I had been thrilled by the thought that I was actually soon to see what I had only read about before, but my upbringing had not prepared me for the sights that met my eyes when we first went ashore in Shanghai.

We could not walk down the street without having swarms of beggars tag along behind us. Some were old, disease-ridden relics of another age; some were dried up, whining women; but saddest of all were the children, especially one little boy. He had a baby in his arms, a baby whose head lolled on its neck like a swollen, rotten pumpkin, its eyes staring, unseeing, as if no consciousness could light them from within.

These sights made me feel ill and at the same time I was conscious of an almost contemptuous aversion for this land where humanity could be so cruelly reduced to such an abject state. The horrifying picture of that baby lingered in my memory long afterward. But instead of trying to understand how this situation had come about and how it might be changed, I continued to recoil from every contact with these signs of poverty all during our first years in China. I felt personally put upon every time I had to pass by the outstretched hands of beggars in front of such places as the French Bakery in Peking where we bought pastries and ice cream. Why did they have to plague my conscience?

When we reached Peking on October 21, 1948, the weather had already begun to turn cold. The sky was dark and as we stepped off the train a chill wind whipped scattered drops of rain across our faces. As we rode from the station to the missionary language school in the northeast section of the city where we expected to live and study, I felt let down by the impoverished grayness of the shops, the streets, even the people. It was in direct contrast to the picture of brilliance and splendor which had filled my imagination from the time Rick had first read to me Marco Polo's description of the ancient capital.

The afternoon of our arrival we went to have tea with an American friend who had preceded us to Peking by a few months. His face was as downcast as the sky above.

"You couldn't have arrived at a worse time," he gloomily remarked. "Everything is collapsing and the Nationalists are on their last legs. Their currency reform in August has done no good at all and inflation is starting to run wild again. Food is expensive and scarce, and the city is filled with refugees. Business is at a standstill. There is so much resentment against the corruption and oppression of Chiang Kai-shek and his Nationalist government that we may be in for some real trouble here even if the Communists don't come in."

As if this welcome had not been discouraging enough, we were further depressed by the hysteria which had gripped the other Americans and wealthy Chinese whom we met. The anticipation of the Communists taking over hung like a giant storm cloud, dominating the entire atmosphere of the city. On the lips of all the foreigners and Chinese we met were the questions, "Are you going or staying?" "When are you leaving?"

As we attended one farewell party after another for people whom we had just come to know, we began to feel as if we had been suddenly dumped aboard a sinking ship. Even so, for us there was no question of leaving. Having just arrived, Rick was not to be thwarted in realizing his youthful dream of studying in China, but we were faced with the practical problem of livelihood in the event of a Nationalist withdrawal which would mean the end of our scholarships. Therefore, hoping to find some security, in mid-November we obtained positions as part-time English teachers at Tsinghua National University, six miles northwest of the city. At the same time we enrolled as students in the Chinese Department there.

It had been with a sigh of relief that we finally settled down in the little house on the Tsinghua campus. There at least we were not so apt to find people stretched out starved to death on our doorstep as we had one day in the city. But still we could not escape from the impoverishment which so characterized the life of the Chinese people in the last days of the Nationalist rule and the unsettled period immediately following the establishment of Communist rule.

How this social decay had affected even the upper strata of intellectuals was brought home forcibly to us one afternoon shortly after we had moved to Tsinghua, when we walked from the home of an American professor living on the campus to visit a Chinese friend a few doors away. We had been struck by the attractiveness of the American's furnishings—wall-to-wall beige carpeting, full beige drapes, beige-covered couches, an aquarium, beautiful flower arrangements, and paintings to blend in with the beige motif. Siamese cats, sprawled on the chairs or prowling the floor, added the last touch.

In startling contrast, when we reached the Chinese professor's house, which was identical in floor plan with the other, we found bare floors, no drapes, and no softly glowing lamps. A single, unadorned bulb hung from the ceiling to cast a garish light, and an ugly, potbellied stove almost in the center of the room looked antiquated and inadequate in contrast to the central heating in the home we had just left.

My first reaction had been, "How can these people live like this? It's so cold and bare!"

This unspoken thought was answered by our Chinese host as he offered us a glass of hot water instead of tea. "Don't let that stove fool you," he said, smiling cheerfully. "I've had it ready and waiting since the beginning of November, but here it is mid-December and I can't afford coal to burn in it. Perhaps you had better keep your coats on while you're here."

A wave of remorse reddened my face. The American professor was living on a substantial Rockefeller grant. As for the Chinese—if there was no money for coal was there any point in thinking about drapes and slip covers?

The insecurity and misery suffered by the Chinese people which had so repelled us at first caused us to sympathize with the students and professors in their open desire for a change.

Students in China have always been more politically conscious than our young people in the United States. They were proud of the fact that much of the revolutionary activity in China from the beginning of the century had been carried on by students, and that they had kept to this tradition in spite of all efforts at intimidation or suppression on the part of the war lords, Japanese and Nationalists.

And now in November and December, 1948, with the end of all those years of struggle at hand, it was almost impossible for them to concentrate on classes. They either came wholly unprepared and sat through the hour in complete apathy, their minds obviously miles away, or they showed active rebelliousness by writing diatribes on Chiang Kai-shek and American foreign policy instead of compositions on the topics we had assigned. Their open hostility to the Nationalists was also manifested on the walls and buildings outside the campus, where they scratched Chiang's name in chalk within the outline of a turtle—an extremely derogatory symbol for the cuckold in China.

On December 13, the Communist forces, moving down from the northwest, swept past the gates of Tsinghua to lay siege to the city of Peking and cut it off from the surrounding countryside. During the initial commotion classes were canceled. A week or so later we tried to resume for a few days, but finally had to give it up until March, when the spring semester started. Somehow, with the line of battle just a few miles south of the campus and Peking itself under siege, the poetry of George Crabbe seemed utterly inconsequential.

In the first flush of excitement the students, like ourselves, wandered around the campus and the surrounding countryside or gathered in one of the class buildings to hear the latest battle reports on the radio. Everywhere we went we met little knots of young people chattering jubilantly, and they would wave to us in friendly fashion or ask us if we had any news more up-to-date than theirs.

The professors were perhaps not so expressive as the students in their excitement over what we all came to call "liberation," but they were just as eager to see it take place. Not only had they been reduced to extreme poverty during the long years of war and corruption which had accompanied the Japanese invasion and the return of Nationalist rule but many of them had found their very lives endangered. At the time we moved to Tsinghua, Jang Hsi-ro, one of China's well known liberal scholars, was almost a prisoner on the campus because of threats made against his life by Nationalist gunmen, and many others told us stories of how they had been beaten or threatened by the secret police.

This excitement on the part of teachers and students was contagious during those weeks of the siege. We felt caught up in the warmth of emotion which met us on all sides and responded with smiles and eager conversation. But there was an essential difference in our attitudes which was to come to the surface very soon after the siege was over. In the first place, we were not sharing to the full the experiences which our neighbors were undergoing. Many of the families on the campus were living on a bare subsistence level, wondering whether they could scrape together enough food to see them through the siege, while Rick and I were eating well on the canned goods, rice, and flour which we had stocked in large quantities before the siege began.

We tended to look on the whole period as a big adventure to be watched from the sidelines. What to the professors and students was a dynamic upheaval in the course of their country's history was for us an interesting situation to be stored up for future table conversation. Being totally incapable of understanding the force of the revolution or the tremendous issues involved, we could remain enthusiastic only as long as our personal interests were not affected.

We had come to China too late to enjoy much of the glamorous social life and special privileges which the foreign population had known in Peking for almost a century, but it had not taken us very long to absorb the philosophy that foreigners had carte blanche anywhere and were rarely held accountable for their actions. When our student friends assured us that we had nothing to fear from the Communists, I had smiled smugly and thought, "Well, I guess things aren't going to change very much."

Thus when Peking itself was finally occupied by the Communists we reacted quite differently from the Chinese to the new regime which was set up.

On January 23 the university was electrified by the news that Fu Tso-i, the Nationalist commander, had made a peaceful settlement with the Communists for the surrender of Peking and the siege was over. The students were so jubilant that they, along with many of the professors, formed a huge torchlight parade that night. It was a wild celebration. A big drum boomed out a hoarse accompaniment to the strident, clattering cymbals. When we dashed out to see what it was all about we found ourselves swept along by the shouting, ecstatic crowd and could not help being infected by their excitement. Some of the students wanted to turn their parade into a triumphal march into the city, but the Communist military authorities put a stop to it, stating that conditions were still too unsettled.

We had received a request from the new authorities, relayed to us through the university, asking that foreigners, in the interests of safety, refrain from wandering around until the area had been definitely secured. This request had some validity, as we knew from the experience of an

American friend living about a mile away. Just a few days before, some heavily armed Nationalist deserters had broken into his home and made off with all the money and jewelry they could find.

However, Rick and I had not felt bound by this injunction. As Americans, why could we not go *where* we pleased *when* we pleased? And so, in the company of some other foreigners in the university, we cycled into town the next morning, January 24. We had no trouble getting into the city, but two days later, as we were cycling back to Tsinghua, we were stopped at the Communist line which was still held in the suburbs, pending the formal occupation of Peking. The guard was very polite and quite friendly, but he had orders that no foreigners were to be allowed past their line and no amount of pleading could budge him. I was furious at being thwarted in my plans and resentful toward what seemed pure unreasonableness on the part of the guard. I felt that I had been personally insulted, but there was nothing to do but go back to the city and try again the next morning. Not until two days later did we finally manage to obtain permission to return home.

This resentment increased as the spring of 1949 wore on. It was a blow to our egos when, during those first few months of the new regime, we, as foreigners, had to show a pass to get in and out of the city while our Chinese friends cycled through the gates without stopping or sat calmly on the bus while a policeman asked us for the proper papers. What a sharp contrast this was to the days before liberation, when we could sit comfortably aloof while the Chinese had to get down from the bus at the city gate and be examined by Nationalist MPs!

Our irritation at being "discriminated against" was not soothed when we saw slogans such as "Down with American imperialism" painted all over the walls throughout the city. We found ourselves more and more on the defensive and often tried to find public excuses for American policies even when we ourselves privately considered them wrong. As Rick jokingly expressed it one day in a conversation with the director of the local U.S. Information Service, "You ought to be paying me a salary. I used to be as noisy as anyone in damning the mess we were making of things in the Far East, but now I'm beginning to sound like the Voice of America."

The superficiality of our early enthusiasm was made clear by our reaction to an incident which occurred about a week after the city was taken over. We were sitting at dinner one evening in the comfortable home of a friend in the American Consulate when we heard voices in the street. It was a group of students, singing revolutionary songs and shouting anti-American slogans as they disbanded from a celebration held in the city. Whereas two weeks before, on the Tsinghua campus, we had watched with enthusiasm and sympathy the torchlight parade in celebration of liberation, now we felt a definite hostility.

Each time we felt a new surge of resentment over what we considered discriminatory actions on the part of the new authorities, I thought longingly of the leaky-roofed, rusty-piped apartment on Chestnut Street in Philadelphia where we had been able to shut ourselves off and let the rest of the world go by.

All through 1949–50, we had tried in a rather blind fashion to enter into the life of the university but, in the divergence of our outlook as well as of our income and standard of living, we could do little more than make a pretense of sharing in the life the professors were leading.

Our Fulbright grants had unexpectedly been paid in a lump sum of American cash, which had been flown in from Nanking while the Nationalists were still holding the city. Altogether we had received about $4,000, which by judicious budgeting we expected to make last for a two-year stay in China. By American standards $150 a month does not seem much, but when one compares it with the about $20 a month which Tsinghua professors were receiving in 1949 it is easy to see how there might be a difference in our outlooks on life.

The glaring contrast in our economic situations made me feel self-conscious. Inwardly, I tried to excuse myself by comparing our standard of living with that of the Consulate crowd. In their eyes we were "poor students" who had to be invited in to a good meal once in a while. Outwardly, my self-consciousness took the form of talking about how simply we lived. I made a great point of telling Chinese friends that we ate millet gruel for breakfast and soup for lunch. That was true as far as it went, but I failed to mention the empty tin cans which kept piling up in the kitchen, waiting for the junk man to take off the cook's hands for a good price, or the cheese, butter, bacon, coffee, etc., which we bought regularly.

To the Chinese, that twenty or so dollars a month salary, usually paid in millet, was their main source of livelihood, but we regarded the millet we received almost as a joke each time we sent the cook to collect it. He would take empty flour sacks to the disbursement office and come back laden down with the golden grain. The problem then was what to do with it, for the little amount we ate for breakfast every morning would hardly make a dent in it, and to keep it for any length of time was to run the risk of mildew. We finally gave a good portion to the cook for his salary, traded small amounts for eggs each week, and contracted to have a twig fence made around our tiny yard for twenty-eight pounds of millet. We managed to "get rid of it," but our Chinese friends had to live on this.

In view of the continuing low standard of living in the university during the first year of liberation, one might ask whether the professors did not soon become as disgusted and despondent concerning the new regime as they had been over the old one. This was far from the case. The professors could not become despondent, because they suddenly found themselves taking their destinies into their own hands.

I had expected, as I believe many of the faculty had, that with the arrival of the Communists administrators would be brought in from the outside, courses would be changed, professors fired, and those who remained told what they could do and say. On the contrary, a committee of seven professors in the university was chosen by the faculty to run the affairs of the school, and the various departments began to meet every few days to work out any problems which might arise.

In June, probably for the first time in the history of the university, faculty members sat down together by departments and rank to discuss salaries. Rick and I, as lecturers, sat with the other teachers in the English department, and for several evenings we took up each person in turn, went over his academic qualifications, length of teaching experience, other positions held, and articles published, gave points to each of these items, and on this basis determined what each individual's salary should be for the coming year. Though the salary still amounted to little more than he had been receiving, each man on the faculty felt satisfied that he had been dealt with fairly because he himself had participated in the process.

They soon found too that, unlike the situation under the Nationalists, they were receiving a higher rate of pay than people in the government. One professor had been offered a rather responsible position in the Ministry of Foreign Affairs and was about to accept when he found that his salary would be only about one-third what he was making in the university. When he declined the job and returned to his teaching position one of our friends remarked, "Well, it certainly shows that this government is going to weed out the opportunists right from the beginning."

All the other problems in the university were settled in the same way as the salaries had been. The question of housing had long been a source of bitterness. The bungalows and two-story houses on the campus had been allocated years before on the basis of rank and pull rather than according to need, with the result that some of the larger homes were occupied by single men while big families were crowded into a few small rooms.

In the summer of 1949 the professors gathered together and discussed the redistribution of all the houses. They then appointed a committee to rate each professor according to seniority and need. One afternoon in early fall everyone came together again and each professor, in accordance with his rating, spoke up for the house he would like to live in. The larger houses were all divided into two homes and, even though the faculty was increased that fall, there was plenty of room for all. There is no doubt that some of the professors were dissatisfied at being ousted from the roomy quarters they had enjoyed before, but the general reaction was one of supreme satisfaction and a growing admiration for the democratic process which had been instituted.

But this democratic process meant more and more meetings. Curriculum, administration, cooperatives, defense, and the hiring of new faculty members—almost every part of the university life was handled through endless discussion. The women organized a women's association which dealt with problems of nursery schools, health facilities, family benefits, running of the cooperatives, and political education.

One of our friends was not the "joiner" type, as she laughingly put it, but in 1950 she told us, "In the beginning I thought it was all a lot of nonsense and the political discussions particularly were a case of the blind leading the blind, but, you know, I began to find that if I didn't go to the meetings I couldn't take part in my friends' conversations when we got together for tea or a shopping trip. I found they were discussing subjects I didn't know anything about. I didn't want to become completely isolated, so I started going to the women's association meetings. And now they've made *me* chairman of one of the committees!"

Her experience in being drawn into group life was not unique. In general, all the people in the university soon became engrossed in the common experience of creating a new life for themselves. We, on the other hand, with the worsening of Sino-American relations, had become more and more hostile to the very ideas which our friends were absorbing. Having nothing in common with them, we withdrew almost completely into our study of ancient Chinese, Rick in history and I in poetry. Our leisure time was spent almost entirely in the company of the small, isolated group of foreigners in the city.

This relationship had been made doubly close by the fact that, from the time of the siege, Rick had been using our trips into the city on weekends to provide Roger, an old Naval Intelligence friend who was a vice consul in the American Consulate, with political and economic information which he had gathered at Tsinghua through his contacts there with important liberal leaders connected with the new regime.

Therefore it was with troubled hearts that we began to watch the gradual withdrawal of the Consulate after January, 1950. On the morning of April 10 I had picked a small bunch of violets in the field near our home at Tsinghua to take to Roger and his wife, Kathy, who were leaving that day, the last of the Consulate group to go. As the train pulled out of the station, taking these people whom we had counted among our best friends, we suddenly experienced a feeling of loneliness and insecurity. After the Communists took over, the Consulate had been rendered powerless but still it had always seemed like a home base to which we could turn if ever we ran into trouble.

To a certain extent this feeling had been alleviated by our rapidly growing friendship with members of the British Negotiation Mission, which had formally taken over the job of looking after American interests in the absence of the Consulate. Since Britain and the United States had a joint intelligence command in London, Rick transferred his espionage relations to them.

Our espionage activities made us feel even more self-conscious and uncomfortable in the presence of our Chinese acquaintances, but it was the Korean war which brought about the final break in our relations with them.

As usual, I had not paid much attention to the Voice of America news broadcast, so I was not prepared that June morning in 1950 to argue with my Chinese teacher when he asked Rick and me very seriously whether we knew that South Korea had invaded North Korea. Rick stepped in to explain just as seriously that he thought Mr. Li had gotten the story a bit garbled, because, as Rick had heard from the very reliable Voice of America, it was North Korea which had attacked South Korea. It was quite obvious that neither could convince the other, so, with slightly embarrassed smiles, the subject was dropped and I got on with my Chinese lesson. To my mind, it did not make much difference one way or the other. In spite of its relative geographical proximity, Korea seemed a long way off and of little concern to us.

However, the next day on the bus from town back to Tsinghua, when I learned from an American missionary woman at Yenching that Truman had sent American troops to Korea and the Seventh Fleet to Formosa, things took on a different light. I realized that this open intervention into the Chinese civil war was bound to lead to strong anti-American feeling, and I wondered if it would not be better to give in to my longing to return home.

One afternoon in early July we spent a rather depressing few hours discussing the problem over plates of watery ice cream in one of Peking's Western-style restaurants. We finally decided that Rick's position as one of the last American observers in Peking was too important to be given up at that time unless it became absolutely necessary.

We had then tried to carry on as if nothing had changed, but as we heard the news of American defeats in Korea and saw in the Peking papers the many pictures of dead American troops our emotions were aroused to a peak of bitterness. Naturally, we were not able to conceal our hostile feelings and it soon became obvious that what little popularity we had enjoyed with the Chinese was rapidly disappearing.

By mid-July we were certain we would not be asked to renew our teaching contracts at Tsinghua for the following year. When an assistant in the Foreign Languages Department dropped in to see us one evening to tell us that we were going to be "fired," we rose up resentfully and said, "Well, we have already made other plans." If we had finished the sentence with a "so there!" and stuck out our tongues our feelings could not have been more clearly expressed.

Our contracts were up on July 31, and though no one in the school said that we had to get out by that date we were determined, in our position as the "aggrieved party," not to give them any cause to find fault with us. We left on August 5 and moved in temporarily with Harriet Mills in the city.

The big question now was what to do next. We thought of taking a house in the city, but that would have meant being cut off from the Chinese almost entirely. We realized how much we had suffered, from the point of view of learning the language, in living so much to ourselves, and decided on a bold step. We enrolled for the fall semester as students in Yenching, which, as an American missionary university, was willing to accept us, and made arrangements to split up and live in the men's and women's student dormitories at the beginning of the autumn term.

This move had an added advantage for Rick. Since the two universities were situated only about a mile apart, he could continue to keep up his contacts at Tsinghua.

All these external factors we had carefully assessed, but we forgot that our own characters had not changed much. Conflicts began to show up almost immediately.

In the first place there was our own marital relationship. We saw each other only at breakfast, which we ate in the home of an American missionary friend, and for a couple of hours during the day when we studied together in a room rented for the purpose in one of the faculty member's houses. By the time Friday afternoon came we were all too ready to jump on our bicycles and pedal into the city to spend the weekend at Harriet's. It was all very well to talk during the summer about how easy it would be to break up housekeeping and move into the dormitories, but, as Rick expressed it to a friend later in the fall, "This monastic existence is getting me down."

There was also the question of food. At Tsinghua our cook, Wang, had been proficient in something which he claimed was Western cooking, and so, out of fear of causing him to lose face, we dared ask only occasionally for a Chinese meal. When we moved to Yenching we thought that, with a Western-style breakfast to start the day, we could manage the simple Chinese dormitory diet the other two meals, so we bought student meal tickets.

However, instead of trying to adapt ourselves to the monotony of dormitory fare, we tended to eat more and more meals in the restaurants in Cheng-fu, the village outside the east gate of the university. Before long we had given up all pretense of eating in the dorms and so ended that attempt to mingle with the students.

I found soon, too, that my optimism about getting along with my roommates and fellow students was misplaced. I shared a room with two Chinese girls, both Christians and neither very progressive. One was an English major, the other a botany major. Presumably we should have had a lot in common, and, since neither spoke English very well, it should have been a good opportunity for me to practice my spoken Chinese. But I felt tonguetied in front of them, and although they were both as polite, considerate, and sweet as they could be we never had more than the briefest exchanges of words. In the morning we all tumbled out of bed silently and went on our respective ways. In the evening, when it came time for lights out, we all returned and just as quietly got ready for bed.

I did try to take some part in extracurricular activities in an effort to become part of the student life but I always felt awkward and on the defensive, both because of my poor command of Chinese and because I felt that people must feel slightly uncomfortable about being too close to me, an American.

As a matter of fact, in the early fall the students in the Chinese department had gone out of their way to make me feel at home. They included me in all their meetings, social and business, and asked me to join them in the October 1 parade on the anniversary of the founding of the People's Republic. Rick's classmates had asked him to take part in the parade, too. After a short consultation, we decided to go.

When we gathered in the big square at Peking University in the city to line up for the parade, the various departments joked back and forth and had a wonderful time together but we stood on the side, incapable of sharing that warmth. The songs which they took turns singing with such gusto were unfamiliar to us, so we could not join in.

As we marched past the reviewing stand the students around us went wild with excitement. Waving handkerchiefs, they jumped in the air. Deafening shouts of "Long live the People's Republic of China!" "Long live Chairman Mao!" mixed with "There he is! He's waving to us! He's the one in gray! Don't you see?" engulfed us like a mighty wave. I tried to make a show of excitement, but the words stuck in my throat. I was really more interested in looking for some of our diplomatic friends among the spectators in the grandstand and wondering how much farther we had to walk.

It was with a sigh of relief that we finally arrived back at Harriet's house late in the afternoon and slipped out of the dusty navy blue slacks and white shirts which we had worn in the parade. That night we went to a dinner at the British Embassy and joked loudly about our day's "adventure."

From that time on it became increasingly difficult to feel any bond with the students. When we finally heard from the police and Rick went to the station I had no feelings holding me to China. As I closed the suitcase and waited for Rick, my great wish was to get back home.

The minutes seemed to drag on endlessly. Would they never return? It was really only half an hour later that I heard them putting their bicycles in the passageway outside. Even before they entered the sound of their dragging steps gave me a premonition that all was not well but I still looked up hopefully and said as they came in, "All set?"

Rick's only answer was a shake of the head, and Harriet glumly replied, "Temporarily denied."

It was a moment before the significance of the words sank in. Temporarily denied! But now there would be no possibility of catching our boat. Still we clung to the word "temporarily" with all the hope and imagination in our power. Perhaps we would be only another week. Could they possibly keep us longer than a month?

Rick wrote out a power of attorney on a piece of note paper, so that my father could take care of our affairs if we were detained indeterminately, and, along with some letters to friends giving his views of the situation, sent it out secretly in the Dutch diplomatic mail pouch.

Harriet attempted through a girl friend, who had connections with people in the Peking Public Security Bureau, to find out why the permits had not been issued, and when this attempt failed she and Rick began visiting all the influential Chinese they knew to solicit help in the matter. Such methods might have worked in the old China where it was always just a question of knowing the "right people," but in the new China we ran into a blank wall.

We had packed and sent off to the shipping company all but the barest essentials. It seemed useless to cart them all back again if our delay were to be only a matter of weeks, so we took out only a few things like our evening clothes—absolute essentials for the embassy parties in the city—and asked the shipper to store the trunks until time to send them off. At the university we wore regular Chinese padded clothes, so with those for every day and a dress and suit for the weekends we felt prepared to sit out the period of waiting. After a few days there seemed no reason for lingering in the city where we could only become more depressed; therefore, the following weekend we decided to return to Yenching and try to resume our work there.

As we approached the stand where we were to catch the school bus, a dilapidated old Dodge which after liberation had been converted to burn charcoal gas, we met one of Rick's classmates. I felt my face flush at the thought of having to face all those people who had said final good-bys to us a couple of weeks before. What would they think of us now, slinking back almost with our tails between our legs?

As the driver cranked the bellows of the charcoal burner in the rear of the bus preparatory to getting under way it seemed almost as if he were fanning a violent flame within me. What right had these people in the government to put us in such an awkward, embarrassing position? I wanted to shout out against them and even thought of getting up on the steps of the administration building where I would tell all the students how unfair their government was in not letting us go home. I was sure I could enlist their sympathies and perhaps start a riot.

Of course, it never occurred to me that the government might think it had some justification for detaining us. None of us at that time would admit that there was anything wrong in what we were doing. We tried to picture ourselves as poor, oppressed students who wanted only to go home. Yet, even while decrying so bitterly the "unfairness" of the Chinese, we continued to collect information about them and turn it over to the British.

2

Rick: As we chugged along on the bus back to Yen-ching, I too was storming inside. The people in the university would be really suspicious of us now that we had not been given exit permits, and I recoiled at the idea of having anything to do with them. What excuses could I give and how could I keep up the pretense any longer? Dell seemed to think we should try to go on with our studies as though nothing had happened, but I was in no mood to putter around translating texts on ancient Chinese philosophy. My only thought was to get back home and into uniform. All during the retreat of the Marines down to Wonsan and Hamhung I had hardly been able to leave the radio. My hatred for everything Chinese smoldered in me like a small volcano and, though it might mean a firing squad in the end, I was determined to find some means of retaliation.

Even before the end of 1948, when the Chinese Communists had entered Peking, I had formed certain opinions about them through extensive reading and talks with a number of well-informed people, including personnel in the State Department, who looked on them primarily as nationalistic agrarian reformers. I could not agree with the interpretation advanced by the China lobby group in the United States that the Chinese Communists were puppets of Moscow. There was no evidence to show that they had received any significant material assistance from the Soviet Union since the failure of the first revolution in the 1920's. Furthermore it was clear to us that one of the dominant forces shaping Chinese society was an intense nationalism.

Ever since the anti-foreign Boxer uprising in 1900, any government in China which associated itself too closely with foreigners was bound to incur the enmity of the Chinese people. It was Chiang's subservience to the United States which as much as anything else had turned the weight of public opinion against him, and whatever government replaced his regime would have to take this into consideration.

Moreover, though the leaders of the Chinese revolution called themselves Communists, there were factors in Chinese society which made me feel that this designation was not applicable, at least not in the Soviet sense. In the first place, the very nature of the Chinese revolution had come to differ considerably from that of the Russians. The latter had based their revolution primarily on winning over the support of a rather strong urban working class. In China, on the other hand, since the working class was very small and rendered almost completely impotent by Chiang's anti-labor repression, the Chinese Communists had had to confine their activity from the 1930's on largely to the countryside. Their chief source of strength, therefore, lay in the peasantry, seventy per cent of whom were either landless or possessed so little land that they were reduced to unspeakable poverty. It was the demand of the peasants for land which had been the principal revolutionary force in China throughout its entire history. Mao Tse-tung and his group, by making it the focal point of their attack, were able to build up a great mass movement and eventually lead the revolution to a successful conclusion.

However, the peasant, as a small property owner, was by his very nature fundamentally opposed to communism per se and its philosophy of collectivism. Moreover, I had thought other aspects of Communist policy, such as general economic control, equality of the sexes, and the elimination of superstition, were bound to come into conflict with Chinese traditional ways of thinking and therefore meet with considerable opposition on the part of the peasants.

The two revolutions also differed in that the Chinese Communists had made a special point of winning the support of the small but influential middle class, the businessmen and intellectuals. Due to China's backwardness these people enjoyed almost a monopoly on the experience and technical know-how mandatory for the running of a modern state. Because of the Nationalists' corruption, suppression of democratic rights, and subservience to foreign interests, this group had more and more come to support the Communists. However, since most of them had been trained in the West, they were inclined to be Western-oriented in their thinking.

For this reason I, along with many people in the State Department and others familiar with China, felt that if the Communists were to retain any mass support at all in China they would have to confine themselves in the countryside primarily to simple agrarian reforms and in the cities to a Western-type democratic revolution. Otherwise they would lose the support of both these elements and eventually go the way of the Nationalists.

This theory was further supported by the fact that the Communists themselves spoke in terms of creating what they called a "new democratic society" which would permit capitalism to exist for some time before attempting to move on to socialism. It seemed to me then that this preservation of capitalism would probably bring the Chinese Communists more and more into ideological conflict with the leaders of the Soviet Union and thus, as the demands of Russian imperialism began to be felt, an irrevocable split would follow. Moreover, since only our country was capable of providing the vast amount of economic and technical aid necessary for reconstructing China's broken economy, not to mention its future industrialization, I felt that as soon as the bitter issues created by American support of the Nationalists were resolved it would be only natural for the Chinese Communists to incline toward friendly relations with the United States.

Having become absorbed with this line of reasoning, I was inclined to look on them rather favorably. This impression was heightened by my first actual contact with them. During the siege of Peking I made two trips through the battle lines from Tsinghua into the city to give information to the American Consulate. As a Chinese student and I were making our way back through the lines to Tsinghua after my second trip, a battle suddenly broke out in full force over our heads. When artillery shells began landing all around us, we jumped off our bicycles and sought the shelter of the ruts in the road.

We were pinned down for some time, but when a short lull came in the firing I fetched my brief case, which contained among other things a few hundred silver dollars and a bundle of registered mail for the university, and suggested that we leave our bicycles behind and start wriggling our way up the road toward the Communist positions.

After what seemed ages we reached our goal. We were taken by a few soldiers to a small house nearby where we were offered a drink of water. The troops were all wearing enormous fur hats, which indicated their Manchurian origin, and seemed quite friendly when they asked us where we were going. The mere mention that I was a teacher at Tsinghua appeared to dispel any doubts they may have had about me but they were curious about my nationality. Their friendly attitude did not change on hearing that I was an American.

In fact, one of them, patting his Tommy gun, laughed good-naturedly, "American weapons are really terrific!"

"And that bandit Chiang Kai-shek makes an excellent supply sergeant," joked another. "These all came through him."

Their boyish faces beamed with delight as they had me look at the American stamp on their guns, which had been captured from the Nationalists. One of them noticed my brief case and wanted to know what it contained. I opened it for them to see. They looked at the money, which must have seemed a fortune to them, but touched nothing and quickly handed the brief case back to me.

As I was leaving I told them where we had abandoned

our bicycles and asked them to tell the local people that we would give a reward to anyone returning them to us at Tsinghua after the battle was over. The words were no sooner out of my mouth than three of the soldiers, running like deer, took off under fire across the fields. In a matter of minutes they were back again, half carrying, half rolling our bicycles with them. My bike was loaded with canned food and other supplies I was taking to Tsinghua, and they insisted that I check to make sure everything was intact. A three-pound can of corned beef hash must have dropped off on the way and they would have gone back to look for it if I had not put my foot down.

I felt I ought to repay them in some way but they wouldn't accept even a cigarette, not to speak of money. Their eyes flashed with pride as one said, "We are the People's Liberation Army. It is our duty to serve the people. If we were to accept anything, that would reflect on the revolution."

This same incorruptibility called forth our anger a few weeks later, when we found ourselves unable to bribe or wheedle our way past the guard when returning to Tsinghua after our trip into the city following the end of the siege. Yet at the same time we could not help but respect their honesty and enthusiasm for the revolution. Feeling as I did, I could see no conflict between this admiration for the Communists' good qualities and my position as an intelligence officer desirous of maintaining American influence in China.

In the first few months of 1949 after the Communists took over Peking there were numerous signs which led me to believe that the rapprochement I had envisaged might well be possible. Acheson's initial attitude of "wait until the dust settles" gave some hope that the State Department was ready to adopt a rather flexible stand.

Through my contacts at Tsinghua I learned that a number of well-known liberals, basically pro-American in their outlook, were to be given high positions in the new government when it was formed. In talks with some of these men I was assured that China would not only want

American recognition but also would need vast amounts of American material to help in its economic reconstruction. These assurances were given credence by energetic efforts on the part of the new authorities right after they took control of Peking and Tientsin to start trade moving again.

During 1949 the United States, in spite of difficulties resulting from an absence of diplomatic relations and a Nationalist blockade, continued to monopolize about 70 per cent of China's trade. This situation was brought to an end only with the institution of the embargo policy and freezing of Chinese assets by the United States after the entry of the Chinese into the Korean war in late 1950.

Moreover, American institutions in Peking such as Yenching University and Peking Union Medical College were allowed to continue their operations as before.

Mao Tse-tung's speech on a democratic dictatorship delivered on July 1, 1949, dealt a crushing blow to my theories. Although I was incapable then of fully comprehending the significance of Mao's speech as a basic program for the development of new China, the one thing which did strike home to me was his statement that in its foreign affairs China would incline toward the Soviet Union. Caught up as I had been in the cold war hysteria of the Truman era, by the time we went to China in 1948 I had already started thinking in terms of a Third World War and categorically putting anyone who sided with the Soviet Union in the position of the enemy.

This reaction to Mao's speech revealed the inconsistency in my former outlook which had denied any conflict between my admiration for the achievements of the Chinese Communists and my desire for the return of American influence there.

Now that they were no longer going to follow the line laid down by the United States, those very achievements which I had formerly admired seemed only to make them a more dangerous enemy. From then on they could do nothing right in my eyes. What I had felt formerly to be an estimable plan to educate China's illiterate 85 per cent of the population I could now look upon only as a diabolical plot to indoctrinate these masses even further in anti-American, pro-Soviet ideologies. The lack of corruption among the Communists was no longer a laudable thing but an insidious means of increasing their control over the country. The attempts of the People's Government to improve living standards became a means to trick the people into following blindly the dictates of their new rulers.

In such a frame of mind I could readily concur with the feeling expressed by everyone around the Consulate in Peking that the time for fencing with the Communists was over and now it was a question of open political warfare.

In the months following I joined in the battle which was centered around China's Western-oriented, liberal intellectuals. Over the years these liberals, under Chiang Kai-shek's tyrannic regime, had gravitated toward close cooperation with the Communists. After the Democratic League—the largest of their liberal organizations—was outlawed by Chiang in the autumn of 1948 they became completely allied with the Communists in a united front to overthrow Chiang's Nationalists. With liberation they were naturally included in the plans for a coalition government sponsored by the Communists. Still, there were many basic contradictions between these people with their concepts of Western bourgeois democracy and the Marxian Communists. It was also quite obvious that, though they were to be given some voice in the new government, the leadership of the new state would be in the hands of the Communist Party.

The State Department, hoping these contradictions would sharpen with the actual assumption of political power, launched its big campaign in the summer of 1949 to separate these liberal intellectuals from the Communists and, by uniting them with so-called reform elements among the Nationalists on Formosa, to patch together a "third force." At that time these "reform" elements within the Nationalist Party were led by such persons as K. C. Wu, former Mayor of Shanghai, and the American-trained general, Sun Li-jen. Both of these men have been ousted by Chiang Kai-shek since then.

In conjunction with this campaign to win over the liberal intellectuals, American intelligence personnel in China expended a great deal of effort in attempting to discover any possible dissident elements within the Communist Party itself who might fit in with this "third force." I was asked especially to note in my reading and conversations with Chinese any references to such people as Chen Shao-yü (Wang Ming), a party leader of the 1930's who had opposed the line followed by Mao Tse-tung.

In July, 1949, the director of the U.S. Information Service in Peking approached me. After a violent tirade against Mao Tse-tung's speech, he asked me to arrange a secret meeting for him with one of the leaders of the Democratic League, who was a professor at Tsinghua. I was a little uneasy about exposing myself by such open anti-Communist activity but I did visit the professor and he finally agreed to a meeting in an out-of-the-way place for lunch. However, the professor was more sensible than I had been, for the USIS director told me later that the man had not appeared himself, sending a substitute instead.

The State Department also increased its propaganda efforts, especially in the direction of alleged Soviet imperialism in Manchuria. To a certain extent this propaganda proved successful, especially after the announcement of the trade agreement between the North East Administrative Area (Manchuria) and the Soviet Union later in the summer of 1949. However, when I suggested to several professors at Tsinghua that, in the face of a general food shortage throughout China, exporting of grain hardly seemed to China's advantage one of them quickly replied, "It is true we could probably use that grain at home, but at this time we need machinery and railway equipment even more to get the rest of our economy running again. These things don't drop from heaven, you know, and your government certainly shows no inclination to help us."

In August the State Department, in its White Paper

on American relations with China, openly called for "the democratic individualism of China" to reassert itself and "throw off the foreign yoke" and expressed the determination of the United States government to "encourage all developments in China which would now and in the future work toward this end." (See State Department White Paper, *United States Relations with China*, p. xvi.) Thus Washington clearly announced its intentions of continuing to interfere in China's internal affairs by fostering the subversion of any government the Communists and their allies set up.

In Peking our immediate task was to sound out the reactions of our hoped-for allies. Since at Tsinghua I was in the very midst of the liberal intellectuals, my activity became even more important. During the summer of 1949, after our first year's teaching in the university, Dell and I had thought of moving to a more comfortable and convenient place in the city but we were persuaded to give up the idea because it would be difficult for the Consulate to get information about what was going on at Tsinghua unless we were there.

I began visiting various professors and inviting them to dinner, as well as pumping my foreign friends and informants among the students. It soon became evident that the White Paper had been a colossal mistake. The Chinese press was able to use it as the basis for an extensive countercampaign, and petitions against it were circulated throughout the universities. Originally many of the intellectuals had remained sitting on the fence and had refused to commit themselves openly concerning the new regime, but now that the State Department had put them on the spot they were forced to take a stand. They were furious at being placed in the limelight and resentful at being treated as pawns in what they considered a sordid political game.

Moreover, the numerous statements which appeared in the American press that we had "lost" China brought forth many bitter comments.

One of my professors in the history department at

Tsinghua, who had spent many years teaching in the United States, remarked sarcastically when I mentioned the subject, "What right have those people to assume that China was theirs to lose? It's time some of your people realized that this country belongs to us Chinese and is not the property of some group sitting in Washington or London."

I too felt a frustrated annoyance with the White Paper and the cries of "having lost China," not because I disagreed with them per se but because they served only to alienate the very people we were trying to win over. This same feeling of frustration increased all through the following year as every major move made by Washington with regard to China seemed to undermine what little good will we had left there. The American policy of nonrecognition, instead of detracting from the prestige of the People's Government, succeeded only in uniting the Chinese people and increased their suspicions concerning the motives of the United States.

President Truman on January 5, 1950, might have done a great deal toward restoring some respect for the United States by the Chinese people when he declared:

> The United States has no predatory designs on Formosa or any other Chinese territory. The United States has no desire to obtain special rights or privileges or to establish military bases on Formosa at this time. Nor does it have any intention of utilizing its armed forces to interfere in the present situation. The United States government will not pursue a course which will lead to involvement in the civil conflict in China. . . .

Unfortunately, there were two things which caused the Chinese to be very suspicious. *Time* magazine very obligingly pointed out that the words "at this time" were deliberately added to provide an opening for a change in this policy whenever it might become convenient, making the whole Truman statement sound like nothing more than a propaganda move to counteract the effect of negotiations then going on between Mao Tse-tung and the Soviet government in Moscow. But even more devastating was the fact that only five days later, on the 10th, the Army announced in Philadelphia it was loading over three hundred tanks, armored cars, and half-tracks on board a Turkish freighter for shipment to the Nationalist forces on Formosa.

What little hope remained for an improvement in Sino-American relations was completely snuffed out by events which took place shortly after this.

Early one morning in mid-January, 1950, the Peking authorities tacked a notice on the gates of the American and other Western Consulates stating that the property which had been seized by the foreign powers for stationing of troops and building of barracks under the Boxer Protocol of 1901 was to be returned to China.

After some deliberation, the other foreign consulates—the British, French, and Dutch—gracefully handed over the property. (The Russians had voluntarily handed theirs over during Mao Tse-tung's trip to Moscow.) Only Washington chose to make an issue of the matter. At home there was deliberately created the false impression that the Chinese were taking over the Consulate itself instead of merely the barracks land. At the same time the State Department sought to exert pressure on the Chinese by threatening to withdraw all diplomatic personnel from China.

The Chinese remained unmoved by any threats, however, and after a few days the Consulate evacuated the barracks. Shortly afterward, all American diplomatic personnel received orders to close up their offices and leave.

For those of us around the Consulate in Peking this decision seemed like the worst case of cutting off our nose to spite our face. The United States was not only leaving itself without any trained observers in China but, more important, its position was completely indefensible in the eyes of even heretofore friendly Chinese. The Boxer Protocol has always been looked on by the people of China as the greatest insult in their history. That we should take such an extreme step as withdrawing our diplomatic personnel in an attempt to preserve the provisions of this treaty was inconceivable from the point of view of practical international politics.

Our feeling of pessimism was further increased during those weeks before the Consulate's withdrawal in April by the final realization that our hopes of seeing a general economic collapse which would force the Chinese to seek American aid had failed to materialize. This was made especially clear to us by the stabilization of prices and the beginning of an over-all economic recovery in March and April, 1950.

The gulf which had been created between us and our Chinese acquaintances by the deterioration of Sino-American relations was further deepened by a growing divergence of views on the ideological level.

At the time of liberation, Marxism was little understood by the ordinary Western-trained Chinese intellectuals. Even afterward, in spite of their great interest in the new ideas and regular attendance at the university-wide lectures and departmental discussion meetings, the professors at Tsinghua remained rather superficial and academic in their understanding of Marxism. They continued to look upon the West as their main source of intellectual and spiritual inspiration. Many of them were quite openly contemptuous toward the new philosophy. After all, having mastered the best that the West had to offer, what could they learn from a bunch of uncouth Communists who had none of the social graces and hardly shoes to put on their feet?

However, by the late spring of 1950 perceptible changes in outlook were taking place which made very conspicuous a big difference between us and the Chinese, both the old die-hards and those who were absorbing the new. The contrast was brought out very clearly one evening when we invited two old faculty friends and their wives to dinner

Mr. and Mrs. Wu arrived first and sat talking with us about their experiences in the United States, where Mr

Wu had spent several years teaching at Harvard during the war. I was just about to ask him some questions about my research when the door was thrown open and in walked Mr. Jao, with his usual air of polished eagerness. Mrs. Jao came trailing along behind him.

As we took their coats, we heard Wu say to him mildly, "I didn't see you at the faculty conference today."

Jao waved his hand with an air of brushing aside a trivial matter. "I was busy in the library all afternoon. I think I've found the earliest reference to the sweet potato in China. It first appeared in Fukien, you know . . ."

For the next few minutes the sweet potato dominated the conversation, until Jao decided to launch off on one of his other great discoveries. In an effort to bring the conversation up to within the last century, Dell mentioned that she had been studying some contemporary poetry and asked Jao if he had read any of it.

With a snort, Jao replied, "Did you say 'contemporary'? Hmmm, I think 'temporary' would be more appropriate. Fifty years from now, no one will ever hear of it." His cultivated Oxford accent emphasized even more strongly his contempt for China's new poets.

We all laughed and then Wu said in his soft-spoken voice, "Some of it's not so bad, and they are trying to write something the people can understand."

"Bah, the people don't understand poetry anyway!"

The announcement of dinner cut short any reply Wu was about to make and the conversation moved on to other channels.

After dinner I asked Jao if he were attending any of the political discussion groups. "Discussion!" he exclaimed. "That's no discussion; it's a talkathon. What they call logic is sheer nonsense. Why, it would make Aristotle turn over in his grave. That goes for all this Marxist thought. There's absolutely nothing in it. Puerile, that's what it is, puerile."

As the laughter subsided, Wu smiled slowly and said, "I don't know. I've come to think that there is something in it."

I was surprised to hear Wu say this, for, with his conservative, scholarly manner, he seemed the last person in the world to be inclined toward communism. I asked him what he meant.

"Well," he replied, "I have come to feel that the development of human society has not been as haphazard, unpredictable, and unintelligible as a superficial glance at history would make it appear. The Marxists claim that there are certain basic laws which govern this development and that by understanding them mankind may begin to shape its destiny. The history of the revolutionary movements in the Soviet Union and China during the past thirty-odd years would certainly seem to bear them out. In any case, of one thing I am certain—it becomes possible for the great mass of ordinary people to live a decent life only when every man takes an interest in what is going on around him and assumes an active part in political affairs."

"But one doesn't have to live in a Communist society to take an active part in the country's affairs," I interposed quickly.

"I'm not too certain about that," he replied. "The United States is supposed to be the most advanced type of what is known as bourgeois democracy, and yet you know what it is like there. For the average person political activity is limited to casting a vote every two or four years and even the man he votes for is limited to one of two parties and is picked in your notorious smoke-filled rooms by professional politicians and people with enough money to have influence. What you actually have is very little democracy for the masses of the people themselves."

"Well," I said, "at least we have *two* parties and we can choose between the lesser of two evils."

"Yes," he replied, "you can pick either Truman or Dewey, but what's the difference? Even their programs are the same. Besides, whether it is one party or a dozen the question is whether that party expresses the desires of the vast majority of the people. You are forgetting that though the Communists constitute the leading party in

China our government is made up of a coalition of parties often representing very different points of view. But what is more important is that in our country today, except for landlords and those who were highly connected with the Nationalists, everyone is encouraged to take an active role in political life whether he has any connections with some party or not."

By this time I was beginning to feel a little warm. "Do you think these people all agree with the policy of simply following blindly after the Soviet Union?"

"I wouldn't say we were blindly following the Soviet Union or anyone else," broke in Mrs. Wu. "It is true that we are trying to learn from the Soviet Union because they have had more experience in developing a backward country like ours, but China is standing on its own feet now, which is something it never could do before."

"I simply don't understand what there is to be learned from those barbarians," grumbled Jao.

"The point is," said Wu, "we Chinese always used to look up to the United States as a model on which to pattern our country, but many of us have come to see now that that is nothing but an idle dream. The period since the Japanese war has shown us all too clearly that we can never expect any real help from the United States in building up an independent China. The American policy since liberation has proved one thing—though the American people may wholeheartedly sympathize with us, unless the entire China lobby in Washington can maintain their special privileges here they'll do everything they can to destroy us."

I thought it was time to change the subject, so I asked Jao whether he was going to accept the chair which Oxford had been offering him for the past two years.

Jao shook his head slowly and said, "No, I don't think so. I don't always agree with Wu, but this is my country. There's a lot going on and I'd rather like to stick around and do my bit."

After Wu and Jao left I had an uncomfortable feeling that, though they were progressing at different rates of speed, they were moving in the same direction while Dell and I were going the opposite way.

Those last days of June, 1950, marked the beginning of the final divergence in our paths, and at the same time the new and dangerous turn in Sino-American relations made our position in China even more difficult. The barrage of anti-American propaganda and the ridicule engendered by the defeats of the American "paper tiger" in Korea made it almost impossible for me to curb my temper and hold my tongue. I found my blood running hot and constantly exposed myself in arguments with Chinese acquaintances.

My frustration was eased temporarily in the days following the Inchon landing when American forces moved rapidly north, and I had begun to feel almost jubilant. At least we could no longer be called a "paper tiger." However, even in that moment of seeming triumph our personal prestige had been dealt another devastating blow. For the Chinese government had placed Dell and me in a dangerous and embarrassing position by refusing to allow us to return home. Well, if that was the way they wanted it . . . With my contacts at Yenching and Tsinghua I probably could still collect information which might be of value to our side. It was not much, but it might help some to even the score.

3

Dell: In mid-January one of our friends at Yenching went in to the police station to pick up her exit permit. We asked her to inquire about ours while she was there. Her face told us the answer on her return, and, over a cup of tea, she went on to explain, "They had a stack of permits there on the desk—there must have been sixty or seventy of them. I asked the fellow, who used to be an English student of mine, by the way, whether yours were in the pile. He went through every one, but they weren't there. I just don't understand it. Why should they keep two students like yourselves from leaving?"

"They're holding them as hostages," broke in another foreign friend. "They want those Chinese students in the United States, and they think they've got a talking point as long as a few students are held here."

"But Bert got his permit and left the day after Christmas," exclaimed another. "He's an American student. It's my theory that their being Fulbrights is the cause. Look at the picture—all three of them were Fulbright students."

"That may be," I said wryly, "but look at all the other Fulbright students who were allowed to leave. I think they're just being ornery. They'll give us the permits when they get good and ready and not before."

I do not think it could have occurred to any of our foreign friends at that time that we might be spies, since on the surface we seemed to be serious-minded students, a little Bohemian as far as the missionaries were concerned, but still students. In true ostrich fashion, we kept hoping that the People's Government would also look on us as innocent scholars and eventually let us go.

We kept in touch with Harriet, who, in the city, continued to try every means possible, through the embassies and Chinese friends, to obtain our permits or at least some news of them. We even discussed writing a letter to Chou En-lai, but by that time Rick decided we would do better to lie low.

Rick: To our surprise, the excitement caused by China's entry into the war actually made it easy for us to return to the campus, for in those first few days people were far too busy with other things and our presence went almost unnoticed. As time went on, most of them seemed to have forgotten that we had ever been intending to leave and we gradually slipped back into the regular routine. It was only our own insecure state of mind and antipathy toward what was going on around us that made those days so unpleasant.

China's entry into the Korean war probably did not come to most informed Chinese with the same degree of surprise that it did to people in this country. Any illusions which some Chinese may have had about the good intentions of the American government had been dispelled by Truman's sending the Seventh Fleet to protect Chiang on Formosa. The Chinese press, which had been telling the people all along not to be taken in by Truman's January 5 statement that the United States would not intervene in Formosa, could now say "I told you so." To the British and Americans in Peking, from the point of view of Western prestige in China, this had appeared to be the blunder to end all blunders.

The American action in Formosa and its crossing the 38th Parallel in Korea in spite of explicit warnings by the Chinese government that they could not permit American troops to approach their borders, combined with the threatening statements of American political figures and the persistent bombing of China's territory along the Yalu

River, had given rise to bitterness among the Chinese. There was a growing conviction among them all through the latter part of 1950 that the real aim of the United States was not to carry on a mere "police action" in Korea but to launch a two-pronged attack from both the north and south against their young republic in hopes of crushing it before it could become really stabilized. Some sort of clash seemed inevitable, but still when war actually came it was a shock and was followed for many people, even those wholeheartedly supporting the action of the People's Government, by a brief period of uncertainty and depression.

To many it seemed unbelievable that China, which for over a hundred years had been kicked around at will by almost everyone and whose backward economy was still in dire straits, could take up arms against the mightiest industrial and supposedly strongest military power in the world.

These doubts even affected some of the liberal leaders in the new government and there appeared signs of wavering among a few of them. One such person in a very high position had paid us a surprising visit in the city several days after it became generally known that we were planning to leave. As we sat in Harriet's cold little study he had become eloquent about his friendship for the American people. It was only the policies of the American government to which he and other Chinese objected. His wording had all been very subtle but his manner had left no doubt that he would be very happy if we were to let the right people in the United States know that they had a sympathetic friend in Peking in case the situation should change and Americans were to return to the mainland of China.

But as the Chinese troops in Korea scored one victory after another these first reactions began to pass away. Perhaps the United States was only a "paper tiger" after all. A new-found confidence grew with leaps and bounds, and with it a determination to win. When the Chinese entered the war, the government called on the people for volunteers to serve in Korea and asked for contributions to support the war effort from those remaining at home.

The students, as usual, were among the first to respond. They volunteered en masse for officer training schools. In the end very few were accepted; they were more needed for reconstruction work at home. Their enthusiasm, however, helped mobilize the people at large. Especially the propaganda teams, which they organized with great gusto to visit the factories and countryside, played an important part in arousing the people.

At first many people, in particular the peasants, were rather apathetic to the whole business of the war. The slogan "Resist America and Aid Korea" failed to impress them very much. America, even with its troops in Korea, seemed a long way off to the ordinary man, and as for the Koreans, throughout history the Chinese had somewhat looked down on them. This feeling had not been helped by the fact that before and during the war against Japan most of the Koreans whom they had known had been either opium peddlers or secret agents for the Japanese. Therefore they had no great feeling that the United States was a menace which must be resisted and certainly there was no enthusiasm for aiding the Koreans.

But their apathy disappeared when press and spokesmen pointed out the dangerous implications of the Seventh Fleet in Formosa, the revitalization of the American alliance with Chiang Kai-shek, the rearming of their deadly enemy, Japan, and the all too striking parallel between the path being taken by the American troops in Korea and that followed by the Japanese in their aggression against China almost twenty years before. It would be only a short step for the Americans to enter Manchuria and then sweep down on all of China just as the Japanese had done. They knew all too well that if the Americans did come they would bring Chiang and his Nationalists with them, and they also knew what would happen then to that newly won land, to their jobs, their unions, and even their very lives. To them the war then became a life-and-death struggle.

On November 21, as I walked across the campus I noticed a large group standing around the newspaper posted on the bulletin board in front of the library. From the stirrings of the crowd I could tell that something was up, so I discreetly edged my way into the group to see what was there. I was afraid it was bad news, but I hardly expected it to be as bad as it was. There on the bulletin board were two issues of the *People's Daily*. One had reproduced a page from *U.S. News & World Report* of October 13, showing a map of North Korea and Manchuria, with arrows pointing from Korea toward the various centers of northern China and giving the exact bombing distances to each. The other was a reproduction of a page from *Collier's* for September 16, containing an article by Brigadier General Fellers and another map with arrows from Japan and Korea, Okinawa and Formosa, driving into the heart of China.

As I stood there I felt my blood run cold and swore under my breath, "Don't those fools in the States think anybody else can read! Now no amount of talking will ever convince the Chinese we didn't intend to invade them!" The fact that both maps had been printed well before the Chinese had entered the war was not lost on the crowd. There was real anger in the murmuring I heard around me. "*Ta-ma-di!*" ("His mother's") swore one of my classmates to his friend. "They had everything figured out." As he turned to leave, his eyes met mine but they seemed to look right through me, and I heard him mutter through clenched teeth, "*Hao-le, wo men kan ba!*" ("Okay, we'll see about that!")

When these people became convinced they were quick to convince others. Thousands of groups of students, office clerks, politically advanced workers, peasants, and housewives spread into every factory, shop, and village to make speeches, display posters, sing improvised songs, and put on skits. These skits usually showed "courageous Chinese People's Volunteers" putting to flight a tall, villainous looking Uncle Sam with caricatures of Chiang Kai-shek and Japanese war lords following close at his heels like "running dogs." As these amateur propaganda teams reached everywhere, they aroused the whole population to form a mighty patriotic movement.

For us in the United States, propaganda is something more or less left to the professionals, who get paid for turning out millions of words for the press, radio, television, and films. But in China, where such mechanical mediums have relatively little currency except in the larger cities, propaganda becomes a business of the ordinary people, especially as they take part in these amateur propaganda teams. By our standards their art often appears extremely crude and simple; yet, because of the fact that it is something which comes from the people themselves and therefore expresses their own feelings, it has an appeal and force frequently beyond our comprehension.

This patriotic movement which swept through China was further intensified by a real sympathy which the Chinese soon came to have toward their Korean neighbors. As letters and reports describing the terrible destruction wrought by American bombing in North Korea came, they quickly related it to what they had suffered under the Japanese, and their former indifference and condescension gave way to the comradeship and admiration which one people develops for another in the face of mutual hardship and a common enemy.

The movement to "Resist America and Aid Korea" then came to affect the life of practically every man, woman, and child in China. In every village the peasants pledged themselves to make contributions of grain, cotton, and other vital materials by increasing production. They also organized themselves to support the relatives of those volunteering for service in Korea by working their land for them while they were away. In the cities almost every worker pledged to contribute a specific amount of his monthly income and at the same time to strive to increase his output and practice economy. The businessmen made large donations and promised to increase production and cut costs in order to support the war effort.

Of course, not all of this was as sincerely voluntary as

appeared on the surface. But, as far as I was able to learn, force as such was never used. In fact, it was not necessary, for in China, where "face" still meant a great deal, there was strong pressure to conform simply because the movement had the complete support of public opinion and anyone who did not go along with it felt like a social outcast.

Dell: At Yenching, the scene was a replica in miniature of what was going on all over the country. The students had all been caught up in a swirl of activity which had risen to such proportions that classes had been called off for a few days.

Though the students returned reluctantly to classes after the first few weeks of mobilization work throughout the countryside, the movement continued to play an important part in the life of the university. One of its most striking manifestations was the emphasis placed on physical education from a patriotic point of view. When the government called on the students to build up their bodies as well as their minds as a patriotic duty, the first gropings toward an active program were made. Extracurricular sports such as volley ball, basketball, track, and gymnastics were carried on every afternoon, and whenever one heard shrieks and embarrassed giggles one could be sure that a circle of boys and girls throwing a volley ball back and forth was in the vicinity.

The regularly scheduled gym classes consisted in part of body-building exercises with a faint flavor of guerrilla warfare practice. I went to these classes with mixed feelings. On the one hand I wanted to show off my skill. I felt that with my long legs, long arms, and years of training in various sports I could far outshine the fragile little Chinese girls. But on the other hand I was not very happy with the idea of throwing mock hand grenades or running with a twenty-pound pack on my back in companionship with people who were practicing these things as part of a "Resist America" program.

My arrogance and curiosity, plus the fact that the whole thing seemed like a big game far removed from any war-like implications, made me decide to participate, and I threw and jumped and ran with the others. What was my chagrin, however, when the final tests were run off in late spring, to find that my young classmates were not so weak and inferior as I had thought! In the 500-meter dash I strained my bursting lungs, but as I lumbered, gasping and redfaced, up to the finish line I found that six girls had come in ahead of me. It was a terrible blow to my ego and at that point I wished even more that the whole "Resist America and Aid Korea" movement would die a quick death.

But as the spring progressed the movement seemed to be intensified. The faculty and staff workers were as enthusiastic as the students, though their activities developed along different lines. One day in late spring Rick and I were sitting in the garden of an American missionary friend when an elderly man walked by with an armful of fans which he told us some of the university workers had made for sale. They were quite cheap and rather pretty, so we bought one made of split rushes and another of bright yellow and blue feathers. Upon closer examination we found that the four characters "Resist America Aid Korea" were imprinted on the fans. Anyone looking at our faces at that moment would undoubtedly have burst out laughing.

"Oh, well, the characters are only on one side," Rick said at last with a shrug of resignation, "and if we turn them over, we won't have to look at them."

The following week, when I went to the infirmary for a routine typhoid shot I was greeted at the door with the smell of doughnuts frying.

"Come on in and sample one of our doughnuts," said the nurse. "We're making them to raise money to buy planes."

I was caught in an awkward position. To have refused might have created an unpleasant situation, which we could ill afford, but I certainly had no wish to contribute a single penny to their old plane-buying campaign. However, since a few pennies spent on a couple of doughnuts would not have much effect on the total war situation, I finally bought two.

It seemed as if everywhere we turned we were reminded of the Korean war, and yet it all seemed to me so inconsequential. As I watched the university busily making fans and doughnuts, and cutting down on expenses wherever possible in order to give to the war effort, I could not help thinking, "What good will that measly little bit do against all the tanks, planes, bombs, and equipment we are pouring into Korea? These people are crazy!"

But what I forgot was that when 600 million people each contribute one penny, they have $6,000,000 to work with. The activities at the university could contribute only a small share to the total, it is true, but they were part of a gigantic movement which had the support of the people, and as such it represented a tremendous force.

Rick: The outbreak of the war had a far deeper effect on the intellectuals than merely rousing patriotic emotions of the moment. It marked the beginning of their final and complete break with the West.

One day in December Dell and I cycled to Tsinghua to visit our old friend Mr. Wu, whom we had not seen since the night he and Mr. Jao had come to dinner before we moved. We were not sure how we would be received, as we had become generally unpopular during the intervening months. As soon as he saw us, however, he threw open the door and shook hands with us with more emotion than I had ever before seen him display.

"Come in, come in," he said. "I heard you didn't get your exit permits and I've been worried about you."

I searched his face for an explanation. Had he heard anything about me? But, without another word, he turned and led the way into his living room. He asked us to sit down and then disappeared, to come back in a moment with three cups of tea. Our conversation soon turned to the Korean war.

Playing upon what I thought was his weak point, I said, "Irrespective of the justification of China's cause, for the country at the present time to become involved in a hopeless war against the United States, and for that matter the entire West, seems to me like national suicide. How will you ever complete the revolution and go on with your industrialization?"

"There wasn't anything else we could do," he replied simply. "We couldn't sit by and see our country invaded again."

I was left speechless, for though I knew that Wu's thinking had undergone considerable change during the past year and a half I had always had great respect for his judgment and knew he was not one to be influenced easily. If even he had been taken in so completely, there seemed little hope left.

If I needed any more to convince me, I certainly got it. A few days later, on December 23, I met Charlie Cheng at a wedding reception. He was an architect with one of the government's planning commissions, and his precise Oxford accent seemed completely out of keeping with his dirty, padded blue uniform and run-down boots. He appeared extremely friendly and willing to talk, so after the reception I invited him to the Peking Club for dinner and a drink.

There was a small dance going on that evening and, after tossing off several martinis and wolfing down the club's best pheasant dinner, he made himself the life of the party by dancing with all the embassy women there. As the club's steam heat, drinks, and dancing began to make themselves felt he tossed his padded jacket aside, revealing several layers of flannel pajamas and woolen underwear.

"It's a little cooler than this in the Planning Commission dormitory," he said with a grin. "In fact, we have no heat at all there now."

"How do you stand it?" I asked sympathetically. "I should think it would be impossible to do any work at all under such conditions."

"Well, one gets used to it, though it certainly isn't like the old days. But, you know, there is something about it—really doing constructive work for a change. When I was in Nanking before liberation all I did was sit around in a big office and draw up occasional plans which I knew never had a chance of developing into anything. Now, for the first time since I returned to China, I can see my drawings being transformed into reality."

"How much chance do you think there will be for any continued building with this war going on?"

"That remains to be seen. They're certainly keeping me busy enough at present," was his answer.

I then began hammering away on the old line that, by going into Korea, China was merely pulling Russian chestnuts out of the fire.

By now Cheng had begun to feel all those martinis a little and, with a flushed face, he said, "My friend, I was in Shanghai when it was liberated. I had seen armies marching up and down China for over thirty years and that was the first time I ever saw troops move through an area without so much as damaging a stalk of grain or taking as much as a stick of wood. I don't know anything about your international politics but I know this, when our government says it is a people's government I believe it and I support it, because only a people's government and a people's army could do the things I saw them do in Shanghai and since. And when our government says we must go into Korea to defend our own land I believe it, and you can jolly well take your Russian chestnuts and st—"

With an embarrassed glance at Dell he stopped talking for a moment. Then, leaping to his feet, he bowed from the waist with exaggerated politeness. "May I have the next dance?"

When these changes came to affect even my closest friends, people whom I had considered absolutely loyal to the ideas I represented, I began to feel the world must have gone mad.

Our best friend at Yenching, George Lee, was an American-born Chinese who had served in the U.S. Army with distinction during the war. He was an anti-Communist liberal and our ideas had always seemed to go along similar lines. He had also been one of my best information contacts at Yenching. He too had been worried about what might happen to him when the Chinese first entered the Korean war, and in November, 1950, while Dell and I were trying to leave he had sweated off several pounds wondering whether he dared ask for an exit permit or not. Finally he decided against it, because he believed that if I were not given one he certainly would not get it. Since the problem of dual citizenship had not yet been settled and he could still be legally regarded as a Chinese citizen, he felt that his position was even more dangerous than mine.

Naturally, his feelings toward the People's Government could hardly be considered friendly, but during the ensuing months something happened to him, with the result that the once friendly discussions we engaged in almost every day turned into violent arguments which often left us both shaking. Formerly we had both damned the Truman administration's policies toward China, but there was a difference which, though at the time seemingly unimportant, now became the basis of our disagreement. I felt that Truman's policies were stupid and had achieved the exact opposite of their intentions—the restoration of American influence in China. George had also wished to see the return of American influence there to a certain extent, especially since, as a citizen of both countries, his own personal interests were involved, but he had damned Truman's policies more for what he considered their basic lack of principle and justice.

A climax was reached one evening in March during one of our endless arguments about the Korean war. I angrily asserted, "By going into Korea the Chinese have brought us to the verge of a third world war, and whatever you may try to say that is good about them is nullified by that."

George's round face flushed slightly as he replied, "Listen, Rick, you know perfectly well that when MacArthur crossed the 38th Parallel he was on his way to Manchuria. The Chinese could not stand for that. Besides, what business had the United States intervening in a completely internal Korean question in the first place?"

"The North Koreans were the aggressor," I interrupted hotly.

"Nonsense! How can a people aggress against themselves? The 38th Parallel was never meant to be more than a line for the demarcation of temporary American and Russian occupation. The problem of Korean unification has been going on ever since the war ended and there has been fighting back and forth across that line for some time. Hardly a week went by without Rhee shouting about marching to the north. Whether it was North Korea or South Korea which made the first push on June 25 is merely academic. They were Koreans settling their own problems. What right had the U.S. to come 6,000 miles across the Pacific to force Syngman Rhee down their throats?"

"In the first place it is not the United States but the United Nations—"

"Nuts! Truman ordered American troops into Korea before the U.N. could say anything about it. The only thing the British and French could do was tag along whether they liked it or not. It's like the business of supporting Chiang Kai-shek all over again. Only this time the brass in Washington decided to throw their own troops in too."

"Yeah, well what about the Russians?"

"Well, what about them? The Russians haven't sent their troops to intervene in Korea, but we sure have. The trouble with you, Rick, is you can't see anything but Russian red. If the Koreans want to kick out an evil old rascal like Rhee and unite their country, it's the Russians. If the Chinese don't like the Americans taking over their territory, Formosa, it's the Russians. If the Indo-Chinese have had enough of the French, it's—"

"I don't care. The Chinese practically set the entire world on fire just when we were about to have peace."

"What peace? If MacArthur could have set himself up on the Yalu he would have been in Manchuria within a year. As I said before, China had to go in for her own protection."

"Fine protection! You know what it'll mean if this war spreads. China will be finished. What could it do in a modern, atomic war?"

George laughed. "In a country like China with no great concentration of industry, what good will your atomic bombs do?"

"By God! They'll do plenty," I exploded. "Maybe there are no big factories, but you know what a few bombs dropped along the Yellow River dikes would do. The Chinese would be helpless. Your guerrilla warfare is no good against that."

As I raged on, George's face went white. "Rick," he said with suppressed emotion, "I am an American and I've always been proud of it, but if the United States were to do something like that—I don't care, I'm through." He then continued, more quietly, "In the past few months I've thought over a lot of things. Here we Americans are supporting every lousy, stinking, two-bit crook in Asia from Syngman Rhee and Chiang Kai-shek to Bao Dai, up and down. And now that the Chinese at last have a government which is really trying to do something for its people—what do we do but try to cut its throat? Just take a look around you. You know what it was like before under the Nationalists, and how much better it is now. They may make a lot of mistakes but I think they're on the right track."

I stamped out of the room and slammed the door. For a moment I stood trembling, realizing I had lost. None of my arguments seemed to faze him or anyone else, and I knew I had gone too far in the business about atomic bombs. I thought to myself, "Why do these people have to get so damned moral about everything? Don't they know there's no such thing in practical politics?"

I was not completely alone in my feeling of hatred toward the People's Government. There were a number of Chinese whose opposition was no less active than mine. Right after liberation the government had adopted a very liberal policy in its treatment of all ex-Nationalist officials and secret agents. Except for those who had committed extremely serious crimes, such as murder, all that was required of them was to register and refrain from any counterrevolutionary activity. By far the greater part of them responded favorably to this lenient policy and soon became at least passive supporters of the new order. I knew at that time several ex-Nationalist agents who became respected members of the new society. One was the head of a large warehouse, another a leader in cooperative work, and a third a well-known writer on agricultural problems.

There were many, however, who merely took advantage of this leniency either to continue their activities on the chance that if they were caught they would be given only light sentences or to go underground while waiting for what they considered the certain return of the Americans and Nationalists in the event of a third world war. When the war broke out in Korea, and especially after the Inchon landing, they began to feel that the time was near, and when China went into Korea they were sure that the war was on.

This brought about an upsurge in counterrevolutionary activity which, by the end of 1950, was rapidly getting out of hand. A wave of killings and sabotage swept the country. Just outside Yenching two people that I knew of were brutally murdered. Shots were fired into the windows of private homes, houses set on fire, and wells poisoned. The government was forced to take drastic action and began to tighten its control of former Nationalist agents. In February, 1951, the Standing Committee of the People's Government passed the Articles for the Suppression of Counterrevolutionaries, under which the death sentence or life imprisonment could be meted out for almost any form of active espionage or counterrevolutionary activity.

This may seem rather harsh, and to me at the time it seemed nothing short of "Red Terror," but to the Chinese who were being shot at or who were finding their wells poisoned and houses set on fire the measure was wholly welcome. Even the intellectuals in the universities, who were by nature opposed to any extremes, supported the Articles.

One day a professor at Yenching asked me if I felt under any strain because of the measures taken to suppress the counterrevolution. Lying through my teeth, I said I felt under no strain myself, but I then took the opportunity to say I felt that the movement seemed to be a reversal of the former lenient policies which had won so much support for the revolution and was the result of the evils of a dictatorship.

He nodded and said, "We must be careful to see that justice is done. We must do all we can to make sure that not one man goes to jail who doesn't belong there. But I'm afraid when you say this is an evil growing out of dictatorship you are rather unfair. In China we have always had a dictatorship. It is just a question of whether it is a dictatorship of the majority or of a small, reactionary ruling clique like the Nationalists. I was in Kunming at Lien-da University in 1946 when Li Gung-bo and the famous scholar Wen-I-do, who had helped found the Democratic League, were brutally assassinated by Nationalist agents. Our public meetings in the university were fired on, many of us were attacked and beaten as we walked down the streets, and I myself, with some of my friends, was forced to flee.

"Our experience has taught us Chinese one thing, that if there is to be any democracy for the people it must be based on a suppression of the White terrorism of the reactionaries. You call us a dictatorship, and quite frankly we are just that. But we are a dictatorship of all the decent people in the country over the scum which would try to force us to return to the starvation and corruption of the Nationalist days."

Other people with whom I talked pointed out that in spite of the harsh provisions of the law relatively few people were actually executed and Article 14 stipulated that those who gave themselves up voluntarily or who made complete confessions and showed some willingness to repent might have their sentences reduced or even suspended. My violent opposition to the law, of course, was more than just academic. It was in accordance with Article 6, concerning specific acts of espionage, that I eventually went to prison.

Dell: As the counterattack against the Nationalist agents and saboteurs gathered momentum, during the spring of 1951, Rick and I began to experience repercussions in our own lives.

When we had enrolled in Yenching we had rented a room on the third floor of one of the Chinese professors' homes, in order to have a place to study together during the day. One day in mid-March, as Rick was climbing the stairs to our room the professor stopped him and, after shuffling his feet embarrassedly for a moment, said in an apologetic voice that he was sorry but we would have to get out immediately. He was being subjected to a good deal of adverse criticism by other people on the campus for allowing us to use the room and he could not afford to have his own position jeopardized by associating with us. It was a blow to be faced with this fresh manifestation of suspicion, but there was nothing we could do.

Then came the problem of what to do with our furniture. We decided to find a house in Cheng-fu, the village outside the east gate of the university. If we had to remain for some time, we ought at least to be comfortable. A servant for one of the missionary groups said a house he had bought and was refinishing would be ready for us to rent in a week or two and we could store our things in a room of his house while waiting. It seemed an ideal solution. The furniture was stored and we looked forward to having a home of our own again. The week or two had long since passed, however, and we seemed no nearer our goal. Our prospective landlord told us that the family still in the house refused to move and we would have to wait until he could find some way of getting them out. It soon became clear that this was only an excuse to cover the fact that he had been criticized so severely in the village for preparing to rent to Americans under suspicion that he did not dare go through with the deal.

It seemed as if we could become no more isolated than we were, and yet all these factors failed to bring us to our senses. That spring we ate all our meals with an American who taught piano at the university. A Chinese friend came in one evening and said to us seriously, "You ought to be more careful when you go to the British Embassy and talk about what's going on in the university with those people. These things have a way of getting known, you know, and I have it on good authority that the security police have just about decided to pull you two in."

My jaw dropped as I was taken aback by the force of this outspoken warning but, recovering myself, I said resentfully, "But what in the world do they think we're doing? It's pretty bad when you can't even go visit your friends."

"Yes, but Dell, whether you realize it or not, when you tell certain people in the British Embassy about what's going on here you are providing them with intelligence and the Chinese don't like it."

Rick said hotly, "That's ridiculous! I'm an American, and those people are my friends. I'll see whom I damn well please. Besides, the British are looking out after American interests and I have a perfect right to go there."

"It's not that," replied our friend. "You can go where you please and have all the friends you want, but just be careful what you tell them. Anyway, I'm just trying to tell you for your own good." He could see that his well-intentioned words had only made us angry and quickly changed the subject.

In spite of this warning, I kept on closing my eyes to the scene around me and tended to become impatient with both Harriet and Rick, who, I felt, dramatized the situation too much. Harriet said to us very confidentially one Sunday morning while we were watching a volley ball game in the British compound, "Some of my friends at Peking University have told me that if we can get through this movement to suppress counterrevolutionaries without any trouble, we'll be okay and won't have to worry."

Trying to hide the exasperation in my voice, I said, "What has that got to do with us? We're not Chinese, you know."

"Harriet's right, though," Rick added quickly. "As far as the Chinese are concerned, there would be no counter-revolutionaries if our government weren't supporting Chiang Kai-shek."

Although I refused to face such realities there was one thing which did disturb me, and it was to play a decisive role in my attitude after my arrest. That was fear of torture. It seemed as if every movie we saw that spring had at least one torture scene in it, either of a Japanese working over a Chinese or a Nationalist agent grilling and abusing an innocent peasant. I could not bear to watch the scenes and invariably closed my eyes until they were over. Then, too, the reading of such books as 1984 did not help matters any.

I dreamed about these painful episodes several times and one day, unable to hold in any longer, I broke into tears and said to Rick, "I don't care whether they put us in prison for the rest of our lives, but I just don't think I could take torture. I'm frightened."

Poor Rick was at a loss to comfort me because he certainly was not in any better frame of mind, but he did say something which occurred to me several months later. "If we are arrested," he said, "the only thing to do is tell the truth, or at least never let yourself be caught in a direct lie."

After it became obvious that we could not find a place to live at the university, we began looking for a house in the city. We asked several friends to keep an eye out for us, but here we met with the same reluctance to rent to us as Americans. It was only by agreeing to pay an exorbitant rent that, near the end of May, 1951, we finally obtained a small place on Hsin Kai Lu in the east city. It was a house built around a tiny courtyard about ten by twenty feet. Just at this time, the couple with whom Harriet had been living obtained their exit permits and we asked Harriet to move in with us.

As soon as we signed the lease we started to collect our belongings and borrowed beds, a sofa, chairs, tables, lamps, pots and pans, and everything else we could think of from friends in the city. When we had at last brought everything together under one roof I sighed with relief and said, "I'm so tired of sleeping in one place, eating in another, studying in another, and having our belongings scattered all over the place, I'd just like to sit down in this house and not move for a month!"

I was to get my wish—and then some!

4

Dell: July 25, 1951, began like any other summer day in Peking. Dressed in shorts and thin short-sleeved shirts, we still felt pressed down by the heat. My arms stuck to the desk and little trickles of perspiration kept running down my face and neck as I struggled over an analysis of ancient Chinese literary criticism. Rick had a class with his Chinese tutor, Mr. Chi, that morning and as they sat in the living room I could hear Rick trying to pump him for some information about the rumored drought in the countryside.

Just before noon the doorbell rang and a moment later our cook, old Wang, ushered a rather shy young policeman into our study-bedroom. After asking him to sit down I explained that Rick was in the midst of a class.

"Should I call him?"

"No," the young man shook his head in reply. "It is nothing important." But he went on to ask several times if this were the house of the American, Li Ko.

I assured him it was and even wrote out our names in Chinese and English so there would be no doubt. With a vague promise to return in the afternoon the officer finally left, and I promptly forgot about the incident. With arrest practically upon us I still felt no forewarning in the visit of this policeman.

We had invited guests for dinner that evening, some British friends, including a First Secretary in the Negotiation Mission and a manager of the Hong Kong & Shanghai Bank in Peking.

At 4:30 Rick rose from his desk, stretched, and said, "I think I'll knock off for a while and make the ice cream.

If I don't get started, that cake of ice will have melted down so there won't be enough left to pack the freezer."

As he started out the door he turned back, as if to ask me something, but at that moment there was a loud knocking at the big front gate.

We watched old Wang, looking hot and peevish, cross the courtyard to open the door, and in a moment the place was swarming with men and women dressed in uniform. I took only a cursory glance at them and then, thinking, "It must be a health inspection group or something like that. Rick is up. Let him take care of them," turned back to my poetry.

I heard Rick go into the living room with some of them and then the low murmur of voices. It was impossible to distinguish what was being said, but with my curiosity at last aroused I knew it was useless to try to concentrate on my work any further. I was just wondering if I should go into the living room too when Rick came back into our room, followed by several policemen. As I looked up I caught a glimpse through the open door of Harriet, standing tense and frightened in the living room.

"I guess I'll have to go with them," Rick said in a strained voice.

I started to exclaim, "Go with them?" but the words stuck in my throat as one of the men said gruffly, "You are not permitted to talk to each other."

Rick changed into his trousers and leather shoes. As he went out into the courtyard and sat down on one of our wicker chairs I noticed a couple of helmeted soldiers with rifles standing by the wall. It sank in finally that this was no health inspection group. Rick was being arrested!

Someone told me to go out and sit on the low narrow verandah which faced the courtyard. As I sat down I gazed at Rick, who looked white and miserable. Movie scenes in which the heroine throws herself on her beloved as he is led away to prison flashed through my mind. But I shrank from making any display and instead smiled what I hoped would serve as a message of encouragement and love. If anything, my smile seemed to make Rick look even more miserable, and I was about to throw all caution to the winds and run over to him anyway when I was told to go into the living room.

"Play along with them. Don't give them a chance to make the situation any worse than it is," a voice inside me cautioned. I followed the guard into the living room and when he asked, "How much rent do you pay for this place?" answered meekly, "1,300,000 JMP." (People's Currency—about $65.)

The man's voice had not been disagreeable but I could not forget the Tommy gun laid across his lap as he sat. I could see nothing of the courtyard from where I sat, and could only speculate on what was happening from the sounds which drifted my way. Soon the front gate banged loudly and a jeep started up. Not long after, the sounds were repeated and things began to quiet down. No one came into the living room, where the guard and I continued to sit in silence. I began to think, "They must have taken Rick and Harriet away, but they've left me. If they were going to take me too, wouldn't they have done so by now? Maybe they're going to leave me here. But why? Rick, when am I going to see you again?"

Rick: I had looked in bewilderment at the small army of khaki-clad men and women who surged into the courtyard as old Wang opened the gate, but by the time I was led into the living room and presented with a warrant I knew the long-expected day of my arrest had at last arrived.

Even back in the summer of 1949 I had begun to realize that my connection with ONI (Office of Naval Intelligence) and the Consulate might some day prove troublesome. But, still quite sure of myself, I had only determined to be a little more careful. I had burned the mass of material I had been collecting to turn over to Naval Intelligence on my return home, and from then on I tried to make all my activities appear like those of any ordinary student. My relations with British and American officials had ostensibly been purely social. My trips into the countryside had been motivated simply by a desire to visit cultural landmarks. When I discussed politics with Chinese it was in the role of a well-intentioned student with an academic interest in China.

This pretense of being a simple student was dealt a shattering blow when in the summer of 1950 the Marine Corps, apparently unaware of the fact that there had been a revolution in China, had sent me my health record and orders to report to the nearest naval hospital or U.S. public health authorities for a physical examination. Before I could get word back to them I was showered with Marine Corps letters and bulletins all addressed to 1st Lt. W. A. Rickett.

From the time of the Korean war on, I assumed that I was being carefully watched, though I had no actual evidence of it. Of course, after we failed to receive exit permits I knew definitely that I was under constant scrutiny. People who had no reason for being friendly with me suddenly became so. I was constantly on the lookout for traps. Some of them I felt I had avoided, but others, I discovered afterward, I had not.

For instance, in June, 1951, just before I left Yenching I received a note from a former student at Tsinghua, who had been one of my best contacts there. I had not seen him for almost a year and was surprised when he said he wanted to see me again. A few days later we invited him to lunch and our old friendly relations were reestablished. In his last days at Tsinghua Deng had begun to turn "progressive," but now he told me that he had changed his mind again, primarily because his father, a Nationalist official on Formosa, had been declared a counterrevolutionary and there was some chance that his property in Peking would be confiscated. This seemed quite logical to me, and after checking up on Deng as well as I could it seemed that he had indeed reverted to much of his original antipathetic attitude toward the new regime. So it was not long before I began using him as a source of information again.

One day in July he told me that he wanted very much to contact his father but was afraid to send letters through ordinary mail. Hoping to cement our relations even further, I told him I had ways of sending letters out secretly and could do the same for him. Deng promised to write the letter and give it to me. But the next time he arrived, he said he had decided to think about it for a while. That day Dell and I had bought a small gift for his new baby girl and, as he was leaving, I gave it to him. From the expression on his face when he took it I knew something was wrong. He left, hardly saying a word. As I walked back to the living room I had a queasy feeling. Now they not only knew I was collecting information but that I had ways of getting it out.

All these things flashed through my mind as I stood looking at the warrant. Where else had I slipped up? Now that arrest had come at last, how was I going to handle it? Trying to pretend an almost calm indifference, I asked if I might change into some suitable clothes. The tall, lean, rugged-looking security policeman in charge nodded his head. I went into our study-bedroom, where Dell was sitting and, as she looked up questioningly, tried to make my voice sound reassuring. "I guess I'll have to go with them." The guard abruptly cut off any further conversation and stepped between us while I hastily slipped into slacks and leather shoes.

My fumbling fingers had barely finished tying the shoelaces when the guard motioned me out into the courtyard and told me to sit down on a chair. Soon Dell came out and sat on another chair on the verandah. At the sight of her drawn face my heart turned over. What had I let her in for? Overcome with shame and remorse, I could only stare at the ground. When I finally looked again in her direction, her faint smile of encouragement served only to increase my despair. Just then a man stepped out and told Dell to go into the living room. I could hear their voices and wondered how long it would be before I saw her again.

In the room back of me I could hear Harriet talking to

some policewomen. She came out shortly and as she passed near me I heard her mumble, "It looks like this is it." She went out the gate and I heard a jeep start up.

In a few minutes the security policeman who had served the warrant came back and told me to come out to the jeep. He followed and quickly climbed in after me. With a jerk the jeep started rolling through the hot, crowded streets toward the northern part of the city. Unhandcuffed and accompanied by only one guard and the driver as I was, for a moment I gave full rein to my imagination. Should I try to escape? In all the spy stories I had read or seen in the movies the hero could easily have taken advantage of such a situation and made a break for it. But I was inclined to hesitate. In the first place where would I go? With my big nose, blond hair, and light eyes, I could not possibly hide. Besides, though my companion was slightly shorter than I and weighed far less, I was sure he could make two of me in a fight. Even more, supposing I did get away, that would not solve Dell's problem.

Finally the jeep entered a long narrow *hu-tung* (lane) and came to a stop before a large red gate. It was quickly opened by some guards and we drove into an enormous courtyard which looked like a drill field. I was told to get out and follow the guard across the field, but just before we reached a small gate leading into another courtyard he ordered me to halt and motioned to a sentry on duty to keep an eye on me while he went off. The sentry, with the point of his gun, directed me into a small garage close to where I was standing and then told me to squat down and wait.

As I squatted there, looking into the barrel of the guard's Tommy gun, there came to me a picture out of my childhood of the St. Valentine's Day massacre in Chicago. These gruesome thoughts were quickly dispelled, however, when the policeman returned and ordered me to follow him into a small office where I was searched, fingerprinted, and told to turn in my watch. The young woman in charge asked me if I needed my glasses. I nodded and she allowed me to keep them.

Another man wearing the faded blue cadre uniform of a government worker appeared and led me out into a courtyard flanked on either side by long one-story whitewashed buildings. Closing the other end of the courtyard from where we entered was a two-story affair with the traditional upsweeping Chinese tile roof. Flower beds ablaze with dahlias, zinnias, and giant cannas lined both sides of a cobblestone walk in the center. The picture was that of a typical rich residential compound and from the courtyard it appeared little different from those serving as dwellings throughout Peking. The only discordant notes were the armed guards and the wooden palisades around the outside of each window. I later learned that this courtyard was known as the west prison compound.

I had little more time to observe my new surroundings when I was ordered to enter the building on the left. Just inside we turned into a long, dim corridor which ran the length of the building and was lined on either side with solid wooden doors. We came to a halt before that of cell No. 3. The cadre threw open the door and motioned me in. As soon as I had crossed the threshold, I heard the door slam behind and the metal bolt shot home with a loud, rasping noise.

I stood peering around while my eyes became accustomed to the gloom. The cell was not large. It appeared to be about ten by eleven feet, with a rough concrete floor and rather dirty whitewashed walls. Most of the room was taken up by a *kang*, a wooden platform about two feet high which, in Chinese fashion, served as a bed at night and a place to sit during the day. There was a rather large barred window in the wall opposite the door, but it did not afford much light because of the wooden palisade on the outside.

Seated cross-legged on the *kang* were five Chinese. Except for one, all were stripped to the waist because of the heat. Three were dressed in old nondescript khaki uniform pants; another, a tall, lean man, was wearing dirty, rumpled, Western-style slacks and shirt, and rimless glasses which immediately typed him as an intellectual. The fifth, a huge, bull-like fellow, was clad only in thin white cotton, Chinese-style, trousers. He was vigorously wielding a palm-leaf fan as the sweat rolled down his giant frame.

Were these men prisoners, or—? Ever since the summer of 1950, when I had begun reading such books as Koestler's *Darkness at Noon* and Orwell's *1984*, my mind had become more and more filled with thoughts of the torture which would certainly follow if I were arrested. The three men in khaki might be security police and the bull looked like someone who had just stepped out of a Hollywood horror story. It seemed as if even an interpreter had been provided in the person of the intellectual.

As I began wondering how much torture I could stand and hoping I could pass out quickly if it came, one of the men, a slightly built, sharp-faced individual of about forty, pointed to the *kang* and told me to sit down. Kicking off my shoes, I sat gingerly on the edge and waited to see what would happen next.

"What's your name?" the man asked in a mild tone, and when I answered he followed with, "Are you a German?"

"No, I'm an American."

His eyes opened wide. "Priest?" he asked.

"No, student."

This excited his interest even further.

"My name's Jeng. The government has appointed me to act as leader of this cell."

Then, pointing to the intellectual who was sitting beside him, he continued, "This is Ju. Maybe you know him. He was a dean at the Catholic University in Tientsin."

I did not know the man, but that spring I had read in the papers about the arrest of some French Catholic priests and Chinese at Tsin Ku University and I looked at Ju with interest.

He smiled at me and asked in Chinese, "Can you speak French?"

"Not as well as I can Chinese."

"Then that isn't very good, is it?" remarked Jeng. "Have you had anything to eat yet?"

"No, I just got here."

"Then I'll get you something."

Swinging his body around and slipping his bare feet into a pair of badly worn Chinese cloth shoes, he shuffled to the door where he shouted for the guard. I certainly did not feel in the mood for eating and started to say "Never mind," but then I thought it might be a good idea to keep up as much of a pretense as possible, and so remained quiet. When the guard came and opened a small window in the cell door Jeng told him a new prisoner had just arrived who had had nothing to eat and asked if it would be possible to get him some food.

As the guard went off Jeng came back to the *kang* and introduced the others. One of the other men, who must have been in his middle forties from the looks of his bald, bullet-shaped head and heavy, tough-looking features, was named Gwo. Jeng introduced him as an ex-cop. The other, about my age, with a pock-marked face and shaven skull, was called Meng. He had been an officer in an underground Catholic youth army which had been organized by Nationalist agents before the liberation. The bull, whom I had pictured as my torturer, was a harmless butcher named Lu. His brother had been a Nationalist agent, and Lu had made the unfortunate mistake of allowing him to use his house as a hideout and thus had been arrested as an accomplice.

While the introductions had been taking place I noticed that both Gwo and Meng were wearing ankle chains. I did not quite dare ask about this, but it did help convince me that they were really prisoners and not security police. Casting another glance at Lu's enormous scarred head and hamlike hands, I breathed a sigh of relief.

For a while we sat talking about where and what I had been studying and how I had come to China. Then Jeng suddenly asked me, "Why are you here?"

I shook my head, pretending I did not know.

Jeng's face became tight and stern. "You don't know?" he snapped. "Do you know what this place is?"

"I guess it's a jail."

"You guess? It's a jail all right, but it's not an ordinary jail. This is the Tsao-lan-dzu Hutung Detention Quarters. The only people who come here are spies and counter-revolutionaries. Discipline is different here from other prisons. You see that fence around the window? That's so you can't look out, and when you leave the cell you've got to keep your head down. Don't look around and don't talk to anyone. If you break discipline, get tough, or insist on lying, you'll end up in handcuffs and those." He nodded toward Gwo's ankle chains. "And let me tell you, when you're called in by the investigating judge for questioning you'd better tell it straight. They've got you cold or they wouldn't have brought you here in the first place. Now do you know why you're here?"

"Well, I came to China on a government scholarship. It probably has something to do with that," I said, hoping to avoid any further argument.

"All right," said Jeng, "but believe me, you'd better come clean. You know what the law is. If you don't confess, they can take you out and shoot you tomorrow."

It was only later that I learned how much Jeng had over-simplified the process of Chinese law, but in spite of this his threat failed to make much of an impression on me. My initial fright was beginning to wear away a little, and now for the moment death and even torture seemed rather unreal, something one only read about in books and newspapers. Still, I felt much relieved when Jeng's lecture was interrupted by the arrival of one of the prison mess men with a bowl of string beans and a *wo-tou*, a type of bread made of steamed corn and bean flour and shaped like a cone. He even provided me with a spoon, but I rejected that for chopsticks which Big Lu brought out from a basin under the *kang*.

Up to that time I had still clung to the illusion that I was taking my arrest quite calmly, but as I took my first bite I realized how I had been deceiving myself. At another time the string beans would probably have been quite palatable, but now they stuck in my throat. So did the *wo-tou*. Try as I would to eat it, the food would not go

down. My attempt to make a good showing had boomer-
anged and revealed for all to see the nervous state I was
in. Finally, with almost a full *wo-tou* and three-quarters
of a bowl of beans still staring me in the face I had to give
up. Shrinking inwardly from the expected blast from Jeng,
I said hesitantly, "I guess I'm not very hungry after all."

Jeng's thin lips twisted into a half smile and instead
of blasting me he merely said, "All right, we can send the
wo-tou back, but you've already eaten part of the beans
and we can't throw 'em away, so you'll have to finish them
tomorrow. Put 'em in that green basin under the *kang*
and cover them over. They won't go bad, don't worry."

I then had a chance to look around the cell a little more
closely. Under the *kang* there were two large, green pottery
basins, which I discovered later were used to carry food
and drinking water. A rice bowl and chopsticks for each
man were piled in one of these basins and the other was
filled with water. Alongside were several chipped enamel
drinking cups with toothbrushes sticking out the tops and
a cake of yellow soap which I later learned belonged to
Big Lu but was used by everyone. Stretched between two
pegs driven into the front wall was a string on which were
hung a number of dirty face towels. On the floor beneath
them was a tin wash basin full of water. A covered bucket
used as a urinal had been placed in the corner away from
the door. Jeng explained that there was a latrine call twice
a day when everyone went out. More serious business was
to be conducted then unless one was ill, and then it was
possible to gain permission to make a special trip.

On a corner of the *kang* there was a large, disorderly
pile of quilts and bundles of personal belongings. The
kang itself, made of rough wooden planks supported on
sawhorses, was covered by a tattered, woven straw mat.
From the ceiling hung a single, bare light bulb, which
could not have been more than fifteen watts in size and
was so covered with dust that it gave off just enough light
to keep one from going to sleep and not enough for working or reading.

After I had put the bowl away we sat around talking.

As Jeng asked me questions about myself it did not take me long to realize that here was an old professional agent. His questions came one right after another, weaving in and out and keeping me off balance completely. At the end of an hour or so I felt that he knew more about me than I knew about myself.

Finally a whistle blew and everyone jumped up. Jeng informed me it was 9:15 and time for bed. Big Lu pulled an old piece of straw matting out from under the *kang* and stretched himself out on top of it on the floor, the only place that seemed to afford enough room for his enormous bulk. Jeng told me to sleep on the *kang* along with him and the others, and we all lay down, feet to the wall, side by side like so many sardines.

Soon I was surrounded by deep, regular breathing. Pulling out a handkerchief and putting it across my eyes to shield them from the light, I attempted to settle down to sleep but the room was still stifling hot and a persistent mosquito droned in my ear. Minutes passed slowly. I could hear the soft pad of the guard walking up and down the corridor outside and then someone placing padlocks on the doors. As he noisily locked our door I had the first feeling of really being in jail. It suddenly came to me that I would not be going home that night.

"I'd better get some sleep," I thought, but my mind kept going round and round. What was happening to Dell? Had she been arrested, too? What an awful thing for our guests, to be met by security police when they arrived for dinner. Why hadn't I been called up for questioning? I wished they would hurry up and get it over with.

After a while I must have dozed off, only to be awakened by the fearful grating sound of the bolt being slid back. The door was thrown open and a voice called my Chinese name, "Li Ko." As I struggled to collect my wits, I felt Jeng nudging me and heard him say, "Get going! The supervisor is calling you to report for interrogation." I pulled on my shirt, slipped into my shoes, and stepped over Big Lu on my way to the door.

The supervisor motioned me toward the entrance of the

cell block where a guard was waiting for me with a pistol in his hand. I was ordered into the courtyard and directed across the big drill field where the jeep had stopped that afternoon. As I walked along, the night air felt chilly after the heat of the room and I began to shiver a little. I knew, though, that the shivering was not all due to cold. It was part nerves. I had been under a strain for a long time and now the big moment was at hand. I kept telling myself to take it easy and, above all, not get excited.

We entered a small rectangular courtyard with a long, low building running the length of one side and a high wall topped by an electric fence closing in the other three. The guard instructed me to halt before one of several doors in the building and shouted a few words I could not understand to someone inside. Waving his pistol, the guard then told me to enter.

I pulled back the lattice screen over the door and entered a large room. Along one side, under several open windows, were a sofa and a couple of easy chairs. At the end of the room were two large desks, behind which sat a young woman and a man about my own age in security police uniform. His strong, squarish face was set off by a small mustache and piercing, black eyes. A single, straight-backed chair had been placed a little way out from the wall opposite the desks. The guard motioned me over to it with his pistol and then, keeping me covered all the time, went to sit beside the man who was to be my interrogator. I stood behind the chair, waiting. After looking me over for some time the investigating judge asked me my name and told me to sit down.

"Why are you here?" he asked abruptly.

"I don't know."

"You don't know? You're here because you're a spy."

"I'm not a spy."

"Don't make me laugh. We know all about you. You're a spy for the American government and an enemy of the Chinese people."

"I am not," I said with annoyance. "I've always been very sympathetic toward the Chinese people and the Chinese revolution. I never liked the Nationalists from the start."

"That'll be enough of that," was his sharp reply. "Stand up!"

"I guess this is where it starts," I thought, and braced myself for what was to come. But instead he proceeded to tell me in firm, measured tones that the government had known about my espionage activities for a long time. I had been allowed ample opportunity to change my attitude but had refused to do so. Since I had persisted in violating the Chinese law I had been arrested in accordance with the Articles for the Suppression of Counterrevolutionaries. I was now in a military court where, if I made a full confession, I would receive lenient treatment. Otherwise—well, I knew what the punishment for espionage was.

"You're young," he went on, taking up a stubby Western-type pipe and filling it from a package of cheap Chinese tobacco which lay on his desk. "You've got a long life ahead of you. Don't make a mistake. It would be a shame for a young man like you to sacrifice his life for that bunch on Wall Street."

At the mention of Wall Street, I almost felt like laughing. I wanted to tell him Roosevelt had taken care of that place long ago and he was almost twenty years behind the times. Fortunately, before I could make any such stupid reply he waved his hand and said, as if he had already dismissed me from his mind, "Go back to your cell and think it over."

Walking out into the open air, with the guard at my heels, I congratulated myself for the ease with which I had come through the first encounter. At the same time I knew that this was only the beginning. Back in the cell I lay down and prepared to go to sleep, but it seemed as if my head had no sooner touched the makeshift pillow than the door was thrown open with a clang again. A blue-clad supervisor appeared with instructions for Jeng to help me write out a list of all the books I had been using and a résumé of my studies, including information as to where my notes had been kept. Jeng had just about finished writ-

ng up the material when I was called out for another trip
to the interrogation room.

After ordering me to sit down the judge began again,
this time adopting an entirely new approach. Where was
I born? What was my family background and what did
my mother and father do? Did I have any brothers and
sisters? What did my brother do? Where had I gone to
school? What books had I liked to read? What about detective stories? How had I become interested in China?
He went into every detail of my childhood and youth,
and kept me going for what must have been a couple of
hours. Then again I was sent back to the cell, but I had
hardly a chance to stretch out on the *kang* next to Jeng
before I was called out a third time. This was repeated
once more before the judge's patient probing had gained
him a thorough picture of my life story.

When I left the interrogation room the last time, it was
already the beginning of another hot, dry day. As I passed
by the wild array of flowers filling the prison courtyard
I could not help but feel struck by the incongruity of their
cheerful colors and the grim purpose of the place they
served to decorate.

Entering the cell door, I found the others already up
and brushing their teeth. Jeng motioned me to the wash
basin on the floor and threw me his towel. The water felt
good on my hot, tired eyes, and I did not care how dirty
it was. As I dried myself with Jeng's towel Big Lu, the
tall, finished brushing his teeth and, after carefully rins-
ing his toothbrush, he handed it to me. I stood staring
down at it not knowing what to do. My ideas of sanitation
made me a little squeamish about taking it, but I was
deeply moved by his show of generosity and rather than
possibly hurt his feelings dumped a little of his tooth-
powder on it and began brushing away. Never had I ap-
preciated the simple morning ablution so much before, and
's simple, friendly gesture made me feel for the first
me in the three years I had been in China as though I
re accepted as part of the group and not some foreign
erloper.

A few minutes later the door opened and we all file out to the latrine. I kept my head down but, under lowered brows, my eyes roved freely. Suddenly I almost stopped dead in my tracks. There was Harriet coming toward us, her hands cuffed behind her back. The good feeling which my fellow prisoners' generosity had stirred in me only a few moments before now vanished in a flash of cold anger. Gritting my teeth, I muttered under my breath, "Someone is going to pay for that," but at the same time I hoped desperately that Harriet would curb her well-known impetuosity. A hot, stubborn temper would solve nothing here.

5

Rick: When we returned to the cell we sat down cross-legged on the *kang* and I felt the former friendliness of my cell mates disappear as if turned off at the source. Jeng, is cell leader, started off in a very businesslike tone by asking, "What did the judge ask you last night?"

"Oh, he just wanted to know about my background."

"Anything else?"

"What do you mean?"

"You didn't end up here because of what you did in our childhood."

"Well, he said I was a spy."

"Are you?"

"No-o-o, I don't think so."

"What do you mean, 'you don't think so'?" growled Gwo, his heavy features scowling. "You are, or you wouldn't be here!"

"Well, maybe they made a mistake," I faltered.

"These people don't make mistakes," cut in the pock-marked Meng. "Now listen, you, we've been here for some ime and have gone through it all ourselves. We've seen lot of men come and go. They all say the same thing at rst, just as we did and as you are now, but you're not urting anyone but yourself. You're just as guilty as we vere."

When I did not say anything, Gwo suddenly let out a oar, "Talk, will you!"

"Well, I'm not a spy," I said defiantly.

Then bedlam broke loose. Everyone began shouting at nce. Big Lu, his former amicability gone, began shaking his huge finger under my nose and repeated over and over "You'd better come clean. You'd better come clean."

I sat silent until the wave subsided. Jeng then altered the approach.

"This isn't going to get you anywhere," the cell leader resumed calmly. "What did you do during the war?"

"I was in the Marine Corps."

"What did you do in the Marine Corps?"

I hesitated and then said, reluctantly, "I, uh, interrogated Japanese prisoners."

"I knew it," shouted Meng.

"Isn't that intelligence?" asked Jeng.

"Well, I guess so, but that's different."

"What's different about it?" someone yelled.

"Well, we were all fighting the Japanese. What's wrong with that?"

"Who said there was anything wrong with fighting the Japanese? It's what you did after you came to China that counts. Are you or are you not an intelligence man?"

"I was during the war, but not afterward."

"You severed all connections with the Marine Corps?"

"Well, no, I was still in the Reserves."

"Ta-ma-di," cursed Gwo. "This character wriggles like a snake. What did they send you to China to do?"

"Nothing," I said, and then hastily added, "They didn't send me to China."

Ju, the intellectual, then took up the battle and asked, "Do you mean to tell us that the United States government spends $100,000,000 a year sending spies to the socialist countries and then lets one of their trained intelligence men wander around China with nothing to do?" He waved his thin, bony hand in disgust. "That doesn't make sense."

Jeng broke in, "Where did you get the money to come to China, anyway? You said you were a poor student and your father was a railroad worker. He couldn't have helped you."

"I had a scholarship."

"What kind of a scholarship?"

I paused, hoping in some way to avoid the question.

"What kind of a—a—whatever-you-call-it?" bellowed Big Lu, shaking his finger with even more gusto.

"Well, it's sort of hard to explain—"

"We've got lots of time. Where did the money come from?"

"From the, uh—" I hesitated again.

"Answer! !" they all roared.

"Well, it was sort of a Nationalist Government and State Department business."

"*Ta-ma-di!*" swore Gwo again. "If you don't stop wriggling, I'll break your neck!"

By that time I was becoming angry enough to wish he would try. Who did these guys think they were? If they thought they could push me around, they were mistaken. Gwo made no move, however, and fortunately I was given a chance to cool down by the call for breakfast. Big Lu and Ju each grabbed a green crockery basin from under the *kang* and, when the door was opened, dashed out. They returned a moment later with the basins filled with *wo-tou* and tomato soup. Meng then began carefully ladling out a bowl for each of us.

In the meantime Jeng pulled out my string beans and, reverting to his friendly manner of the early morning, told me, "You can eat as much *wo-tou* as you want, and if you'd like there's a bowl of soup, but you must finish these beans. You can't let them go to waste."

Waving aside the soup I started in on the string beans, but I cared no more for eating than I had the night before. After nibbling a few, I ended up with the bowl still over half full.

"What's the matter?" asked Big Lu, with his mouth full of *wo-tou* and his huge hand already reaching for another. "Don't you like string beans?"

"Oh, sure, sure, but I'm not very hungry right now."

"Well, you'd better eat them. You can't waste them. Somebody worked hard to grow those beans."

"I'll save them till tonight," I compromised.

"Aren't you going to eat any *wo-tou*? I brought you two," he persisted.

"No, thanks. I'm really not hungry."

Big Lu, who was now working on his third, shook his head. "They're mighty good. You'd better try and eat some. We eat only twice a day. That's the custom in the countryside, you know."

"Yes, I know," I replied, wishing he would change the subject. I wandered off and stood facing the wall. A few names had been scratched into the whitewashed clay. remembered a book I had read about prisons under the Nazis in Europe, where the condemned prisoners had scratched pathetic messages on the walls. With my finger nail I involuntarily started to trace Dell's initials. "I'm getting dramatic and stupid," I thought, and hastily rubbed it out so the others would not see.

Turning back, I found the others finished and starting to do the dishes. When I asked if I could help, Jeng told me to go sit down and think things over. I had hardly settled myself on the *kang* under the window where a slight breeze gave some relief from the heat when the door opened. I jumped up, hoping it would be a call for me. Anything to get out of that room. But Big Lu picked up one of the green basins and dashed out again. This time he reappeared carrying hot water. Jeng poured me a bowl.

"Drink it," he said.

I picked it up and set it down again. "It's too hot. I'll wait till it cools off."

"Cold water's bad for the stomach," said Big Lu seriously.

"Foreigners always drink it that way," explained Ju with a certain amount of condescension in his voice for Big Lu's ignorance. "They even put ice in it."

"Yes, I heard once they even put ice in tea," interposed Meng.

Big Lu choked over his bowl of water. "In tea?" he gasped. "No wonder they all go around with such sour looking faces. Their stomachs must be tied up in knots."

Just then the supervisor could be heard blowing his

whistle. The bowls were hastily put away and everyone climbed back on the *kang*. An air of seriousness descended on the room. "Now begins round two," I thought glumly.

As usual, Jeng started off, but this time his manner was less harsh than before. "You must realize," he explained, "that you are in a dangerous situation. Your only way out is to come clean. We know. We were once in your position. That's why we want to help you. In the new society, everyone helps everyone else."

"Help?" I thought. "That kind of help I can do without."

Jeng went on, "If we didn't do everything we could to help you straighten out your case and you were shot for refusing to confess, we'd feel morally responsible."

"Of all the hypocrisy," I fumed inwardly. "Why don't you admit you're just trying to get in good with the Communists in order to have your sentence reduced?"

As if he had read my thoughts he continued in a quiet voice, "We know you can't understand all this now. You're probably thinking that we're just out to get you, but it's not true. We really want to help you, because we see things a little more clearly than you do now. You see, I am an old *te-wu* [special agent]. I worked with Japanese intelligence outfits all during the War of Resistance, and after the Japanese surrender I entered the *Jun-tung* [Special Service Section of the Nationalist military intelligence].

"I had so many things against me that I was sure I would be killed when the Communists came, so just before liberation I escaped to Nanking. From there I ran to Hangchow, then down to Canton, always only a few steps ahead of the Liberation Army. Then, because my money was gone I was unable to get to Formosa. I had just enough to make my way back to my wife and child in Nanking. I found them almost starving, but I didn't dare go to anyone for help. Finally we had sold everything, even my clothes, except for a pair of shorts and an undershirt. I was in torment. The baby and my wife were always crying. When I couldn't stand it any more I used to beat them. One day the police came. I tried to escape and they could have shot me, but instead of doing so they chased me until I was finally caught. They sent me back here to Peking to settle my case.

"At first when they questioned me, I, like you, refused to say anything. I thought, 'I'm going to die anyway. Why should I confess? Besides, if I did confess and the Nationalists came back I'd certainly be killed then if I weren't now.' As for dying, it all seemed so hopeless I was past caring. But I soon found that the People's Government was not what I had expected. They patiently explained to me that there was no need for me to die. I had committed too many crimes for them to be overlooked, it is true, but the People's Government was not out for revenge. If I were willing to change and become really a good and honest citizen, I too would be able to enjoy a happy life in the future.

"At the same time they gave me clothes to wear, and when I had one of my attacks of amoebic dysentery they gave me special food to eat and medicine. I decided then that there might be some hope, after all, and so I confessed a little. But there were some things I didn't tell, because I was still suspicious. Maybe they were treating me well just to get a confession and then it would be all over.

"The months dragged on. I was worried also about my wife and baby. What had happened to them? One day I received a letter. To my surprise, it was from her. When I was arrested she could hardly write her name. The People's Government had found her a job working in a cooperative and she was going to school to learn to read and write. This was the first letter she had ever written. When I finished reading it I cried and began to think about all the rotten things I had done in my life. I had sold out my country to the Japanese and many innocent people had died because of me. And now the People's Government was not only taking care of my wife and child but also offering me a new life where I could live like a decent human being. I decided to make a full confession and put my trust in the People's Government."

His thin, pointed face worked with emotion as he spoke

"You have no idea what a wonderful feeling it is to get that all off your chest. And now if I did not try to help you save yourself I would feel that I was betraying my own self again, not to speak of harming you and our country and helping its enemies."

While Jeng talked I could not but feel that he was sincere, at least when he spoke about himself, but his words left little impression upon me. My thoughts kept turning toward Dell. They must be questioning her, too. Would she be able to fence with them? Sometimes she could be rather stubborn. What if they put handcuffs on her, too? A wave of sick anger swept over me. Both my wandering thoughts and Jeng's speech were interrupted by the opening of the door and I was called out again to the interrogation room. I was a little groggy from lack of sleep but the judge went right to work as if being up all night had not fazed him one bit. The only show of strain was the nervous way in which he paced up and down while firing questions at me.

This time he wanted to know how I had come to enter Naval Intelligence, what I had done during the war, and what connections I had had with them after the war. This was getting on dangerous ground and when it came to the last question I flatly denied I had had anything to do with them at all. After well over an hour of close interrogation I was sent back to the cell again, to find that everybody was already having the summertime two-hour noon nap.

I heaved a sigh of relief and thought at least now I would have a chance to rest a bit; but once I lay down I found my mind in such a whirl that I could not sleep. I kept going over my past, trying to remember if I had mentioned to anyone that Naval Intelligence interview in Seattle. If that were known, they really had a case against me. Dell knew about it, but I could not remember whether Harriet did or not. Why had I not settled on a story with Dell beforehand? Worst of all, I had told her not to be caught in a lie. She might tell, and she might not. If she did and I did not, I was in for trouble. But if she refused to give in and I did, what would happen to her? Could I get away with admitting the meeting but denying any espionage orders? After all, they could not prove I had had any contact with Navy organizations in China. Thus my mind spun on. Before the whistle to rise had blown I was called out again for a repeat of the earlier interrogation.

When I returned I saw that Jeng was not in the cell. The others were seated in a semicircle on the *kang* and Gwo, the ex-cop, seemed to be in charge. They waited in impatient silence until I had slipped off my shoes and sat down against the wall next to Big Lu who, as ever, was wielding his fan vigorously. I had hardly crossed my legs when Gwo started in. "What was your interrogation about this time?"

Afraid not to tell the truth, I answered reluctantly, "It was just about my connection with Naval Intelligence during the war."

"What about afterward?" The words hissed through Gwo's chipped, blackened teeth.

"*Bu-lao-shr* [dishonest]," added Ju, in the same tone he must have used when disciplining his students.

"He wanted to know that too, but I haven't had any since the war."

"Weren't you in the Reserves?"

"Yes, I've already told you that, but I was inactive."

"Since when is *spying* called *inactive?*" interposed Ju again.

"Where did you get the money to come to China?" Gwo demanded belligerently.

"I had a scholarship."

"Scholarship? That was expense money for carrying on your filthy spying."

"Nonsense!" I said, impatiently, my temper beginning to show. "That was an ordinary scholarship and nothing more."

"Are you calling me a liar? I say it was!" he shouted.

I did not answer.

"Answer me. Are you calling me a liar?" His ugly, threatening face was thrust close to mine. I still said nothing.

Suddenly his fist shot out and caught me on the side of my jaw. My head snapped back, hitting the wall with a crack. That was too much. With fists clenched I was ready to go after Gwo. I heard the others shouting and then the door swinging open with a crash. Everyone froze and a dead silence descended on the room. We were like a group of schoolboys caught in the midst of some mischief.

I turned my head and saw one of the supervisors standing there. He glared at us for a few moments and then brusquely told Gwo, "Don't hit him." Turning to me, he said, "You straighten up and start telling the truth or I'll put you in handcuffs and ankle chains. We don't treat liars politely here!" With that, he swung out the door, slamming it behind him.

Gwo sat glowering at me and Meng took up the battle. "Why did you come to China?" And on it went until Jeng returned. As soon as Jeng entered the door Big Lu burst out with, "Gwo clipped him!"

"Clipped whom?"

"Li Ko," answered Big Lu, surprised that there should be any question about it.

"What did you do that for?" asked Jeng. "You know it's against regulations."

"Well, we were helping him and he got tough and called me a liar."

"Is slugging the only way you can think of to help somebody? This is not the old days of the Nationalists, and this is not your old precinct headquarters where you could kick people around at will. You write a statement of self-criticism and hand it in to the supervisor."

He then turned to me with a withering glance. "You still want to play stupid, huh? We're trying to help you and you try to get tough. You'd better remember that the Chinese have stood up in the world and no lousy imperialist is going to walk on us any more. Now apologize to Gwo."

I practically choked, but did manage to murmur a reluctant "*Dwey-bu-chi* [I beg your pardon]."

"Now Gwo has to write a self-criticism," continued Jeng sternly. "You ought to do one, too, but you can't write Chinese well enough. What do you propose to do about it?" He paused expectantly.

"Let's punish him," suggested Ju. "Make him stand with his hands over his head for a while."

"That's a good idea," agreed the pock-marked Meng. "It will teach him to behave himself."

"No, we don't have to do that," said Jeng. "Let him punish himself." And to me, "What would you suggest?"

I searched for something that would satisfy them and yet be easy on me. "How about not eating any dinner?"

Jeng gave me a disgusted look. "You ought to know that the People's Government would never stand for that. Besides, you don't eat anything anyway."

Seating himself on the *kang*, he asked, "Who were your friends in the Consulate?"

I named a few of them.

"Did you ever give them any information?"

"No," I said, "we were just friends."

"What did you talk about when you were with them?"

"Nothing much, just parties and—"

Gwo hit the *kang* with his fist. "*Ta-ma-di*," he shouted, "so help me—"

Motioning him to be quiet, Jeng went on. "Did you ever talk about the political situation?"

"Occasionally," I replied, "but not very much."

"What in particular?"

I mentioned a few innocuous topics which we might conceivably have touched on in normal conversation.

"Nothing else?"

At that moment we could hear a commotion in the hall and a thump as the huge vats used to carry in the food struck the ground. Big Lu and Ju scrambled down from the *kang* to get out the basins, and the session ended for the time being. "Saved by the bell," I thought. I pulled out the bowl of string beans, but they looked no more appetizing than they had at the first meal. I even turned down the offer of some tomato soup proffered me by Jeng.

After the dishes were done and we had returned from the evening latrine call Big Lu and Meng took out a chessboard and began to play, while Gwo labored over the writing of his self-criticism and Jeng read a book. Ju just sat on the edge of the *kang*, knees drawn up under his chin and back propped against the wall. I walked aimlessly up and down the cell in the space in front of the *kang*, thankful for the rest period which gave me a chance to collect my battered thoughts. Suddenly I looked up and was appalled to see Ju staring at me from behind his rimless glasses with a look of cold hatred in his eyes. He must have realized that I had caught him off guard, for he immediately covered himself by asking, "What university did you go to?"

"Pennsylvania," I replied. "Where did you go?"

"Bern. I took my Ph.D. in philosophy there."

Jeng looked up from his book and said in a biting tone, "Reactionary philosophy. The only thing he learned was how to serve his foreign masters well."

Ju looked away and did not make any comment.

Just before the whistle blew for the evening session a note arrived ordering me to write out a list of all the people I knew in Peking and what my relations with them had been. I took a sheet of paper and began writing down a few names. Since most of the foreigners I had known had already left China I had no qualms about putting them down, but when it came to listing the Chinese and those foreigners still in Peking I hesitated. I had been under surveillance for so long there could be no secret about my acquaintances. If I did not mention them it might create more suspicion. Knowing full well whom I knew, the government might be setting a trap to see whether I was going to be honest or not.

Suddenly my thoughts were interrupted by a curt question from Jeng, "What's the matter?"

"Nothing."

"He's just stalling," said Ju, his beady eyes fixed on the list I had been writing, "He needs a lesson."

But before he could add any more suggestions Jeng

simply waved him down and told me to get on with my writing. Finally, a few minutes before bed time I finished the list, after putting what I hoped were sufficiently ambiguous remarks like "personal friend," "business acquaintance," "fellow student" beside each name to explain our relationship. I gave it to Jeng, who called to the guard to come and get it. As the guard turned away with the paper the whistle blew and we all began to prepare for bed.

I asked to sleep on the floor, which I thought would be cooler and less crowded. Jeng hesitated, but Ju said, "Let him. He stinks, like all foreigners."

"You ought to know," interposed Gwo. "You've been around them enough."

Ju's eyes blazed, but before any trouble could start Jeng ordered, "Get to bed, all of you," and we all lay down, I on the floor beside Big Lu.

Writing that list had set me to thinking about my friends on the outside. The British must have sent the news home by now and maybe action had already been started to get me out. I knew the British and other friends in the embassies would do everything they could, but somehow I did not have much hope.

The door opened and I was called out again. In my nervous haste to get out the door, the sleeve of my shirt caught on the bolt and was badly torn. When I sat before the judge his dark eyes looked at me sharply as he said, "How did your shirt get like that?"

"I tore it on the door as I came out."

He fixed me with a level gaze for a moment, as if trying to ascertain whether I were telling the truth or not. Then, apparently satisfied, the matter was dropped, but his obvious concern over any mistreatment I might have met with in the cell gave me an uplift and from that time on I was never worried about being tortured.

He began firing questions at me in rapid succession, as he had done before. Why and how had I come to China? What relations had I had with the American Consulate? The systematic probing into every facet of my past went on all night, interspersed with short rest periods back in the cell. The painstaking thoroughness of my interrogator made my experience in questioning prisoners during the war seem like child's play. Sometimes he sat patiently smoking his pipe; sometimes he paced restlessly up and down, giving release to his suppressed energy. Occasionally, when he thought I was lying his eyes would flash, but he usually managed to keep his voice calm. The man's stamina amazed me, and all the time the little secretary sitting next to him busily took down everything I said.

With the dawn the interrogation came to an end. I returned to the cell to fall into an exhausted sleep, only to be aroused by the whistle and the feel of Big Lu's rough hand shaking me. I awoke with a terrible headache. After washing quickly I sat down on the *kang* with my head in my hands. Jeng noticed me sitting there and asked if there were anything wrong.

"Just a headache," I replied.

"You can get some medicine if you want. There's a sick call every morning. All you have to do is write out a slip and hand it in during latrine call. Here, I'll fill it out for you."

He tore a small piece of paper out of an improvised notebook and wrote down my name and the fact that I had a headache.

The "helping" began again and, except for breakfast and a welcome trip to the dispensary where I was given some aspirin, it went on all morning. When noon came not even my troubled thoughts could keep me from sleep and this time I was dead to the world for the whole two hours. I awoke feeling oddly refreshed and realized suddenly that the bad cold I had had the day of my arrest had long since disappeared.

The discussion began again with Jeng delivering another long lecture on how I ought to confess for my own good, telling me to think of my family. It would be a terrible thing for them if I were shot just because I refused to confess. How would they feel? He was just about to get down to questioning me again when the supervisor called him out and Gwo was left in charge. It was with mixed feelings that I saw Jeng leave the cell. I was afraid of him because he was too smart, but at the same time I had come to look upon him for protection against Gwo's third-degree methods. When Gwo began talking I knew immediately I was in for trouble.

"Are you going to come clean or are we going to have to get nasty?" he said belligerently.

"I've told you all there is."

"You've told us nothing," said Ju. "To whom did you give your information?"

"Nobody. I didn't have any information."

"You're a liar," shouted Meng.

Ptfu! I winced as Ju spit in my face.

"Who was your superior?" yelled Gwo again.

"I didn't have one."

"Take off your glasses and stand over there against the wall."

As I moved to obey, Gwo followed me down from the *kang*, his ankle chains rattling on the cement floor.

"Now are you going to come clean or am I going to have to slap it out of you?" he demanded in an ugly tone, his body pressing close to mine.

"Hey, Gwo," Big Lu called from the *kang*, "if you hit him you'll have to write another self-criticism."

"That's all right. I'll hit him first and write the self-criticism afterward."

With that he drew back his fist and let go. I turned my head to avoid the full impact of his blow but it caught me on the jaw, and for a moment my brain flashed black and white and my knees turned to rubber.

"Now are you going to be good?" he asked. "Get back on the *kang* and start talking. If you don't tell it straight, this is only the beginning."

I sat down again. A cold rage was boiling inside me. At first I made up my mind not to answer any more questions at all, but then as I looked at Ju, Gwo, and Meng sitting across from me I could see that they meant business, and though Big Lu was obviously against any rough stuff he certainly would not try to stop the others, if for no other reason than that he would be afraid of being accused of having sympathy for me.

As the others started throwing questions at me again I decided it might be better to play along and stall for time until Jeng returned. I deliberately began talking in circles or pretended lack of comprehension of the questions put to me on the plea that my Chinese was too poor. When Ju then tried to speak to me in a combination of French and English I managed to kill a good deal of time discussing the meaning of the words he used. This, of course, meant a loss of face for Ju and I could see his eyes becoming darker and darker behind his sweat-stained glasses. Suddenly his face was livid with rage. He grabbed a straight pen and tried to jab its point into my foot. I drew back hastily and he missed. Before he could try again Meng seized his wrist, but at the same time they all started swearing at me for my trickery. Then Gwo told me to get down from the *kang* and stand up against the wall again with my hands over my head.

"Now," he said, "you can stand there till you get ready to talk." Turning to the others, he said, "Let him think it over in that position for a while."

In just a few minutes my arms began to ache and I started dropping them down a little, but every time I did so one or another of them shouted at me to get them back up. Fortunately, it was not long before the door opened and in walked Jeng.

When he saw me standing there he asked Gwo, "Now what?"

Gwo replied, "Li Ko's been *bu-lao-shr* again and we've had to help him."

"What did you do? Hit him again?" asked Jeng in disgust.

"Just once," said Meng. "Gwo made him take off his glasses first."

"*Ta-ma-di,*" swore Jeng. "I thought I told you not to hit him. Can't you get it through your head it's against regulations?"

"Well—" said Gwo.

"Well, nothing," interrupted Jeng. "You were arrested because you couldn't keep from beating people up, you filthy *te-wu*. And now here you are in the people's prison, still in ankle chains, and you think you can go right on doing it."

Then turning to me he roared, "Who told you you could take your arms down?"

When I hastily shot them up again he ordered, "Get back up on the *kang*."

I had hardly sat down when we heard the welcome sound of the food vats hitting the floor in the corridor. Big Lu and Ju jumped up. So ended another session.

Thus it went on morning, afternoon, and night. I had little chance to sleep, but with my nerves keyed up to such a pitch I really did not seem to need it. At the same time, the tension had tied my stomach up in such knots that I could hardly stand the sight of food. By the third day I had managed to finish the bowl of string beans, with the help of some soup mixed in, but the *wo-tou* was still beyond me. On the fourth day, after Big Lu and Ju had returned with the steaming basins, the door opened a second time and I was ordered to bring my bowl for some rice gruel and take all I wanted. I helped myself to only a little because I did not think I could swallow it either, but as soon as I tasted it I wished I had taken more. It was good and I finished it quickly.

Reaching for my bowl to put it in with the dishes he was washing, Jeng said gruffly, "That's better, huh? I told the People's Government you weren't used to eating *wo-tou*, so they sent you some rice. Usually only people who are sick get that. Now will you believe that the People's Government really looks out for every person?"

"Yeah," I thought. "I used to give cigarettes, candy, and even brandy sometimes to Japanese prisoners to get them to talk. If you think I'm going to give in for a little rice gruel, you're crazy." But to Jeng I said, "Yes, the People's Government is very kind."

"You'd better say that," snarled Ju, his face twisted. "Lousy filthy imperialist. You ought to be shot." He moved away from the rest of us and sat sulkily on the edge of the *kang*.

"What's on your mind?" questioned Jeng, getting up from his dishes to stand before Ju.

"Well, they don't give food like that to us. Here my stomach can't digest that *wo-tou* either. Why should he get special treatment? If it weren't for stinking imperialists like him I wouldn't be here. And they don't even put him in handcuffs and ankle chains." With that he took off his glasses and started to cry.

There was a sharp smacking sound as Jeng slapped him across the face with the palm of his hand. "So that's it, huh? I've been noticing you these past few days. You've been trying to get him. So it's his fault you're here. Why, you turtle's egg! I suppose everyone who's had anything to do with a foreigner has landed in prison. Who forced you to sell out your country? Now, get this straight. In this place we're all equal. He's a spy and you're a *te-wu* [secret agent] and nobody gets special privileges. The People's Government will put him in irons if he deserves them, and if he is given rice it's because he needs it. As soon as his stomach straightens out he'll be eating *wo-tou* along with the rest of us. If your stomach is as delicate as you say, how is it you can manage to eat two *wo-tou* every meal? You can criticize Li Ko all you want for his sneaky lying, but if I catch you picking on him again to satisfy your own revenge against foreigners you're going to end up in irons yourself and for a good long time. You'd better begin to realize that one of the things you're here for is to come to an understanding of yourself and stop putting the blame for everything you've done on someone else."

The rest of us had stood around half-embarrassed by the naked emotion displayed in Ju's outburst. As Jeng turned angrily back to his work we all made a pretense of busying ourselves in preparation for the evening latrine call. Ju continued to sob quietly to himself.

I cast a furtive glance in his direction. Now I knew why he hated me so. He was taking out on me all his hatred against the government and the foreigners who he felt were responsible for his ending up in prison. It was a reaction which I was to meet again later. In fact, the most difficult people I had to contend with all during my stay in prison were those very men I thought should be most friendly because of their past pro-Western attitudes and connections with foreigners.

Ju's explosion ended all threats of violence from the other prisoners, but it did not relax their pressure on me. If anything, it was intensified. They shouted, cajoled, threatened, pleaded, argued, and even gave me the silent treatment, but since I obviously welcomed this latter they soon rejected that method.

In the meantime the pressure from the interrogations themselves was rapidly becoming unbearable. The questions came one after another. Who were my contacts in the Consulate? What were my relationships with them? What had been the subject of our conversations? How often had I visited there? What were the dates? Who else was there? Who else did I know in Peking? What was our relationship and when did we meet? Time, place, frequency, witnesses? What did I do at the universities? Had I taken any trips into the countryside? Why had we become so friendly with the British?

The exhaustive, systematic probing seemed unceasing. Whenever my interrogator thought I was about to balk he quickly changed the subject to something I was willing to talk about, thus always keeping me off balance and never allowing me to come to a crisis, yet not relaxing his pressure. I found myself being led into a maze of truths, half-truths, and outright lies. Often I was unable to remember what I had said before and kept tripping myself up on details. Several times I tried flatly denying any knowledge of a person, only to give in later when I realized my relations with him must have been known. Sometimes, too, I really could not remember details which might have occurred three years before. Then, under the cynical, accusing stare of my interrogator I often felt even more uncomfortable than if I had been telling a lie. All the while, the haunting realization that a large part of what I said could be checked against the facts already in the judge's hands made me feel even more insecure.

To make matters worse, I constantly felt the cold, rational force of my interrogator's arguments dragging me down. At almost every session he stated in a matter-of-fact tone that the government already had enough evidence against me to give the maximum penalty. To refuse to confess was pointless. It would help no one and only bring on dire consequences for myself.

The strain was such that I knew I could not hold out much longer. Finally, on the fifth day I admitted that I had supplied information to my ex-Naval Intelligence friend, Roger, and others in the American Consulate, but I tried to maintain that it had not been deliberate and that such information had been revealed only during ordinary conversations. If I had thought that this would satisfy my interrogator, or, for that matter, the prisoners in the cell, I was mistaken.

As Jeng put it, "Do you mean to say that with all your experience in intelligence work during the war and close relationship with that Naval Intelligence friend then, you could provide him with information in Peking and not even know what it was? It doesn't make sense."

And so they kept at it. Soon I had to give way on this point, too, because it was so obvious, but I was determined to do everything I could to avoid the question of my interview with ONI in Seattle. I reasoned that if I could hold to the story that whatever I had done in Peking had been purely spontaneous and had no official connection with any intelligence organization, I might get off lightly. But if I were dubbed as a Naval Intelligence agent there was little chance of ever being released. For some strange reason I still looked upon the Consulate's intelligence activities as less serious than those of the military organizations. However, again there was a strong chance they knew all about that interview and if I did not tell about it it might go even worse with me.

More disturbing were Jeng's frequent questions about such groups as Office of Strategic Services (OSS), the Army's ESD, and other organized American espionage agencies in China. His implication was that I must have had relations with them also. Although I knew this to be part of the standard technique of interrogation, I could not help giving way to fears that I might be accused of a multiplicity of relationships which would prove even more serious. The fact that I was frightened by such inferences gave me added proof that I was weakening. If there were only some way of gauging how much they really knew and how much it was expeditious to confess.

From the moment of my arrest I had been speculating as to why we had been picked up just when it looked as though the Korean situation were going to be settled. With my usual propensity for guessing wrong, I had decided it was because the Chinese authorities needed a propaganda stunt to counteract their defeat in Korea. It was not until four years later that I learned our arrests had never been mentioned in the Chinese press.

At the time, however, I reasoned, "Probably all they want is a confession. If they get what they want, they may just deport us as they did a number of foreign priests who were arrested in Tientsin and other places."

Perhaps the best course was to make a full confession and in that way secure escape from the country for Dell and me. When we arrived in Hong Kong I could deny everything. Thus I would still be on good terms with Naval Intelligence; and then, remembering the case of Robert Vogeler who had been released from prison in Hungary in May of that year and been extolled as a great hero, I could see myself in a similar position. I would become an expert on Communist China, write a book, and make a lot of money. Everyone would sympathize with me, and a position in a university would be assured.

I was feeling very sure of myself that night, about twelve days after my arrest, as I stood before the judge and said, "I've decided to tell the truth."

I then spent several hours making a fairly accurate confession of what I had been doing, although wherever possible I tried to avoid as much of the responsibility as I could.

When I had finished, the investigating judge relaxed in his chair. It was only then I realized that he was almost as tired as I was. But he paused for only a moment and then, leaning forward, asked me a curious question, "Why did you confess?"

After some hesitation I finally replied, "Because I knew you had too much evidence against me, and if I didn't I would probably be shot."

He nodded slowly. Then, looking out the window, he seemed suddenly to notice that it was already light. "You can go back to your cell and rest," he said. "You must be tired. You can sleep during the day if you want."

When I returned to the cell I found the others up. I told them what had happened. Everyone, except Ju, expressed happiness. Jeng even offered to wash my shirt, which by now was reeking.

Big Lu said, "We can get a needle and thread and mend that sleeve for you."

After breakfast the others sat in a circle at one end of the *kang* and discussed a book they were reading, and I lay down to take a nap but I could not sleep. Now that I had finally decided on the course of confession I found myself wanting to tell everything, in order to be certain there was nothing about my activities which the government could say I was holding back. I kept going over every detail. There were so many points that had to be cleared up, because I had made a great number of contradictory statements in the past two weeks. For the next couple of days the judge went over and over my story to clarify the details. By this time there was no particular strain for me. I was telling a straight story and it came out easily.

The afternoon of the second day after my confession I arrived in the interrogation room to find several Chinese there, both in uniform and civilian clothes. I was asked to repeat my story for them. As I left the room I noticed a car outside and I thought, "Maybe they're going to let me go now and that car is to take me home."

As soon as I reached the cell I dug out the socks I had put aside earlier, to save from becoming worn on the *kang*, and started to put them on. Ju looked at me suspiciously and asked, "What are you putting those on for?"

I was stopped for an answer, but Jeng immediately came to my rescue with, "His feet probably sweat in those leather shoes. If he wants to wear his socks, that's his business."

The minutes seemed to drag interminably as I sat waiting for the door to open, but when dinner came and it gradually began to get dark I was forced to realize that leaving here was not going to be that simple. It was not until the next morning that I was called out again. This time I was given a stack of paper and an outline for writing my confession.

With a feeling of triumph I returned to the cell and showed Jeng the outline. However, as soon as I sat down to work I ran into more trouble. It seemed that "helping," to my cell mates, not only applied to convincing me I should confess but also to the writing of the confession itself. I would write in English and then make a clumsy oral translation into Chinese for them to hear. When I could not translate properly, Ju would help. Everyone sat around and discussed whether what I had written was right or not.

The first question dealt with my history and education, and a fight started even there. Jeng insisted that I should bring up the fact that I liked to read detective stories, because they had influenced me toward becoming a spy. Ju wanted me to include a statement that in school I had been taught to look down on all other races. I would not agree and my exasperation knew no bounds. How was I ever going to finish this and leave here if they kept butting in? By the end of two days I had exactly two pages written and I was called in again for interrogation.

"How's it going?" asked the judge.

When I told him what had been happening, he said seriously, "This is your confession. You write it as you know it and don't let anyone else try to tell you what to say. Try to be as honest and realistic as you can."

With that he waved me back to my cell. I was just starting to tell a rather crestfallen Jeng what the judge had said when the supervisor came in and ordered me to get my things together. A few minutes later I was ushered into cell No. 9 across the corridor, a room very similar to the one I had just left, except that, being on the south side of the building, it was much lighter. Seated on the *kang* was a group of about six men, some wearing ankle chains and one in handcuffs. The leader was a tall, handsome Chinese who looked about my age but who was actually several years older. He introduced himself as Liao. After telling him my name I explained that I was supposed to write my confession. He promptly ordered one of the other prisoners to clear a place by the window so that I could use the broad sill as a desk.

As I sat down to write I felt a conflict of emotion. I was glad to get away from Jeng's unceasing questions, Ju's hatred, and Gwo's bullying, but still during those weeks I had developed a certain attachment for them all. They were the first Chinese I felt I had ever really known, and Jeng's sincerity had left a deep impression on me. It seemed strange, but I had actually come to look on cell No. 3 as a sort of home. Now I was in a new place among strangers again, with a new set of relationships to be worked out. I wondered why I had been moved. Only later did I learn that it was the government's policy to transfer a prisoner after he had passed a crisis in order to give him a chance to start fresh in new surroundings. However, for the next few days I was so busy writing that except for the exchange of a few words at mealtime I had little to do with the others.

Finally I completed my confession, altogether seventy-six hand-written pages, and gave it to the supervisor. I was now ready to leave and my mind was filled with what I would do when I reached Hong Kong. My story for the press was all prepared—how I had been unjustly arrested, mistreated, and forced into making a confession. I wondered if I would be asked to go on a lecture tour, maybe even appear on the radio. My spirits soared as I thought, "This is turning out to be the best thing that ever happened to me."

6

Dell: Several hours had passed since Rick and Harriet had been taken away in the jeep. The shadows were beginning to lengthen in the courtyard but still I sat on in the living room, my hands folded in my lap, not daring to move under the watchful eyes of the armed guard. Our guests were expected at eight o'clock and I fidgeted inwardly. "If there were only some way of telling them not to come. What a thing to be involved in!"

My thoughts were interrupted by the entrance of a cadre who asked me, "Aren't you going to have your dinner? It's getting late."

"What time is it?" I asked hurriedly.

"Quarter to eight."

"I've got guests coming in a few minutes. I suppose I had better wait and eat with them," I said, hoping to find out from his answer just what my status was.

"Suit yourself," he replied indifferently.

"Well, if I'm going to eat with them—" I paused to see if he would say anything, but he met my questioning gaze with a blank stare. I tried again from a different tack to find out what I could without asking a direct question. "Uh, well, I had better get dressed. I can't receive guests in these clothes! And I had better tell Wang to start setting the table."

I made a move toward the door and called, "Wang! Wang!"

"Never mind, never mind," said the cadre hurriedly. "You don't need to change. We'll take care of everything. You just sit down and take it easy."

My short-lived hope flickered out as I took in the significance of his words. It was plain I would not be allowed to see our friends. When the doorbell rang at eight, the guard motioned me to go into the little room over the kitchen which we had been using as a pantry and catch-all for odds and ends of furniture. There was a small boudoir chair in the room and I sat on that in the dark with the guard standing just outside the door to the living room.

The first to arrive were the two couples from the British Embassy, and they were ushered into the room which I had just vacated. A few moments later the bell rang again and I heard the bank manager's voice asking in bewilderment, mixed with a trace of fear, "Isn't this the home of Mr. Rickett? I'm looking for Mr. Rickett. This must be the wrong house."

He was assured by the guard that he had come to the correct address and was asked to sit down in the courtyard. The cadre had just started to converse with him when one of the British walked boldly out of the living room and, standing in the doorway, called in a clear voice, "Rickett's been arrested." He then walked calmly back into the room and to my amazement I heard the four of them start to play bridge.

The poor manager sputtered for some time in the courtyard about how he had hardly known us; really we could not be considered his friends, just chance acquaintances seen at the club once in a while. After an uncomfortable two hours, he and the others were allowed to go. I wondered if they had realized that I was there, but in a way it did not matter much whether they knew or not. They seemed utterly remote at that point.

Not long after they had left I was asked to step into the living room again. Two young men in blue cadre uniform, who looked as if they had just finished college, were sitting on the couch. One, a man with a broad, high-cheekboned face and unusually pasty complexion, accentuated by snapping black eyes and a thick shock of black hair, motioned me to an easy chair and asked if I had eaten.

I smiled wryly, "I'm really not hungry."

"Would you like a glass of water?"

I nodded and the cadre told a guard standing nearby to fetch a glass of water.

Meanwhile the pasty-faced cadre went on to explain that Rick had been arrested because he was a spy. Evidence had been gathered which proved this beyond the shadow of a doubt.

He continued in a quick, central China accent which I sometimes found difficult to understand, "We have not placed you under formal arrest because we haven't decided to what extent you were involved in your husband's crime. We know that many wives are forced by circumstances into becoming accomplices of their husbands, without realizing the implications of their actions. In such cases the government tries to be extremely lenient. If in the course of the investigation it should be made clear that you were as responsible as he, you will probably be arrested too, although your attitude in the investigation will have a lot to do with deciding your future. If you are honest and do not try to hide the truth, the People's Government will be very lenient with you. The People's Government felt that, as a married woman, you would be more comfortable at home. Now, tell me, what did your husband come to China to do?"

I explained carefully that Rick was a student of ancient Chinese who was interested only in Chinese history and philosophy. He had come to China to study and wanted to return to the United States to promote good relations between the Chinese and American people by teaching history. As I spoke, the young man tossed his head impatiently as if my words hurt his ears. The curl of his sensuous lips and the quiver of his nostrils revealed a hot temper which he was obviously suppressing with difficulty. Shifting my glance to see the reaction of the cadre at his side, I took stock of him for the first time. He sat there almost phlegmatic. The darkness of his complexion stood out in striking contrast to that of the broad-faced one. His features were small and delicate and the eyes which peered out from behind rimless glasses were calm and somewhat friendly.

Feeling slightly reassured, I waited for my interrogator's comment. He ran his hand impatiently through his thick hair and said coldly, "All right, but we aren't interested in listening to fairy stories. You think about it anl we will talk with you again. You had better get some rest now; it's already quite late."

A young girl in cadre uniform entered and told me I could sleep in Harriet's room. As I passed our study-bedroom, I could see two or three men and women going through our belongings. "Oh, my heavens," I thought, "that report Rick was writing to send out in the Dutch diplomatic mail pouch—was it out on the desk or in one of the drawers? I've got to think of some way to get in and grab it. If need be, I could chew it up and swallow it, or flush it down the toilet."

As I dropped down on Harriet's bed, I realized I was being ridiculous. That report must have been discovered first thing. They would certainly have started with Rick's desk. It must be in their hands by now. "But," I thought, "what shall I do when they ask me about it? Better play dumb and say I never heard of it. Thank goodness it was still in rough form and I hadn't typed it up yet. I can probably get away with denying any knowledge of it."

The next morning, after refusing breakfast, I sat down alone in the living room and stared blankly into space. When the search of all our belongings was concluded, the slow-moving, bespectacled cadre brought me a number of papers, photographs, and cards and asked me to count them and sign a chit to the effect that they were being taken into the custody of the People's Government. My heart jumped when I saw the report in the little pile, but I made no sign that I had an idea what any of the material was as I signed the receipt. I had decided to take my cue from the interrogators. If they thought I was not seriously involved in any questionable activities I would certainly do my best to keep them thinking that way.

After he left I relapsed into my semi-stupor, to be suddenly roused by the thought that Harriet had asked one of her student friends for lunch that day. Yang Miao-jung, a young Chinese girl whose mannerisms, ways of thinking, and habits were as American as any college student in the United States, had been one of Harriet's most valuable contacts and over the lunch or dinner table would be bombarded by all of us with questions about the organization in which she worked—how was their study going, how responsive to the new regime were her coworkers, what did the government stress in their study, what was the hierarchy in her organization, what did they eat in the mess, etc., etc.

As noon approached I waited nervously for her knock. I had asked Wang in a whisper if there were any way we could warn her not to come, little realizing that, as one of Harriet's informants, she was bound to be picked up for questioning sooner or later no matter where she was. But Wang shook his head disconsolately and said "No." The bell rang several times toward noon as people came and went, and then the sound I had been dreading could be heard loud and clear through the courtyard.

"Da de de da daa, Da da!" (Shave and a haircut, two bits!) It was the special knock we had taught her as a joke because she was too short to reach the bell pull that Rick had made.

As soon as Little Yang entered the courtyard I was told to go back into the small room over the kitchen. (I spent much of the next six weeks there.) Little Yang was taken into the living room and questioned. Her relationship with Harriet was well known. Old friends and acquaintances at work had warned her more than once, so she had told us, that she ought not see so much of Harriet, that no good would come of it, but she, in her fiery little way, had retorted that she liked Harriet and would continue to see as much of her as she wanted. It was quite obvious that under these circumstances she would have to undergo some investigation. I wondered if she would be arrested, but it soon became apparent that she was going to be detained in our house. She took up quarters in Harriet's room and wrote to her father, who sent her extra clothes, bedding, toilet articles, and money, which she used for the food bought daily for her by the guards.

We were in close proximity but were not allowed to talk to each other, although for a couple of weeks we passed notes back and forth by putting them in each other's soap dish in the bathroom. When we were caught the hot-tempered cadre who had taken the lead in my investigation told me sternly that we would not be punished since this was the first time, but I should understand that in prison note-passing was a very serious offense and I would not have been let off so lightly there. It was comforting to have Little Yang there. Though we could not talk we did smile and give each other encouraging winks or gestures as we passed from one room to another during the day.

The interrogation was centered on Little Yang the first two days, and it was not until the third day that I was asked to go into the living room again. The two cadres were seated on the couch as before. The dark, bespectacled little man said nothing, while his partner began the questioning. Running his hand through his heavy, black hair in what I came to know as his most characteristic gesture, he asked, "What did your husband do during the war?"

"He was in the Marine Corps."

"What part of the Marine Corps?"

"He was a line officer."

"What was the exact branch?"

"Well, I don't remember. I just remember that he was in a branch where they were called line officers."

He looked me squarely in the eyes and asked coldly, "You don't know what that branch was called?"

My gaze was equally level and cold as I replied, "No, I don't know."

"Well, I'll tell you. Your husband was in . . ."

He paused, and I thought to myself, "Good. You tell me what you know and I may be able to keep one step ahead of you."

But he did not finish the sentence. At the time, it never occurred to me how ridiculous it was to deny knowledge of such open facts about our past. The fact that Rick had been an interpreter during the war had come out back in 1949 when we had applied for residence permits. I could only make the interrogator suspicious of me by playing dumb on such points, but I was determined to say nothing that would incriminate Rick or involve me.

The cadre, with a look of impatient disgust, soon terminated the questioning and told me to write out a list of the people we had known in Peking, our relationship with them, and what we had talked about with them. As I turned to go, he said, "This is our method. If you are honest, that's all there is to it."

I went back to the little room with mixed feelings. All those months past I had been dreading arrest and the torture which was sure to accompany it, but now that arrest had finally come it did not seem so bad after all. The guards walked up and down the courtyard with their guns in full view, it was true, but they had not molested me in any way. I had not been shouted at or treated roughly. Moreover, Wang had been instructed to cook whatever I wanted and to serve it to me on the card table in the little pantry room. On the second day, when I told the girl cadre that I was dirty and would like a bath, she had said that I should have one whenever I wanted. She and the other cadres stopped by my room from time to time to ask how I was getting along or to make some friendly comment, such as, "My, but you're thin!"

And now the interrogator had told me that their method was simply to ask questions and have me write material. "I'm really in luck," I thought, "and if I can keep them thinking I'm a harmless housewife maybe they'll let me go home."

My old longing for home had come back with redoubled force now that I was alone. My greatest fear was that I might be allowed to live on my own in Peking. I had read A Room on the Route some months back and had been profoundly influenced by the story of the American woman stranded in Moscow who could not get a passport to return to the United States but who at the same time could find no work there. With no one to turn to she was gradually starving to death. I could envisage myself in a similar position. I wanted to stay near Rick, but at the same time I wanted desperately to get back where I could find some security. I knew from hearing the experience of other foreigners arrested in Peking that we would not be allowed to see each other, and I began to reason I could wait for him just as well in Yonkers as I could in Peking. As long as he was behind barred doors, ten miles or ten thousand miles did not matter.

With my hopes up for an early settlement of our case, I set about writing the list of the people we had known. I said in the case of our conversations with people in the Consulate and British Embassy that we had talked mostly about American and British customs, books, places we had been, and so on. In mentioning a couple of our friends, I said that "they went around most of the time in an alcoholic haze."

I was elated when the guard, watching me through the window as I wrote, said admiringly, "Gee, you write fast, and with your left hand, too!"

I had written thirty-five pages by eleven o'clock that evening and turned them in, thinking I had written with style and taste! The People's Government would probably tell me to pack up and go home in a couple of days. Two days passed and still no word from the interrogator. When I was called into the living room on the third day he was brusque.

"We have read what you wrote," he said, "but it is not realistic. We want the facts, not a lot of irrelevant matter. I'll tell you this quite frankly." His tone became coldly severe. "The People's Government is lenient with people who tell the truth, but we are not polite with liars. If you insist on lying we will not hesitate to put you in hand-cuffs. That is the first step, and if you still continue to be dishonest the ankle chains come next. Now, you think it over. We hope you won't be foolish."

I went back to the pantry room, my mind in a whirl. Was this the extent of their torture? Handcuffs and ankle chains? But what was the torture in that? Were these people really so naïve and childlike? I almost laughed out loud. If that was all it amounted to, I guessed I could take it. I took out my crossword puzzle book and tried to relax over the word game.

Again I was left alone for a couple of days. I read through a few of Jane Austen's novels and started on *An American Tragedy*. I limited myself to two crossword puzzles a day, and estimated that, with the reading matter at hand, I could keep myself occupied for a couple of months at least.

I was getting ready one evening to lie down on the cot which had been set up for me in the pantry room when I heard a jeep draw up in front. A few moments later the tall cadre, named Lu, who had been assigned to take charge of the house came in and said that it would be more convenient to ask me a few questions in another place, so would I please come along. I changed from the shorts which I had been continuing to wear at home every day into a skirt and fresh blouse, and then put on my leather shoes. If I were going to jail or forced to make long marches, I was going to be sure of being comfortably dressed.

After a short drive across the city I was led into a large room with two desks at one end. A small chair was placed in the center and I was told to sit on it. The informal atmosphere of the questioning at home was lacking here. I faced the same two interrogators, but their manner was more formal and businesslike. This time they both asked questions, to which I answered a straight "I don't know," or gave evasive half-truths or downright lies. The quiet-mannered one maintained his phlegmatic calm, but the hot temper of the other began to show signs of exploding, though he tried to keep his voice level. Eventually I was led into an anteroom and told to rest for a few minutes.

As the questioning started again I answered with a lie and continued to maintain that I knew nothing about Li Ko's connections with Intelligence.

The interrogator, unable to control himself any longer, suddenly interrupted me, anger and loathing in his voice, "Move your chair back away from us!"

I moved it back a few inches and started to sit down again.

"Farther!" he roared.

I complied, thinking, "Well, I didn't ask to come here. If you don't like me, why don't you let me go home?"

But I was not to be let off that easily.

"Why did you and your husband come to China?"

"We came simply as students and nothing more. We wanted to study Chinese and impart some—"

"That's enough," he roared again. "Stand back by the window."

I moved back to the wall opposite the desks and stood defiantly, my fists clenched.

"I tell you this," he said more calmly, but firmly, "if you lie once more we will put you in handcuffs. We have tried to be patient with you, but you must realize that this is a serious matter. You've got to wake up to reality— that there is only one way and that is to tell the truth. The People's Government wants to give you every opportunity possible and will be lenient with you up to a certain point, but if you continue to be so defiant we will certainly not be polite."

He looked down at the desk for a moment as if to compose himself, and then asked, "What did your husband do in China?"

I stuck out my chin and answered, "He was a student."

At that moment I glanced at the young girl who was taking down the record. She was gazing at me with exasperation and astonishment, as if to say, "How can you be so stupid!"

The interrogator motioned to her and she came over to me with the handcuffs in her hand. "Put your hands behind your back," she said gently, and as I obeyed I felt the cuffs snap into place around my wrists. The interrogation went on as before. Finally, as dawn came creeping through the window the officer said, "You go back home now and think things over. Just remember, think of your-self and your husband. It is to his interest, too, to get this case cleared up, you know."

In spite of the anger and temper he had displayed dur-ing the course of the questioning, it seemed now almost as if there were a note of sympathy in his voice. The young recorder then came over to me and started to fumble with the cuffs. As my hands came down to my sides again I began to congratulate myself on having won this round, but she motioned me to put my hands forward and to my amazement the cuffs were snapped back on again.

"Maybe this is just for the ride home," I thought, but when we entered the courtyard at 48 Hsin Kai Lu she said to me, "When you eat or want to go to the bathroom, just tell the guard and he'll take these off for you. He has the key."

For the first time since Rick had left I had a feeling that they might possibly mean business after all. It might not be as easy to fool them as I had expected. In fact, this might call for a reassessment of my position and realign-ment of tactics. Was it possible that they knew more about our activities than I had thought?

Handcuffs locked on in front do not curtail hand and arm movements to any great extent. I could still wield a pencil to work my crossword puzzles, and reading books was no problem at all. I asked to have them removed every afternoon so that I could take a bath, and I managed to stretch every meal out for about half an hour to have that time free of them. I was determined not to show the least sign of discomfort and mentally I maintained such a dis-dain for the whole affair that I could not even feel hu-miliation because of them.

I had been told to "think things over," but the only thinking I was doing was the heroic tale I would have to tell in Hong Kong about how I had been kept in chains. On the second day the quiet-mannered cadre, who seemed to serve as the assistant interrogator, came to see me. He asked me if I had anything further to say. I merely replied that I had told everything I knew, which was nothing. He looked at me almost pleadingly for a moment and then went back to our bedroom-study, which had been taken over by the cadre and guards.

I could hear him say to Cadre Lu, "She still won't talk. What are we going to do?"

"That's fine," I thought. "Maybe you're ready to give up now and let me go home."

On the third night I was taken in the jeep to another courtroom. This time the interrogator asked me about my background and the things I had studied in the Chinese universities. I felt I could afford to tell the truth about such matters and before long he said, "You seem to be more honest tonight. We shall take the cuffs off this time, and I hope you will try to tell the truth from now on. Now I shall give you three questions to think about and next time we want straight answers. 'What were you doing in China?' 'What was Li Ko doing in China?' and 'What was your relationship with the American Naval Attaché, Williams, and his role in China?' " With that I was taken home.

When the handcuffs had been put on I had begun to doubt that my play at ignorance would work, but with the removal of the cuffs my confidence returned in full force. "What can they do if I say I know nothing?" I reasoned. And so I paid little attention to the three questions.

It was at this point that I developed a queer train of thought for a short time. I remembered Evelyn Waugh's *A Handful of Dust* quite vividly and suddenly likened myself to the young hero who maintains a completely detached manner through the dramatic pattern of his life. I placed myself outside the situation for the moment and looked at what was happening as if it were on a stage. "This is just one interesting event in the whole process of my life," I thought. "As long as I look on it as such I cannot be hurt by it."

Thus, a few nights later, when the interrogation started again I carried on with "I don't know" to all questions. In the case of Williams I was telling the truth when I said we had had no relations with him and that I knew nothing about him, but, mixed in with the lies, this little bit of truth remained insignificant.

It was not long before the handcuffs were brought out again and snapped on behind my back. This time when I went home they remained behind my back. I was also told that I would not be allowed to read any more.

It was uncomfortable trying to sleep on my stomach. My face felt as if it were being pushed into the pillow, and I had difficulty working the sheet up around my ears to cut out the buzz of the mosquitoes. But I eventually squirmed around into a half-way tolerable position and slept until late in the morning. As before, I would in no way show that I had any feeling about the cuffs at all, and so, when I wanted to eat or go to the bathroom I very nonchalantly backed my way up to the guard and waited patiently for him to unlock them. I really think they were more worried about my situation than I was, for each time they put the cuffs back on they would leave them so loose on my wrists I could almost have slipped out of them.

With no books to read I found the hours dragged by with interminable slowness. I thought about Rick. I thought about the interview he had had in Seattle, and then quickly tried to forget it. I thought of all the information we had given the Consulate and then rationalized, "But we didn't mean anything by that." I thought about our Fulbright scholarships and our connection with the Nationalists. I went over all our activities, and every time my mind touched on the answers to the questions I had been asked I felt a tremor in my heart. If I could only blank out my mind and really not know anything, how simple it would be!

The assistant interrogator appeared at the end of the second day and talked with me for a few moments in the living room. I could not help but be moved by the gentle earnest tone of his voice, but at the same time he made it quite clear that the People's Government would not stand for any nonsense and that if I did not straighten out it would not go well with me.

All that night I pondered his words. To me they could mean only one thing. If I continued as I had been, the interrogators might really start to work with torture. It was quite clear they were not going to be satisfied with my "I don't know" routine much longer, and I might as well give up any idea of waiting them out. They had all the odds on their side. I began to think of things I might be subjected to, and I finally came to the conclusion that they would certainly force the facts out of me sooner or later if they applied torture because I would never be able to hold out to the end.

"If that is so, why go through all that pain? I might as well give them a few facts now. Maybe they will take that and I will be finished."

Thus I began thinking of what I could tell them without mentioning the ONI or Rick's Seattle interview. I reasoned that our relationship with Roger and some of the other Americans in Peking was well known to the police and I could gain their confidence by "confessing" to having given those people information about Tsinghua. With my mind made up to try this new tactic, I waited almost eagerly for the next interrogation. Basing on my last experience, I was sure that if I presented a few facts the handcuffs would be taken off.

My arms had been pinned behind my back on Tuesday night. On Friday night the jeep came for me. The chief interrogator, whom I had come to dislike intensely for his outbursts of temper and stern manner, started out by asking me if I had anything to say.

I replied, "Yes, Li Ko and I did give information to some Americans."

My arms were immediately released and I was told to sit down. The cadre asked me a few more questions but no mention was made of ONI at that point. As I stood up to leave he said, "What you have said tonight we shall examine more thoroughly. It does not agree in entirety with the evidence we already have, but you seem to be trying to be somewhat honest, so we shall compare the facts. You think about your relationship with other foreigners in Peking and try to remember as many details of your activities as possible, your conversations, etc."

As I lay down to sleep I felt partly relieved, but at the same time fear gripped my heart. It had been easy during the first three weeks when I had been saying "I don't know" and keeping completely detached from it all. Now I had embarked on the road to partial confession. Would I be able to keep the ball in my own hands and stop when I wanted, or would I find myself getting into a spot from which the only way out lay in disclosing all I knew? And what did the interrogator mean by saying that what I had talked about did not entirely agree with what they already knew? Was he referring to Rick's connection with ONI? A month had passed since Rick's arrest. Had he made a confession and were they comparing my statement with his?

Sunday night two days later, the quiet of the courtyard was broken by the sound of the jeep driving up. A moment later my name was called and I hastily changed clothes. I was taken to still another interrogation room this time and told to sit in a straight-backed chair in the middle of a large, pillared room that looked as if it had at one time been a reception room in a private mansion. The soft-spoken assistant interrogator sat at the desk, while the chief interrogator sat in an easy chair to one side.

"What was Li Ko's and your relationship with the Dutch?" asked the cadre behind the desk.

I told them how we had often visited in the home of a Dutch friend, how she had helped us find the house at Hsin Kai Lu and loaned us money. The chief interrogator gazed at me quietly for a moment and then said in a more gentle tone than he had ever used before, "Li Yu-an, did this woman help you out in any other way?"

I stared at him, then at the little girl recorder, and then at the assistant interrogator. The seconds ticked by as I weighed the question. If I denied any further relationship I would destroy the little bit of confidence I had built up in their minds about me two nights before. And yet, if I confessed would I not give Rick and myself away completely? The three of them sat without moving a muscle. I felt as if my whole life depended on the way I replied. Finally I took a deep breath as if getting ready for a plunge into the unknown and said, "Yes, there was something else."

"What was it?"

"Li Ko gave her letters to send out secretly in the Dutch diplomatic mail pouch and I typed those letters for him."

I could hear a sigh of relief as the three of them relaxed in unison. They knew as well as I that a turning point had been reached. My decision to tell about that key point was the beginning of my total confession. I had listened to them telling me over and over that the only way our case would ever be settled was for us to tell the whole truth about it but I had fought against it those first few weeks. Their willingness to investigate the statement I had made two nights before had begun, somewhat superficially it is true, to penetrate my mind as a manifestation of their avowals that they were looking for the facts in an effort to clarify the case. If I denied a fact which they obviously knew about, I could not expect them to treat anything I said again with credulity. Thus the only way out was to tell the truth. I had finally begun to realize that I was involved in a serious business of court investigation and not just a bit of play acting. In the weeks that followed I still tried to shy away from any mention of the Seattle incident. However, their repeated questions about why we had come to China and what we had done in the United States made it clear to me that they knew about this also, and in the end there was nothing for me to do but admit that, too.

I went out for interrogation every night for the next two weeks and finally was told to write up my full confession. I thought surely this was the end of the case and that when I had finished I would be told to go home. It was about the 12th of September that I started to write up the material. On that day I was moved into the living room, where Cadre Lu said I would be more comfortable.

Less than a week later I handed in the forty-four-page confession and sat waiting for whatever was to follow.

The next day Cadre Lu came bounding in with his characteristic excited manner. Ever since he had appeared a few days after Rick's arrest he had taken charge of the house. He could not have been long out of high school but he seemed determined to carry out his duties with a zealous regard for detail which could overcome any problem. We got on very well although his quick, Shansi accent was sometimes unintelligible and he often had to repeat a sentence two or three times before I could understand. This time, however, it did not take long for the meaning of his words to sink in.

"Li Yu-an," he said breathlessly, "a letter has just come for you. It looks as if it might be from Li Ko."

I gazed at him in astonishment, and then grabbed the envelope out of his hands.

> Darling,
>   I think from now on I had better write to you in Chinese. I am fine but I need some clothes and a few other things. Will you please send me the things listed below.
>
>   I love you,
>   Rick

I read the clumsily written Chinese characters over and over and then ran my finger over the three words, "I love you."

The list was a long one and included, besides clothes and toilet articles, some history books, notebook paper, and pencils. My heart soared as I thought of him studying in the prison. At least he could not be having too hard a time of it. Then my eye caught on another item on the list. Eyeglasses. Could his others have been broken? But how? Maybe he was knocked around and they broke when he hit the floor. With this gruesome thought I began collecting the things he needed. Since I was not allowed to go out of the house I sent Wang after whatever had to be bought. While I was waiting for him to come back I mended the holes in Rick's only two sets of winter underwear. We had been talking that spring about buying some new ones, but as usual had procrastinated. Now, with my store of money shrinking, I did not dare spend any more than was absolutely necessary. By the next day everything was ready and the cadre loaded the bundle into a pedicab and took it off to the prison.

On his return I asked, "How much was the pedicab? Since you were taking Li Ko's things, I ought to pay for it."

"Never mind, never mind. You don't need to bother," he said, tossing his head with embarrassed impatience.

That night I put Rick's letter under my pillow, and from then on kept it in my pocket where I could touch it whenever I wanted to.

I had expected that I would be called in for a final interrogation the next week and then told that our case was finished, but as the days dragged on nothing happened. Up to that time my eyes had been dry and my emotions bottled tight inside me. Though I had long since dispelled the *Handful of Dust* frame of mind, I had still kept myself from any outward display of emotion. But finally one day the hopelessness of the whole affair weighed down on me and I thought, "I've made such a mess of it all. They are certainly not satisfied with what I wrote. How am I ever going to make them believe me?"

As I sat thinking, the tears began to trickle down my cheeks. I wiped them away surreptitiously, hoping that the guard or Wang would not discover me crying. Someone must have noticed it, however, because in a short while Cadre Lu came in and sat down on the chair opposite me.

"What's the matter, Li Yu-an?" he asked embarrassedly. "Are you thinking about Li Ko? Are you thinking about home? Don't worry. The court has to work over all the facts in the case and when it is all straightened out and they have determined whether you are telling the truth or not, everything will be all right. But don't worry."

I smiled weakly and told him I was sure he was right but I just felt a bit despondent. He left me alone and I tried to stop crying. But once the dam had burst it was no easy matter to check the stream. By evening I was beginning to worry about myself and cast around for some method to stop the flow before I became ill. I finally started to tell myself *Winnie-the-Pooh* stories. As I concentrated on the delightful nonsense of Pooh Bear and his animal friends my system gradually relaxed, and by ten o'clock I had lulled myself to sleep. The next day I spent in bed with a raging headache, but when that was over I went back to my former calm.

During the days prior to my initial confession I had been told that I could not read. After I had finished writing what I considered to be my final story I thought I would probably be allowed to take up my books again, but I was sadly mistaken. The assistant interrogator and the recorder came one evening to talk with me. The young cadre looked tired as he sat on the couch across from me. He lit a cigarette slowly and asked, "Do you feel that you have finished, Li Yu-an?"

"Yes," I replied, "I can think of nothing more."

"Well, we feel that there are some points you have missed, and we would like you to go on thinking a bit more. After all, we realize that there are some things which you have forgotten that Li Ko has remembered and some things you have remembered that he has forgotten, but it is to the interests of both of you that you get all possible details cleared up. We will not force you in any way, but we would like you to think about your history and your activities some more. Is there anything in your history that you have failed to make a clean breast of?"

I stared at him hopelessly for a moment. "But I have thought and thought these past few weeks and there just isn't any more. Can't you give me a hint, or some line toward which to direct my thoughts?"

"That would be no help. You just think if there is anything at all that should be cleared up."

With that he and the little recorder stood up, buttoned their coats, and left. I remained sitting, my thoughts in a whirl. "I've brought this all on myself," I thought. "I said 'I don't know' so much in the beginning when I was lying that they can never possibly believe me now when I really don't know."

For the next six weeks I sat and thought. I noted with envy that Little Yang was reading again, and every time I remembered Rick's letter asking for books I imagined him reading, too. Was I the only one not allowed to read? But what more was there to say? One or two minor details came to my mind and I jotted these down, but the basic story had already been told. I wondered how long this would go on. If I could think of nothing new in, say, ten weeks would the interrogation officer consider that enough of a guarantee that I had told everything and let me go? But if I came up with nothing new, might they not come to the conclusion that I was giving them the run around and holding some things back on the pretense of ignorance?

And then another train of thought started me off on a fresh tack. I had all along had no feeling that I was an espionage agent such as one reads about in paperback books. From the time Rick had been contacted by ONI in Seattle I had never taken that part of our story in China as anything criminal, mainly because my mind had shrunk from the implications of such an understanding. I certainly could not deny the facts, but I rationalized them wherever possible. However, I realized quickly that the People's Government considered our activities as distinctly of criminal intent, so I began to try to look at our actions from the standpoint of the Chinese. Perhaps there were points which I had never thought of as wrong but which the People's Government felt were. In order to satisfy their law and clear up our case from their point of view, I ought to go over our history again. In other words, I tackled the problem from the standpoint of what I felt they wanted about us and not from what I considered wrong myself.

But even then I could think of nothing new. The facts were still the same, and I had given the facts. And so I spent the days alternately thinking of Rick, my family, home, and our case. Round and round, round and round. Mending, meals, exercise, occasional radio programs, and watching the comings and goings of the cadres and guards broke the monotony, but I longed for my books. This longing had a twofold implication. On the one hand I wanted to read to help pass the time and on the other I felt that the restoration of my books would signify the end of my interrogation and at least partial recognition of the fact that I was not holding back anything.

November 13 was a very cold night. We had not turned the heat on yet in order to save on coal, and I had burrowed under the blankets, though it was still early for sleep. I did not hear the jeep come and was startled to see the little recorder come into the room and ask me to get up. I hastily put on my old Wave overcoat and, teeth chattering—partly from excitement and partly from cold—went out to the jeep with her. We drove to the courtroom, which was in the old mansion. There was a stove in the room but it could not begin to have any effect on the cold. I sat shivering with my hands in my pockets.

Both interrogators were there that night. After being asked the usual question as to whether I had anything new to say I was told to write a brief summary of my history and activities. It came to about four pages. When it was finished I signed it and then sat again on the chair in the center of the room.

The chief interrogator sat puffing on his cigarette for a moment and then said, "Li Yu-an, you and Li Ko have been fairly honest. We recognize that fact. What do you honestly feel about all this?"

I hesitated a moment and then said, "I feel this way. I feel that you consider that our spying activities were the main emphasis in our work in China and that they were the most important. I admit that there was definitely that side to it, but I also contend that our studies were an important element and that we were committed to that activity before there was any question of our spying. You know now, after seeing the evidence, that we had decided to come to China years before we actually did."

He nodded slowly, and then asked, "What would you eventually like to do?"

"There is one main thought in my mind. I want to go home. If I could only go home and stay with my family and wait for Li Ko there I would never, never do this kind of thing again for any kind of government. I don't care who they are."

After gazing at me a moment he spoke again, this time almost as if each word pained him. "You know you can't go home now."

As the sentence penetrated my consciousness, tears involuntarily spilled over and fell on the front of my coat. I pulled out a handkerchief and wiped them away almost mechanically.

He finally broke the silence that ensued by saying, "Well, you go on back now and tomorrow you start to read again. You have a lot of strange ideas about new China. Why don't you read a bit and see if we are really as bad as you've been led to believe? See what we've done and what we want to do in the future. You're willing to look at two sides of the picture, aren't you?"

As I nodded in agreement with the logic of his statement he stood up and walked out of the room, accompanied by the assistant interrogator.

The young recorder came over and sat by me as we waited for the jeep to come to take us back. She smiled at me and said, "What is your viewpoint toward humanity?"

I thought wildly, "What in the world does one answer to a question like that?"

Without waiting for me to reply, she said, "I believe that we should all try to help each other and think of others before ourselves. In that way we can grow to be an unselfish, happy people."

And then, changing the subject abruptly, she continued, "You know, you mustn't worry about Li Ko. He's been getting along very well. He has been honest and has been treated very leniently. So don't worry about him."

The jeep had arrived and we went out to it. As I lay down to sleep that night I thought with excitement of the morrow. I could start reading again. As long as I had books to read I could wait an eternity. Besides, it probably was almost over. They had finally believed me. Home did not seem so far off.

7

Rick: It had taken me several days to write the seventy-six pages of my confession, and during that time, except for joining the others for meals and latrine call, I had taken no part in the activities of cell No. 9. Unlike the men in my first cell who had insisted on "helping" me write every detail of my confession, my new cell mates, apparently assuming that I knew what I was doing, had left me completely alone. When the document was finally handed in it was with a mixed feeling of hesitancy and curiosity that I sat down cross-legged along with the six other men in a semicircle on the *kang*. I leaned back against the dirty yellow whitewash of the wall as if in hopes of physical as well as moral support.

For a few moments no one spoke, while the cell leader, Liao, busied himself with a small notebook he had made of crude brown squares of Chinese toilet paper. The faces around me were expressionless masks, made even more forbidding by the grotesque shadows cast by the dim light emanating from the dust-covered bulb overhead. It was obvious that everyone was waiting to stand in judgment on what I was about to say, and I felt a nervous tension rising in my stomach. Finally Liao finished shuffling his notes and, clearing his voice, gave a sign that class would begin.

"You've been here several days," he said, turning to me, "but we still don't know much about you, nor you about us. Why don't you tell us a little of yourself?"

In an unsure voice I gave a résumé of my background and told them why I had been arrested. The others remained as impassive as before until Liao, apparently satisfied I had made a complete confession, nodded his approval. At this the features of the others began gradually to relax and my tension began to abate.

After introducing the others Liao informed me that everyone in the cell had made at least an initial confession and was waiting to be sent to one of the prison farms or factories or back to his home district to await charges there. In order not to waste time while waiting the days were spent in study.

He hesitated for a moment and then, brushing back the long lock of hair which kept dropping down over his eyes, and with a boyish smile that belied his thirty-five years, went on talking in a smooth, friendly tone.

"In the old days under the Nationalists, a person in jail just sat and rotted, and if he had been sentenced for more than three years his chance of coming out alive was very slim. If slow starvation didn't get him, sickness usually would. Now, under the People's Government, it is different. We are all criminals undergoing punishment, but the purpose of this punishment is not revenge, as it was in the old China, but education, so that some day we can return to society and start anew. However, this means that we must change our outlook on life so we won't try to repeat the mistakes we made before.

"Most of us became counterrevolutionaries and ended up here because we had spent our lives trying to get something for nothing at the expense of others. There is no place for such people in the new society. We must therefore re-examine our old ideas. In other words, we must reform our thoughts. The only way to do this is through study and mutual criticism in order to clarify in our minds right from wrong."

While he talked I sat listening intently and nodded my head as though I understood everything he said. But such terms as "outlook on life" and "reform our thoughts" were as meaningless to me as they had been on the outside, where I had heard them many times before. From the time the Communists had first entered Peking I had come to know a number of persons who claimed that their thoughts and outlook on life had been reformed. Mostly young students, graduates of short-term indoctrination courses at the revolutionary colleges, these people had become fired with an evangelistic zeal for the revolution, and there was no doubt about their changed attitude. However, I had not been inclined to take any of them very seriously at the time. It seemed to me that their change in outlook was a temporary one stemming from immature personalities.

Even when the influence of Marxism began to spread among the Western-trained intellectuals whom I knew and respected in the universities I still did not consider this to represent any profound change but merely a superficial compromise with the doctrines of the new regime. I felt that, with their solid background of Western training, it would not be easy to sway them from a deep-seated loyalty to Western ideals. Therefore, after the Chinese entry into the Korean war in October, 1950, when my close friends such as George Lee and Wu and Jao turned against the West so completely, I was profoundly shocked, frustrated, and embittered.

Particularly from January, 1951, on it was with loathing that I watched the long series of public self-criticism meetings held by the students and teachers at Yenching. In both departmental and schoolwide meetings, before small groups of close friends and large crowds, they decried their former intellectual servility toward the West as manifested in everything from a love of American detective stories to helping American imperialism by working in the United States Information Service. Many had become so emotionally worked up in their self-criticism that they had broken down and sobbed. What had made all this even more incomprehensible to me was the fact that no force appeared to have been used other than the dynamic pressure of a group experience and the emotional patriotic upsurge produced by the Korean war.

And now here I was about to witness this very same process of self-criticism and thought reform at much closer range, but with one difference. Liao, by talking in terms of our being criminals who had been guilty of living by exploiting others, was implying the need of a much deeper change than the mere rejection of a servile attitude toward Western cultural influences. I felt a faint stirring of uneasiness as he seemed to include me with the others in talking of our need for reform. Could I be expected to take part in it? Clearly I was not a criminal and they had no right to ask me, an American, to reform. But then, as I compared Liao's high-sounding phrases with what I had already seen of this so-called study as practiced in cell No. 3, my fears began to subside.

During those first few weeks, whenever Jeng, Gwo, and the others had not been helping me with my confession they had sat in a circle on the *kang* and discussed the history of the Communist Party, a topic which apparently had been assigned for general study during that period. I did not pay much attention, but from what I overheard of their conversation while I was writing or thinking about my problem they seemed to spend most of their time talking about different battles between the Communists and Nationalists, or against the Japanese, or the exploits of some spy.

Whenever they thought the guard or supervisor might be listening at the door, they would, in an obviously forced manner, praise the People's Liberation Army to the skies and loudly damn the Nationalists. Sometimes they would start out with at least a token regard for the form of a serious discussion, but usually within a short time the talk degenerated to plain gossip, the kind one would hear around any barracks. With this lapse into informality the stilted phrases of praise for the Communists disappeared almost entirely. This was especially true when Jeng was out of the room.

With the possible exception of Jeng, the hypocrisy of their attitude was apparent not only in the study period but was inherent in their every action. One afternoon, instead of *wo-tou* we had millet cooked dry, like rice, for dinner. Quite a bit of it had been spilled on the *kang* and Meng had just told Big Lu to brush it onto the floor when the supervisor happened to open the door and call me. Immediately Meng and Gwo turned on Lu with great recriminations, shouting, "What do you mean by wasting all that millet? Don't you realize that every grain of it represents the toil and sweat of some poor peasant? Not one grain of the people's food should be wasted." At the same time they began busily picking up the remnants and putting them into their mouths.

Afterward Jeng criticized them for their dishonesty, but it did not seem to faze them. Thus I felt that if the attitude in cell No. 3 could be taken as typical of thought reform in prison I was capable of handling the situation. By the time Liao had expounded in more detail the need for all of us to reform the whistle blew and it was time for bed.

During the days which followed I quickly became familiar with the study routine. Every cell, except those in which a new prisoner was being helped to make his confession, spent its time in study. The daily schedule which we followed varied little from the time I entered the prison until I left:

6:15	Rising (6:45 in winter)
6:30	Latrine call and start study
8:00	Breakfast (8:30 in winter)
9:00	Study
12:00	Noon nap (1½ hours recreation in winter)
2:00	Study
4:30	Dinner (4:00 in winter)
	Latrine call
	Recreation
7:30	Study (7:00 in winter)
9:15	Bed

During the recreation periods we read, played cards or chess, sewed, or just sat around talking. Sunday was free from breakfast until evening.

The content of the study program was under the direction of the prison authorities, who assigned general topics for discussion and occasional books to use as a basis. The study itself was organized and conducted by the prisoners in their individual cells under supervision of the cell leader. The latter had been picked by the authorities from among those prisoners who had demonstrated some desire to reform and some ability to lead a discussion and maintain order.

Once every few days or week, depending on the need, the cell leaders were called out individually or in groups to report on the activities in the cell—what they were studying, what problems had arisen, and the attitude of each prisoner. The supervisor would then make suggestions as to how to improve study in general or solve individual problems. To counteract any prejudiced opinions the supervisors would also often call in other prisoners for reports, but, outside of this general supervision and discipline whenever anyone got out of hand, our only direct contact with the authorities came through occasional prisonwide broadcasts to explain the policies of the government and to answer questions that had been brought to light in the reports of the cell leaders.

It was only natural, therefore, under these circumstances that the level of study and degree of progress varied from cell to cell, depending on the ability of the cell leader and composition of his group.

When I joined the discussion in cell No. 9 the group had just been issued a small pamphlet written by Mao Tse-tung in 1926 called *Analysis of the Classes in Chinese Society*. Liao read it out loud and then handed it to the man next to him, a thin, wolfish-faced indivdual wearing ankle chains, whom I had come to know as Ma. The latter read it again in a quick, unintelligible Shansi accent and, almost before he had finished the last sentence, tossed it with ill-disguised impatience to the next man. And so it was passed among the four literate members of the circle to read out loud. Afterward Liao went through again paragraph by paragraph, explaining any part which might be unclear and asking for questions which could be used as a basis for discussion. For example, how did the landlords come to own the land; why was the capitalist treated differently from the landlord; was the peasant a member of the proletariat?

As discussion on the first question started, Liao turned to a fat old man clad in a black silk gown and wearing a black skull cap which typed him immediately as either a landlord or country merchant and said, "You're a landlord, Wang. What do you think about it?"

Wang peered over his tinted glasses and, after clearing his throat several times, began as though reciting a piece, "All landlords are parasites and oppressors. They've stood on the neck of the poor people of China for thousands of years. Only under the glorious leadership of Mao Tse-tung and the Communist Party have the Chinese people been able to stand up in the world. When I think of the crimes that we landlords have committed I want to beat my head on the floor. I deserve to be shot."

"Chü ni de ba [Go soak your head]!" broke in Liao. "Who do you think you're going to fool with that hog-wash? You deserve to be shot, all right, but it's not just because you're a landlord. It's because you and your hangers-on tried to sabotage land reform by terrorizing the peasants. When are you going to learn you're not here to mouth pleasantries but to come to a true realization of yourself and what you've done?"

He paused a moment to shake back his unruly lock of hair, and then continued smoothly, "If you think you're fooling the People's Government with that kind of talk you're sadly mistaken. They just laugh at it. We want to hear what you really think. You think the landlords were being terribly persecuted when the People's Government divided up the land and you could have only the same amount as everyone else. But the question we're discussing now is, how did you obtain that land in the first place? It didn't always belong to you. It was only over the years that you people have squeezed it out of the peasants who worked it."

Wang blinked his little pig eyes and remained silent. It seemed as if, having been forbidden to recite his prepared speech, he could think of nothing to say.

Liao waited a moment as though hoping someone else would continue the conversation. The silence that followed was broken only by the rattle of Ma's ankle chains as he picked them up to recross his legs. Then, glancing at Liao, Ma said with a smile intended to appear amiable:

"I can tell you where most of them got it. In the old days anyone who had any surplus and was clever enough to make a few well-placed loans was on his way up. During the *ching hwang bu jye* [period in spring when the old grain has given out and the new has not yet come in] he could lend grain to a peasant who had to put up his land as security. With interest rates of 40 per cent or more, the latter had a difficult time paying it back, with the result that the land quickly passed into the hands of the creditor. The former free peasant then became his tenant. Once a man had a few tenants he could squeeze them for 50 per cent or more of the crop each year and build up even more surplus. He could even go into the grain business—buy it up cheap at harvest time and hoard it until shortages came. That's how my father got his start as a grain merchant.

"Of course, we weren't landlords," he added quickly. "During the war my father gave up most of his land and concentrated on trading, so by the time of land reform we had only enough to be classed as middle-class peasants. Besides, when he did rent out land, he never charged his peasants more than 40 per cent of the crop."

Turning to another man in ankle chains, Liao asked, "What was it in your district, Sung?"

Sung looked up sullenly and replied in a low voice, "It depended on the land. Usually 50 to 70 per cent."

I was curious about this man Sung, whose handcuffs had just been removed the day before. He was about thirty-five, with a small, tough, compact build. I had never seen him smile and he usually sat in surly silence, his rather light eyes staring straight ahead without the slightest flicker of emotion in them. Across his shaven skull there was a long scar.

"Where is your home?" I asked.

"Up near Shanhaikuan," he replied shortly. (Where the Great Wall comes down to the sea.)

"How did the peasants live under such conditions?" I questioned.

"Many of them didn't," spoke up Liao again. "He and his family had their own petty kingdom up there and they did as they pleased. You should have seen the statement this fellow wrote. It's a wonder they took the handcuffs off him at all. Why, he's killed over twenty men—that is, those that he can remember. And he has no idea how many women he's raped, except that one of them was his younger sister."

Sung lowered his head and said nothing. Liao went on, "He and his brother used to carry their pillows along with them. Wherever they saw a girl they wanted to sleep with, they just spent the night there and nobody dared say anything about it. If you've never been out in the countryside you have no idea what it was like. This fellow's family controlled a whole group of villages up there. The land all belonged to them. During the war against Japan, when the guerrillas took over the area they forced his family to cut down on the rents and interest rates.

"After the war, when the Nationalists came back, the guerrillas were forced to retire to the hills. Sung and his older brother organized their own private army and bought a Nationalist unit number for it. That made it all nice and legal. Then they started out to collect all that back rent and interest. They didn't care how they did it. The peasants paid, or else. Tell him how you wiped out most of the Jang family, Sung, the one whose younger son ran off to join the guerrillas when he couldn't stand it any longer."

Sung kept picking at the straw matting at his side, but refused to say a word.

"Yes, go ahead and tell him the way you told us when you were making your confession," said Ma.

Sung still remained silent. Finally Ma, who, I was to learn later, had a penchant for gory details, told the story himself. Pointing to Sung, he said, "One day this character and his brother took some of their men down to the Jang house. When they arrived they found the old grandfather out in the melon patch, watching the melons."

"He was too old and feeble to do anything else," explained someone.

Ma continued, "When they found him there, they asked him how the melons were. He was so scared his mouth just hung open and he stared without saying a word. Sung took out his long knife and asked the old man if he wanted to see how sharp it was. One of the gang picked up a melon and threw it up in the air. As it came down, Sung cut it in two with one swipe. The old man was shaking so hard by that time that he would have fallen over if they hadn't held him up. Then Sung bet his knife could do the same with the old man's head. He tried it, and it did. After that they went up to the house and took care of the old man's son and wife. Luckily, the rest of the family were away that day."

"His brother was a nice person, too," said Liao. "He even outdid Sung here as far as killings were concerned. One time he used a five-year-old child for a football and kicked her to death when her mother tried to make a fuss about being raped. It was especially that little business which infuriated the other peasants so much. When they got their hands on him after the Liberation Army came in, they tied a rope around his feet and dragged him to death through the streets. Sung would have ended up that way, too, if he hadn't managed to escape by jumping off his horse and diving over a cliff—with his hands tied behind his back—while they were bringing him in that night. That's where he got the scar."

"And some people like Wang here think the landlords got a raw deal. Huh!"

"Of course, they're not all like Sung and his family," said Ma.

"Naturally!" snorted Liao. "Otherwise there wouldn't be any Chinese left. But, then, very few of them ended up like Sung and his brother. Most of them were let off pretty easy. They received a piece of land and a house—as much as anybody else, besides being able to keep their personal belongings, all of which represent the blood and sweat of the peasants. In all China there were few districts where the peasants didn't have to eat chaff or the bark and leaves of trees during at least part of the year in order to give these leeches their 50 to 70 per cent rent and 40 to 60 per cent interest."

Another man, who seemed to spend most of his time searching for the lice which infested his dirty, ragged peasant clothes and then cracking them between his broken teeth, leaned forward. As he spoke, in a thick country accent, his eyes, set deep in a face grown gaunt with years of smoking heroin, scowled their hatred for the entire world. "Until I turned bandit at sixteen," he said bitterly, "I had tasted meat exactly three times in my life. And those times were at New Year's when we usually ground up a few old bones and corn meal for a feast."

"I suppose you think that's an excuse for turning bandit and working for the Nationalists," snapped Ma. "And why don't you stop cracking those lice? It's disgusting."

Then, turning to me, he said, "He and his gang ran a kidnapping racket. Of course, after they got the ransom, none of their victims ever went home again. Ning here himself strangled three of them that he admits to. Now he's trying to claim that he was really helping the Communists because the people he killed were all landlords."

"The government doesn't quite see it that way," broke in Liao, "but what he says is right. A lot of peasants turned bandit in the old China because they couldn't find any other way to live. Unfortunately, they usually ended up working with the landlords, Japanese, the Nationalists, or anybody else who would pay them for doing their dirty work. That's why he's here."

Though I knew well, through my reading in Chinese history and sociology, that such conditions had existed in the countryside, this personal contact with landlords and bandits gave me a stronger feeling of their reality.

In the weeks that followed, our discussions covered every phase of China's present, past, and future, with little regard for the limits set by the framework of Mao's text. Every man was quite willing to criticize that part of the old society with which he had little connection, but when the discussion approached his own interests he quickly fell silent or, like the landlord Wang, made such a bad pretense of beating his breast that the others turned away in anger and disgust.

Liao tried often to place our talk on a rational, analytical plane, but for the most part his efforts were in vain. Only Ma, who like Liao seemed to have had some education, showed any interest at all. The others remained completely apathetic unless they were engaged in swapping stories about what was quite obviously to their minds "the good old days."

One might very well ask why it was that these men who were all violently anti-Communist and often unregenerate bandits and murderers were willing to submit to study at all. Naturally, for them it was not voluntary, at least at first. The authorities, in accordance with the Articles for the Suppression of Counterrevolutionaries, put the choice clearly before every man who was arrested. He could refuse to confess and refuse to reform, in which case he would be tried immediately. If found guilty by the military court he would be given the maximum penalty provided by law. For many this would have been death or life imprisonment. If, on the other hand, he made a complete confession and demonstrated by his actions that he was willing to reform he was assured of a lenient settlement of his case and the chance later on to become a respected member of society.

By the time I went to prison in the middle of 1951 there was little doubt in the minds of the vast majority of prisoners that the Communists meant exactly what they said. On the one hand, the well-publicized public executions of the preceding spring had made it clear that the government was quite capable of shooting those who refused to comply. On the other hand, there were many well-known examples of people with a long history of destructive activity under the Nationalists who had decided to change their ways and had not only been allowed to go free but had been given responsible positions in the government and other organizations.

Many were worried about what might happen if they confessed and the Nationalists should come back. Others were also hesitant about involving their fellow-conspirators. But since the present danger of immediate execution was, after all, much more real than the hypothetical revenge which might come from the Nationalists and since, contrary to popular belief, there is really very little honor among thieves, most of them decided to cooperate with the government as their way out. Thus, by the time a man had made a full confession and was ready to take part in study, he had already advanced so far along the road he had chosen that there was very little chance of turning back.

At that time we all had a ridiculously simple conception of what was meant by reform. At first there was a general feeling that it merely involved a willingness to "turn Communist" and memorize a few stock slogans which we could repeat over and over. When our proficiency had reached a certain point in this we would be considered to have passed the test. For those of us who had been involved in political activity for any length of time this seemed like the simplest of the simple. If the Communists wanted "Long live Mao Tse-tung" or even "Long live Stalin," we would give it to them, but what we thought was a different matter.

When we started to take part in study almost all of us began by saying what we thought our wardens would like to hear. Land reform was wonderful. The Korean war was just. America was imperialistic and Chiang Kai-shek was a dirty traitor. It was a long time before most of us came to realize how much we had underestimated our captors.

In the meantime, after the terrible strain I had been under during the first few weeks in prison, life in this new cell seemed almost pleasant. The schedule broke up the day enough so that time went rather quickly. It was especially a relief no longer to be the object of "help." This time the attention of the cell was centered on the landlords, Wang and Sung, or the bandit, Ning. My greatest worry was that I still did not know for certain what had happened to Dell. The other prisoners assured me that she had not been bothered. After all, they said, she was only a housewife, completely inconsequential—but I was not sure.

A few days after having made my confession I was called before the investigating judge to sign a Chinese translation. When I finished, I decided to seize the bull by the horns and ask the judge whether Dell had been arrested or not. He looked at me steadily from under his heavy eyebrows for what seemed like a long time, and then said, "Did she do anything she should have been arrested for?"

My stomach turned over with fear and, as I fumbled for an answer, I wished to heaven I had kept my mouth shut. Hesitantly, I said, "Well, I forced her to type those letters which I sent out."

Then, to my surprise, he waved his hand as though brushing aside the entire matter and said perfunctorily, "What you forced her to do is no crime. No, she hasn't been arrested and you can write her a letter asking for whatever you need here."

With that he dismissed me and as I left the room I was almost floating on air. Short of being told that I could leave, this was the best news possible.

When I returned to the cell I wrote out a long list—blankets, winter clothes, soap, toothpaste, and as many books as I thought I dared ask for. A week or so later the things arrived with a brief note from Dell letting me know she was all right. I was set now to make the most of my time in prison. I began using every spare minute to improve my Chinese and learn what I could about China, because I soon found that the opportunities for collecting information in prison were better than I had ever had outside. More and more I looked upon my arrest as a stroke of luck. My capital for becoming an "expert on China" was growing daily, my dreams of Hong Kong and after even more expansive.

I decided it would be best to appear as much a model prisoner as possible. Outside of class I complied with the rules of discipline and tried to act the "good Joe" by encouraging the others to use my soap and toothpaste when they had none themselves. I also made up my mind to forgo the rice gruel which the authorities had continued to give me and which I no longer needed but had been continuing to eat simply because it added a little variety to the usual *wo-tou* and millet.

Actually, my action was not so hypocritical as it might have been, because I had already begun to feel that there was something wrong in the way we foreigners insisted we were something special and could not live like the Chinese. This had been one of the main factors in forming the gulf which had always separated me from them before, and I could sympathize to a certain extent with Ju's resentment over my special treatment. If hundreds of millions of Chinese could live on *wo-tou*, why couldn't a strong, healthy person like me do it?

In class it was also easy to act the model prisoner, since we mostly discussed problems far removed from me, such as the Communists versus the Nationalists, or land reform. There was little mention of such things as the Korean war, where I was liable to encounter trouble. The ease of my position was further enhanced by the fact that, since I was the only one in the group who had made a formal study of Chinese history, I was able to expound at great length about the evils of the pre-war foreign exploitation in China, the unequal treaties, military intervention, extraterritoriality, etc., as well as the dastardliness of the war lords and the Nationalists.

One day the door opened as I was talking and Supervisor Shen strode brusquely into the room to slouch in un-gainly fashion on the edge of the *kang*, back against the wall. The roughness of his movements was in contrast to the patience he displayed while listening to me with half-closed eyes. When I had finished he looked vaguely at the ceiling for a moment; then, fixing me with his gaze, he said in a hoarse, rasping voice:

"You're very clever. You've read a lot of books, but just repeating things you learned in school isn't going to solve anything. You'd do better to start telling what you your-self really think about the problems of today. Do you really believe imperialism is bad? Obviously you don't, or you wouldn't have come here. You must reveal your own opinions."

With an awkward, sweeping movement of his hands, as if to emphasize his words, he continued, "Put them out there on the table for everyone to take a look at. See whether they are right or wrong. Only in that way are you being honest. You think all we want to hear is a lot of nice things about the Communists. That's where you're wrong. What we want to hear is what you honestly think. Nobody has ever been reprimanded here for being honest. But if you lie and hedge and try to pretend to be something you aren't, then we don't like that.

"On the other hand, of course, we don't allow this place to be turned into a platform for spreading Nationalist or Voice of America propaganda. It's your attitude that counts. If you really want to solve a problem and find out what's right and what's wrong we'll give you all the help we can. If you can't come to a conclusion here, Liao can report it to us and we'll see what we can do. And another thing—don't get the idea you'll be leaving here soon. Your coming here wasn't simple and your leaving here won't be a simple matter either. You've committed a serious crime and you'd better start thinking about whether it was right or wrong. Now talk it over among yourselves."

After the supervisor had gone Liao turned to me, "Well, what do you think of it?"

I tried to smile in order to cover my chagrin, but my words revealed my ill temper. "I don't understand it. I thought we were supposed to study. How can you study without books?"

Liao chose to ignore my petulance and replied, "I, too, once had the same question and I was told that books wouldn't solve many problems for people like us. There are prisoners here who've even memorized Marx, but that didn't keep them from being counterrevolutionaries or committing the filthiest crime. You're here to learn why you turned out to be a criminal and how you can become a decent person. That's a personal problem and you won't find the answer to it in any book. Of course, books sometimes help increase your understanding, but they are secondary. You've got to think it out yourself."

Every time he and the supervisor had used the word "criminal" I had winced inwardly. It was bad enough having to admit I was a spy without any crime involved in it. However, I said nothing and we turned back to our original discussion. But for the rest of the morning the supervisor's concluding remarks remained uppermost in my mind. I had been thinking all along that at most I would be out in about six weeks. That would certainly be long enough for them to review my case and make sufficient propaganda use of my confession. Now it looked as thought I were going to be in for some indoctrination. That might take a little longer—perhaps even as much as six months.

Preoccupied as I was with the idea of leaving, and having no conception of what thought reform actually entailed, I was unable to grasp the real point of the supervisor's speech. I could only search his words for some indication as to how I should act in order to gain my release in the quickest way possible. He said I should express my true thinking. Perhaps I could give the impression of being sincere by revealing a little of what I thought. But not too much—I was certain I would be shot on the spot if I revealed the hostility I had felt toward the Communists during the past year, notwithstanding what the supervisor had said.

I accordingly drew up an elaborate plan. For two months I would pretend to be unconvinced; for another two months I would appear to be changing my ideas; then for the final two-month period I would be completely changed. Arriving at this conclusion I settled back and tried to concentrate on the droning voices around me.

8

Dell: A few days after Rick's arrest, as I was sitting in the little pantry room, young Cadre Lu, who had already taken charge of the house, came hurrying in.

"Hey, did you have some money in the house?" he asked loudly, as if hoping that by shouting he would make his Shansi accent more easily understood.

I replied, "I know my husband had just taken 500,000 JMP [People's currency—about $23] out of the bank a couple of days ago but I'm not sure how much of it he had used."

"Well, a packet of 500,000 JMP and some loose bills were found in the desk drawer. That must be yours. Here, count it. You'd better keep it with you. You'll need it to run the house."

At that time 500,000 JMP seemed like a large sum to me. In my hopes for an early settlement of the case I felt that it would be more than enough to carry me through. It was not long, however, before the little packet had grown quite thin. At that point I was wearing handcuffs, and the prospects of an early departure were not too good. In order to pay the rent, Wang's salary, etc., I finally wrote a note to a Dutch friend and borrowed enough for another month. "That will surely be plenty," I thought. This again proved an erroneous calculation, so I borrowed once more.

By the third month I decided to become crafty. I would make of myself an unsolvable problem by refusing to borrow any more money from my friend. I reasoned that if I had no money on which to live the People's Government would let me go home, as the only solution. The thought crossed my mind that if I had no money they might send me to jail, but I felt it was worth a chance. So when the time came to pay the rent I told Cadre Lu that I could no longer borrow from my friend since it was too much to ask of her every month.

"Well, what will you do?" he asked seriously, his usual whirlwind exuberance dimmed before a problem of such magnitude. "Do you have any money in Peking?"

"No. Our money is back in America, but we can't get it now because the United States Government has prohibited the transfer of funds to China. I don't know what to do."

I gazed at him helplessly. He went off without a word. As I heard the front door slam, I thought, "Now he's going off to headquarters to confer. Maybe they'll finish up the case and release me."

But when he came back a few hours later he had quite a different solution. "Since you don't have any money," he said, "the People's Government will lend you enough to get along on until you can find some way to pay it back. How much do you need?"

I calculated enough to last me another month and was immediately given the sum, 500,000 JMP. This was more than the salary of even a relatively high-placed official in the government, but at the time I was too concerned about being thwarted in my scheme to appreciate this.

From that time on, as soon as the money I had borrowed was running low I would write out a slip asking for an additional sum. The rent was taken out of my hands completely and, I found out later, was paid by my father. For all other household expenditures I used the money borrowed from the government. I was eventually in debt over 5,000,000 JMP (about $230), but I was not particularly worried about it because I felt that I would be able to pay the amount back when I could get funds from the United States.

I tried to live as simply as possible, but I still ate as a foreigner, operating on the myth that an American cannot live on a Chinese diet. I spent 5,000 JMP (23¢) a day and maintained a balanced diet of milk, meat, eggs, fresh vegetables, sweets, fruit, etc. The guards and the cadre cooked their meals in the house also, but they worked on an allowance of 3,000 JMP a day each. In Chinese fashion, both they and Little Yang were eating only two meals a day but, even though a schedule was worked out, the kitchen was hard put to handle us all.

Toward the end of December the jeep drove up late one night and Little Yang was taken away. I wondered whether she were on her way home or being taken to prison, but I knew I would not be surprised if it were prison, in view of her connection with Harriet.

The cook, old Wang, had continued to come every day to prepare my meals and clean the house. There was little for him to do, however, and I would gladly have let him go, but I did not dare bring the matter up because I thought Cadre Lu would certainly have something to say about my doing someone out of a job. On the other hand, it was quite obvious that Wang was not very happy in this situation. Added to this was the fact that, being advanced in years and in ill health, it was difficult for him to make the long trip back and forth every day from home.

When the Chinese Spring Festival came at the beginning of February, I told him that if it was all right with the Cadre he should take a day or two off. It was settled, and on the holiday I went down to the kitchen and cooked my own meals. Cadre Lu came to me the next day and in a slightly incredulous tone said, "I didn't know you knew how to cook."

He then asked if I would like to let Wang go and prepare my own meals. "We can buy your vegetables for you," he continued. "Old Wang doesn't seem to be in very good health, and by letting him go you can save money, too."

I was in complete agreement, with the result that a few days later Wang packed up the few odds and ends which belonged to him and left. He had struck up quite a friendship with the guards and in the next month he came back a few times to chat with them.

From that time on I would write out a slip in Chinese each morning listing the things I wanted to buy that day, and one of the guards would go out for me. One morning I listed a tube of toothpaste. It had been snowing and the streets must have been a bit uneven, for, when the guard returned, he found that the toothpaste had dropped out of the knapsack as he jounced over the road on his bicycle. I told him not to worry about it and gave him another 5,000 JMP (23¢) to buy me a second tube the next morning.

"But I can't take that money," he said, looking at me aghast. "That was my responsibility. If I lost it, I've got to replace it. Put your money back."

I tried to press the bill on him because, though it seemed a small sum, I knew it would take a major portion of his monthly allowance. But he was firm in refusing to accept the money. Later that day, while I was making dinner in the kitchen, one of the other guards came in.

"Did you think that you ought to give him that 5,000 JMP?" he asked straightforwardly.

"Sure," I replied. "After all, it wasn't his fault that he lost it. The ground was slippery and bumpy and he couldn't see the knapsack on his back."

"Well, we all feel that he shouldn't take your money. It was definitely his responsibility and if he lost it he should replace it. The People's Army is responsible to the people and when we are given a job to carry out it is our duty to see it through. If he had accepted your money we would have criticized him severely."

Though I felt uncomfortable at being the cause of the guard's loss, I could not help admiring the honesty with which they dealt with the problem, and I felt a new respect for them because of the incident. All along, however, I had been impressed by the conduct of the guards in the house. They were rotated about every two months and sometimes there were two, sometimes three, stationed in the house together, so that in the course of fourteen months I had an opportunity to observe about twenty young soldiers. One might raise the point of the possibility of my being abused since I was one woman alone in the house with them, but at no time during my entire detention at home did any one of the guards ever bother me in any way. They were friendly as far as chatting with me, asking me to help them use a dictionary, teaching me to cook Chinese food, and asking me to teach them the English alphabet, but that was as far as it went. They were there to guard the house and me, and they took their job seriously as a patriotic duty.

A few of them had come from the city, but most were young country boys who still loved to talk about their villages. One rosy-cheeked, sparkling-eyed young fellow, Yang Ming, seemed to feel that talking was not enough. He wanted some tangible tie with the farm, and so one day he came back from a shopping tour with a live hen.

"Look what I bought for 20,000 JMP [90¢]," he said proudly. "This hen will lay eggs."

"You idiot, what did you buy a hen for? Now you'll have to spend most of your time cleaning up after it. Besides, where are you going to keep it?" said his tall buddy, Liu Shr-lung, disgustedly.

"Yeah, it'll freeze outside in this weather. Who ever heard of buying a chicken in the middle of February?" added the third guard, Jin Hua, a mild-mannered, soft-spoken fellow who seemed slightly older than the other two.

"I don't care," said young Yang Ming, doggedly. "I just wanted a chicken, that's all. I'll fix up a box for it right outside the kitchen window. And you don't have to worry about the droppings. I'll clean up after it."

In the days which followed he did keep the yard quite clean, but the chicken soon became sick. Yang Ming would then take it tenderly out of the box and set it in the courtyard, but it would stand dejected, head down and refuse to move.

"If it doesn't move around, it'll never get well," said Liu Shr-lung wisely. "It needs exercise."

And so all three of the guards would prod it from behind, all the time making "shoo, shoo" sounds of encouragement and inspiration. Nothing seemed to do any good, however, and eventually it died. Poor Yang Ming was teased unmercifully for some time about spending all his savings on a sick chicken.

When the great Three Anti's movement to eliminate corruption, waste, and bureaucracy got under way in early 1952 I had a firsthand view of the movement in action. After liberation, former Nationalist officials, clerks, and army personnel had been taken into the new government en masse and, since many of them brought their old habits with them, bribery and corruption were threatening to become a serious problem in China again. To counteract this everyone in the government and army was ordered to make an accounting of himself, including the guards in the house. If they had not stolen, bribed, or extorted anything while they were in service they had nothing to worry about, but anyone who had been dishonest was expected to make a clean breast of it and, if possible, right the wrong. This applied not only to cases which involved millions of dollars but even to the smallest example of cheating.

To many people in the United States padding an expense account or taking office supplies for one's own use is not considered a serious crime, but in the new China the People's Government impressed upon its workers that such acts were actually cheating the people, since everything belonged to the country as a whole. The movement was designed to clean up any of the corrupt practices which had held over from the Nationalists and to educate the people in a new way of thinking, in which dishonesty had no part.

The guards took turns attending the meetings held in their unit, and there was a great deal of coming and going. Yang Ming and Jin Hua were plainly in the clear and chattered excitedly about the statements others were making. Liu was curiously silent during all this and finally withdrew almost completely from the group. During the day, instead of sitting around with the others as he usually did, he went into the room which had once been Harriet's, saying he did not feel very well and wanted to take a nap. Apparently he had a problem and was worried about the outcome.

It turned out that he had obtained a sum of 50,000 JMP ($2.30) under false pretenses, whether extorted or stolen I was never sure. When the movement started he realized it would be best to own up to the affair, but then he began to worry that his fellow-soldiers would ostracize him or that he would be punished for what he had done. The others could see he had a problem, but left him to work it out himself. Finally he went off one morning and was gone for several hours. When he came back, he retired again to the little room. I heard Yang Ming telling Jin Hua the outcome. He had confessed and, because he had done so voluntarily, he would not be punished, but his unit had urged him to think about how he could pay the money back.

Yang Ming said they all felt that since the emphasis of the People's Government was on exposing evidences of corruption in order to prevent their recurrence, owning up to the affair was the important thing. This showed that Liu was at least trying to be honest. Paying back the sum could be worked out later.

When later in the afternoon Liu Shr-lung had still not appeared, Yang Ming called across the courtyard, "Hey, Liu Shr-lung, how about going to the movie tonight? We're all going together."

With much coaxing, Liu was persuaded to go, but for the next few days he was a very deflated, despondent person. The others made a determined effort to make him feel part of the group again, and even Cadre Lu joined in. As they were discussing getting dinner one evening, Lu said, jokingly, "Jin Hua seems to think he's the only one who can knead bread. How about it, Liu Shr-lung, I'll bet you can make the dough as well as he can. Why don't you give it a whirl?"

Liu Shr-lung laughed embarrassedly. "I don't have as much experience as Jin Hua, but if you don't mind taking a chance I'll try."

Friendly relations returned once more to the little group and on a much more solid basis than ever before.

In the spring of 1952 the army launched a big campaign to wipe out illiteracy and began using a shortcut system of learning which had been worked out by one of the soldiers. The program was designed to teach adults to read and write several thousand characters in a few weeks. When I first read about it in the newspaper I did not believe it. After all, Rick and I, as well as most of the foreign students we knew, had spent years learning to read Chinese; and when we studied in the Navy Japanese Language School during the war memorizing 250 characters a week was considered a fast pace. Yet here were young people with no academic training whatsoever professing to learn 2,000 characters in little more than a month. I was sure it was all propaganda. In May, however, I had a chance to see the process in action, for the three guards stationed in the house at that time all started the literacy course.

Classes took up most of the morning, and in the afternoon they practiced together. This consisted of repeating the phonemes over and over while relating them to the proper symbols. "Bo, po, mo, fo; de, te, ne, le," on and on at the tops of their voices. They kept at it all afternoon and evening. At the end of a week they had mastered all the phonetic symbols and were beginning to relate them to characters. They were transferred soon after, so I was for a while unable to keep up with their progress; but during the summer two of them were transferred back. My curiosity about their ability to read was soon satisfied as I watched them in the courtyard reading the newspaper aloud. They pronounced each character in an expressionless, halting manner, but there was no doubt about it, they could read. Once in a while they would come to me and ask for the pronunciation of a word, but their command of the printed page was phenomenal, considering that two months earlier they could barely read their own names.

When I expressed my astonishment to Cadre Lu, he said, "Well, you know, we feel that if a person has the will and enthusiasm, nothing is impossible. These young men see their country growing and developing into an industrialized nation and they want to be part of it all. They realize they're going to be left out of many things if they can't read and write, and so they crave it. That's one side of it. The other is that they all help each other. None of them feels alone in this. They are carried along by each other's enthusiasm. If one of them gets discouraged, there is always someone to help him out and start going again."

The young cadre himself was a living testimony to his words. His thirst for knowledge was insatiable. He would sit at Rick's desk night after night devouring all the books he could find in the house about the history and culture of China. He maintained this devotion to study and responsibility to his job all through the time he was in charge at 48 Hsin Kai Lu. Saturday night and an occasional Sunday were the only times he allowed himself recreation, but at that time he would put on a freshly pressed uniform and take off in a rush. One Saturday he spent some time pressing his jacket. Finally, when he was ready to go, he stood in front of the guards, put on his hat, and asked with a jocular air, "How do I look, fellows?"

He turned around for them to get a full view, and upon being assured that nobody could rival him and that he would surely make a hit with all the girls at the dance he laughed delightedly and left.

He was quite concerned about my outlook on life and emotional state all through that year. When I started to read after the interrogation period had ended, he often talked with me about my point of view on Chinese history, foreign policy, etc. He also recommended books on history and Marxist philosophy for me to read. When he discovered that I could write Chinese he suggested that I write a page every night on the thoughts I had had during the day concerning what I had been reading, hearing on the radio, or any problems that bothered me about my daily living.

Though I could not help respecting the cadre for his

honesty and obviously sincere desire to help me solve my problems, I did not feel that I was in need of any help. My thoughts were my own and I was not prepared to share them with anyone. I agreed to write the diary, but I looked on it merely as a way of passing time and of practicing my written Chinese. For the most part the content was determined by what I thought he would like me to say. The chief interrogator had said that I knew very little about the new China, so in my diary I would make comments on articles I read in the newspapers, as if I were terrifically impressed by discovering the wonderful aspects of the new society. I felt somehow that if I played along in this way and waited patiently the People's Government would eventually conclude our case and let me go.

However, the true state of my thoughts sometimes showed in what I wrote. In April I dreamed three nights in a row that Rick had died, each night in a different way. I wrote about this in my diary and handed it in to Cadre Lu. Next morning he dashed into the room and said excitedly, "You mustn't think such things. Li Ko has committed a crime, it's true, but it's not anything he'll be executed for. You shouldn't worry about it like that. Everything will come out all right."

I smiled through my tears at the concern on Cadre Lu's face, and said I would not worry any more.

A few days later, he came in again. "How would you like to write a letter to Li Ko? Tell him about yourself and what you're doing."

I hardly waited for him to leave the room before I had grabbed up paper and pencil and begun to write. The letter was a simple one, but it relieved the tension, and I never had a recurrence of the troublesome dreams.

My life at home had taken on a definite pattern over the months. I got up about 6:15, made my breakfast, cleaned the room, and then sat down to study. Some mornings I washed or ironed, but for the most part I spent at least three hours reading. At noon I had a simple lunch and afterward usually bathed. From early afternoon until five I studied again. At five I listened to Radio Peking,

and when that was over went down to the kitchen to prepare dinner. After the dishes were done I took a cup of
tea back to the living room and sipped it while I thought
out what I would write in my diary. It usually took about
an hour and a half to finish the page, and I would then
read for a short time until I turned in, about 9:30. It was
curious that this schedule, worked out by myself, was almost a duplicate of the prison hours.

As the months wore on I began to feel that a change
would have to come eventually. It would be impractical
to keep me very long in the house, where I seemed merely
to be marking time. In the early months I had still clung
to the idea that I might be deported, but in the spring
of 1952, as I continued to be kept under strict surveillance, I began to realize the seriousness with which the
government viewed our crime, and felt that sooner or later
I would be sent to a regular prison.

I had already gone to bed the night of September 20
when I woke to the voice of the guard calling from the
door, "Li Yu-an, get up. Someone wants to talk with you."

When I had finished dressing, my two interrogators,
whom I had not seen for months, entered. The one who
had taken the lead throughout my investigation said very
quietly, "Li Yu-an, we have decided to arrest you, since
it has been definitely determined that you were guilty of
espionage along with Li Ko."

I murmured, "That's quite all right."

My first reaction was one almost of relief. The long
period of waiting was over and a definite decision had
been made about me. If I sat in jail for a while, my sentence would be served and I could certainly go home. At
that point I felt no fear, probably because I knew the interrogation had been completed, and, having observed the
cadres and guards for over a year, I no longer had any
qualms about mistreatment or torture. I made a bundle
of bedding, clothes, toothbrush, comb, and brush, etc.,
and when I asked if I might take along the 170,000 JMP
($8) which still remained from the last time I had bor-
rowed from the People's Government, they agreed.

As we drove to the north central part of the city I remembered the address which had appeared on Rick's letters, and thought, "I'm going to the same place." Thus it was almost with a feeling that some progress had at last been made that I went to prison fourteen months after Rick had gone.

9

Rick: All during the fall and winter of 1951 the composition of cell No. 9 changed continually. People came and went. The landlord, Wang, went off to the prison farm where he could learn how to work. The bandit, Ning, his body ruined by heroin, became ill and was transferred to a cell for the sick. One night Sung was told to pack his things and get ready to leave. We wished him good luck and I hoped that, since he had begun to show some signs of regret for what he had done, he would be given an opportunity to reform.

However, as he went out the door, Liao shook his head. "I'm afraid Sung is going to be sent back to his local district to face charges. He has too much against him to get off easily. The people there simply won't stand for it. They can forgive a great deal, but once a man has spilled that much blood he must pay for it."

I nodded glumly. It was grim to think that a person I had come to know as well as Sung was perhaps on his way to be shot, but at the same time I knew that if I had been one of the peasants who had suffered at his hands I would undoubtedly have felt differently.

No matter how I felt about Sung personally, I had come in these few months to realize that these men in prison were no champions of democracy unjustly persecuted by the People's Government, as claimed by the Voice of America. Undoubtedly certain injustices arose. No system is infallible, especially when tempers run as hot as they do during a revolution, but in my over four years in prison I knew thirty-five or forty prisoners, and there was not one who did not belong there. Furthermore, of all the hundreds who passed through there during my four years I heard of only a small handful who were finally executed.

Much misinformation concerning the number of people killed comes from Chiang Kai-shek's propaganda agencies on Formosa and Hong Kong and from some individuals in our United States who have not stopped to study the somewhat free use made by the Chinese of the term *hsiao-mieh*, usually translated as "liquidate." When the Chinese speak of liquidating a class, they mean depriving that class of its ability to exploit others. The landlords, as a class, have been liquidated, but that does not mean that they have been killed. Their class status has been wiped out by depriving them of control over the land, the basis of their power. But they themselves have been allowed to live on, unless they have committed too many crimes to be forgiven. The percentage of the latter, compared with the total number of landlords, is very small.

Gradually, as people like Sung left, the old steadies in the cell were reduced to Liao, Ma, and myself. By December, 1951, there was only one other, a man named Jou. He and his four brothers, constituting a family gang, had operated as bank robbers and had held up a number of banks in Tientsin and Peking over a period of many years. In 1932 they had killed a teller in a bank in Peking and escaped with almost $30,000. They had concealed themselves by acting as pedicab drivers, and probably never would have been caught if they had not started working for the Nationalists as an assassination team. Jou's last fare was a young man who asked to be driven to the detention quarters. When they arrived Jou was surprised to find that instead of being paid he was being placed under arrest.

With just the four of us, our study became even more insipid, especially since Jou, who was illiterate, had adopted the tactics of playing dumb to everything. When asked a question, he would roll his eyes and wave his hand in front of his face, claiming he knew nothing about politics. That had all been handled by his brothers.

During the big three-day holiday at New Year's, 1952,

things livened up a bit. We were told to enjoy ourselves, and Liao took it upon himself to see that we did if it killed us. We played cards and children's games, sang songs, and for once I found an appreciative audience for my card tricks. What we enjoyed most, however, were the feasts of Chinese meat-filled dumplings, rice, and steamed bread accompanied by a pork and cabbage dish. When the Chinese Spring Festival came, about a month later, there were another three days of revelry and feasting. This time Supervisor Shen even came in to play rummy with us for a while, and to top it off the last night I attended a variety show put on by the prisoners. Every kind of talent, some of it professional, was displayed, and, though I could not understand much of the Chinese operatic singing and dialogue, I enjoyed it immensely.

During the holiday season my spirits ran high, not only because I felt a definite comradeship with my cell mates in playing games and talking over some of our problems but also because being allowed to see the show seemed like a good sign for my quick release, for not everyone was allowed to attend.

About this time the great Three Anti's movement was launched throughout China. In connection with this the cell leaders were called together one day and told that in view of the evils arising out of the practice of having cell leaders they should make a public accounting of their previous conduct.

Under the traditional prison system in China it had been customary for one man to set himself up as leader of the cell. Usually this had been achieved through bullying and intrigue among the prisoners and conspiracy with the authorities. The old-style cell leader was practically king in his own domain. Any contact with the outside had to go through him and had to be paid for. Whatever came into the cell in the way of food, money, or clothing had automatically belonged to him, and he would portion it out as he saw fit. Woe betide anyone who tried to dispute his authority.

After liberation, because of necessity, the government

had appointed certain of the more able prisoners to be in charge. However, many of these men gradually came to take on the habits of the old-style cell leaders. It became customary that anything which came into the cell in the way of soap, toilet paper, etc., was immediately taken over by the leaders for the use of everyone, whether the owner liked it or not. The excuse given was the popular misconception that under communism no one had any personal property and everyone shared equally. This would have been bad enough, but many cell leaders extended their power to the expropriation of clothing and anything else they wanted for their own use. There followed a vicious system of favoritism, even to the point of concocting fraudulent reports about the conduct of the other prisoners. Slugging and corporal punishment were also quite common in spite of the fact that the prison regulations forbade it.

For this I blamed the prison authorities because they knew very well what was going on, but at that time were too busy or at least did not take the trouble to do anything about it. The Three Anti's movement, however, called attention to these things and the authorities, after criticizing their own previous attitude, took steps to correct the situation. One of their first moves was to call the cell leaders together. Those who admitted their wrongdoings were told to go back to the cells and make an accounting before the other prisoners. But it was necessary to put several of them in handcuffs before they were willing to admit the error of their ways.

Liao, though a rather easygoing person, was forced to admit that he had sometimes been arrogant and bullying in his treatment of others. Our main problem in discussing his conduct in the cell, however, was to make clear that even under communism personal property belonged to the individual, to be disposed of as he saw fit. Prison regulations forbade any prisoner to use the effects of another without the express permission of the authorities. But it was well over a year before the habit of "borrowing" was brought under control, and even in late 1952 it was necessary to call a general prison meeting and severely reprimand some of the cell leaders who had continued to brow-beat and abuse their cell mates. Then, even swearing at other prisoners was absolutely forbidden, and for hitting another man one could have one's sentence considerably increased.

Though at the beginning of the Three Anti's movement in the first months of 1952 attention was centered on the cell leaders, it was very quickly extended to include all of us. One day in early February the warden announced over the loudspeaker system that we should all embark on a self-criticism, reassess our attitude toward imprisonment and our conduct since we had been arrested. We should also bring out all the grievances we had bottled up inside us, see whether they were justified or not, and in this way provide a fresh basis for reforming our characters. Only if we knew where we were wrong could we proceed to rectify our mistakes.

During the following week the four of us in cell No. 9, Liao, Ma, Jou, and myself, sat huddled in one corner of the room, which now seemed far too large with the coming of winter's severest cold. Hands buried in the sleeves of our padded jackets, we pressed close together, trying to gain some corporate warmth. None of us wanted to subject himself to a really thoroughgoing self-criticism. Thus, with an unspoken agreement not to probe too deeply into each other's thoughts, we kept the mutual criticism as super-ficial as possible. We all talked in turn, trying to make unimportant matters sound like grave errors which we now sorely repented.

A few days later this relaxed atmosphere was suddenly shattered by orders to pack up our things and move into cell-block A across the compound. Lugging our bedding and numerous bundles, we entered our new cell to find three men sitting cross-legged on the *kang*.

One of them, a slightly built man of about thirty whose shaven head, close-set eyes, and buck teeth gave him the appearance of a weasel, stood up and announced in a surly, authoritative voice, "My name's Bao. I'm the cell leader. Toss your junk over there."

His overbearing manner immediately touched off Ma's hot temper and, throwing his bundle on the *kang*, he exploded, "Who do you think you are?"

"I'm the cell leader, that's who I am."

"You're an officious bully, if you ask me," shouted Ma, ankle chains clanking on the packed earth floor as he moved threateningly toward Bao. "Don't you know you're here to change that sort of attitude?"

Bao started to shout something in return, but just then one of the supervisors entered with a roar that silenced both of them. "What do you think you're doing?" Then glaring at each of us in turn, he added, "All of you behave yourselves or you're going to find yourselves in real trouble." With that he walked out, slamming the door.

Bao and Ma continued to glower at each other, but they were sufficiently cowed to say nothing more. The question of who was to be cell leader then arose. All of us from cell No. 9 wanted Liao, of course, but it was evident immediately that he was to take second place. Bao had been a member of the People's Police until he had accepted a bribe in late 1950 to give information to an American agent in Peking about the latter's impending arrest. Since he was senior to Liao as far as length of time in prison was concerned and presumably of a higher political consciousness, he took command. But from the very first the cell was divided into two cliques, Liao's forces and those of Bao.

Of the two men with Bao, I recognized one immediately. His name was Jin, and he had been connected with the Democratic League. I had seen him often at the Peking Club where he had been known as a big businessman and promoter. I was curious about his reason for being here. The man had lost much of his polish. Now his face was covered with a scraggly beard, and instead of his imported British tweeds he was wearing a much too small suit of cotton padded clothes. One of his socks had a large hole, out of which thrust his big toe. I was willing to bet that, were he to mend it, it would be the first time in his life that he used a needle. The other man was rather a nonentity whom I never came to know very well since he was transferred shortly after our arrival.

We agreed to begin all over again with our self-criticism and it was decided that Jin should start. Most of his talk was simply a retelling of his story. He had gone to the Soviet Union during the 1920's as a student, but became homesick and returned after six months. Then he had gone to law school and afterward practiced law in Manchuria, where he took a Russian wife. When the Japanese came in he gained favor with them by acting as one of their purchasing agents and finally became a personal adviser to Henry Pu-i, the puppet emperor of Manchukuo. When the tide began to turn against the Japanese, he made a quick switch and joined the Chinese underground.

After the war he entered the Democratic League and became a big business promoter in Peking and Tientsin. Through his trade relations with the Soviet Union he obtained information which he supplied to an American OSS agent in Tientsin; at the same time, feeling that a Russian wife might prove a handicap, he divorced her and married a well-known Chinese actress.

When liberation came he entered, through his contacts with the Democratic League, the new government's Ministry of Foreign Trade, where he gained a very high position. However, with the deterioration of Sino-American relations and the outbreak of the Korean war, he decided that in cooperating with the Communists he might have bet on the wrong horse. Consequently, taking a few secret documents with him, he went to Hong Kong, where he turned them over to the American Consulate in return for the promise of a visa to the United States. However, after pumping him for all he was worth, the Consulate brushed him off and he was left stranded on the beach. His money began to give out and, what was worse, in the spring of 1951 it became evident that he had made a mistake. The Americans were not going to make a comeback in China. What was he to do? Finally he decided to return to Peking where, knowing that the People's Government was usually extremely lenient toward anyone who made a voluntary confession, he would throw himself on the government's mercy.

On arrival, therefore, he told them how he had become frightened and had run off to Hong Kong. One thing he did not mention was his theft of the documents. He was certain that no one could have known about them, and there was no point in testing the government's clemency too far. He was subsequently given his old job back, and there was even talk of sending him to Hong Kong on business for the Ministry of Foreign Trade.

On several occasions, however, he was approached by various people who asked him if there were nothing more he wanted to confess, but his reply was always in the negative. Finally in July, 1951, he boarded a train for Hong Kong, reveling in his success. Much to his surprise, just after the train left the station two men in security police uniform appeared and told him to prepare to get off at the next stop. Instead of going to Hong Kong he was being arrested. Jin knew then that he had made the mistake of his life by not making a full confession before. At that moment he tried to confess everything on the spot but it was too late.

His self-criticism ended with him smacking himself on the head and saying, "Oh, why didn't I tell the truth when I had the chance?"

Bao, as the new cell leader, kept the ensuing criticism of Jin to a minimum, and, after he had pointed out the moral of Jin's story, I volunteered to speak next. I began with a great deal of confidence. It was a story I had told many times before—how I had been an imperialist spy, how I had been justifiably arrested, and how I now thanked the People's Government for treating me so leniently. I continued by admitting that I had recently been rather lax in my observance of discipline, and ended with the promise that I would not do it again. Just the week before in cell No. 9 this pretense at self-criticism had passed without a murmur from the others. I was therefore hardly prepared for the blast which now came from Bao.

"Do you call that a self-criticism?" he cried. His close-set eyes, squinting with anger, appeared almost crossed. "Here you are sitting in jail and you're trying to tell us that everything is fine and you're so thankful to the People's Government. *Ta-ma-di!* You're supposed to reveal what you really think so the rest of us can help you with our criticism. We're not playing games. Now start talking sense."

I was so taken aback, for a moment words failed me. Then, in a voice which sounded hesitant even to my own ears, I began a confused repetition of some of the innocuous things I had said before. This served only to increase Bao's fury and he pressed even more relentlessly his demand for my "true thoughts."

Finally, driven to a point of angry desperation, I exploded, "Well, I don't see why I couldn't have had a lawyer."

Immediately shouts came flying from all sides. What did I want a lawyer for? What had I to defend? Was I or was I not a spy?

"The only reason you want a lawyer," broke in Liao, "is so you can avoid having to pay for your crimes. That's the way it is in a capitalist society. If a man has money he can hire a lawyer to get him out of almost anything, while the poor man goes to jail. And what's more, if this were the old China you wouldn't even have had to hire a lawyer. All you'd have had to do was call your Consulate friends and they'd have had you out in no time."

I was silent. How could I answer such an attack? What they said might be true, but to my mind it was irrelevant. According to our traditions, whether a man is guilty or not he had a right to a lawyer.

As if to answer this unexpressed thought, Liao went on, "If you had committed an ordinary crime and this were a civil court, you would have a right to a lawyer and organized defense. But you're forgetting that we're not only living through a revolution here at home. There is also a war going on in Korea. You have been guilty of counter-revolutionary espionage. That puts your case under martial law, and before a military tribunal a person has little in the way of normal legal rights."

Academically speaking, I could see his point. A revolution by its very nature is the antithesis of formal legality. It is a social explosion which takes place when one part of society rises up and forcibly asserts its will over its former ruler. To disagree with such a situation is like disagreeing with the universe. However, when it was a matter of my own life being involved, academic logic seemed cold and barren, and I could find little satisfaction in it.

"Incidentally," spoke up Ma suddenly, "since you seem to have so much resentment about not having a lawyer, what about it? Was your confession true or not?"

I vehemently denied that there was any question about the veracity of my confession. Heaven knows the government had been painstaking enough in searching for the truth during those endless hours of intensive questioning. Every point had been gone over and over, yet the investigating judge had never tried to put words in my mouth. In fact, once when I had tried to accept the blame for an affair in which I had been involved but for which I had not actually been responsible, he had reprimanded me for not taking my confession seriously enough and had crossed that part out of my statement.

My quick response to Ma's question seemed to satisfy him, for the moment at least, but he had no way of knowing what was seething in my mind. Actually what I objected to but did not dare put into words was the very idea of having to make a confession. To me this was a violation of basic civil rights, without which there could be no safeguard for justice. Supposing I had not been guilty but had been arrested on the basis of false evidence? If I had refused to confess, what would have happened? I would have run the risk of being shot. Under the pressure of knowing this a person might very well decide to play safe and confess to something he had not done, in the hopes of pleasing the authorities.

This same point has often been raised by people we have met since our return home. Actually, as I came to realize later on, the court did not determine a person's guilt on the basis of his confession alone. It had to be substantiated by extensive outside evidence. Furthermore, his case was reviewed once a year until final sentence was passed, and even then every prisoner had the right to appeal.

Especially from the latter part of 1952, the government seemed to become increasingly aware of the danger of false confessions. Not only was every confession checked and rechecked for corroboration of the facts, but, in order to avoid undue pressure, prisoners were no longer allowed to "help" each other with their confessions or even discuss the details of their cases in the cell. The use of handcuffs and leg irons as punishment for those people who refused to confess to what the government felt it had substantial proof of was also greatly reduced. Prisoners were frequently encouraged to think over their cases and make any rectifications which would bring their statements more in line with the facts, and it was stressed that any deviation from the facts, whether by way of exaggeration or concealment, was equally dishonest.

It became clear to me that the confession itself served not so much to verify a prisoner's guilt as to give him a chance to make his first step toward reform. That is one of the reasons why the authorities were so careful to see that it adhered strictly to the facts, for only if the prisoner made a really accurate confession could he begin to appreciate what he had done. If he admitted to something he had not done, then, to excuse his reluctance to reform, he would certainly use the rationalization that he was being treated unjustly.

My four years' experience in prison led me to the conclusion that, in spite of the tense internal situation which led to counterrevolutionary and espionage cases being handled by military courts—with the resulting restrictions on normal legal rights—the Chinese government sincerely attempted to see that justice was done. Injustices certainly occurred, as has been admitted by the government itself, but as the internal situation has improved many of the more severe restrictions have been done away with, and at the recent meeting of the National Congress in the summer of 1956 the Chief Justice of the Chinese Supreme Court asserted that the treatment of counterrevolutionary cases was being further liberalized.

At the time of my first serious self-criticism under Bao, however, I could hardly be expected to view the subject with the same amount of detachment I have today. Since it was obvious I still had problems, Bao wanted to know immediately what else was bothering me.

"Well, I don't see why I can't write to my parents," I said finally. "They are certainly worried about me."

"Did you ever ask the judge whether you could or not?"

"No," I admitted, "but then I know it would not do any good."

"How do you know," went on Ma, "if you haven't even asked? You wrote to your wife, didn't you?"

"Besides," broke in Liao, "even if the government said you couldn't, you must realize that yours is not an ordinary case. You're in for espionage. And in any country, during wartime spies are kept under strict security. You've already admitted you had one code. How does the government know you don't have another that you haven't told about?"

Bao then said impatiently, "This isn't getting us anywhere. The real problem is, what do you think of your crime?"

"My crime?" I asked, a little puzzled. "Well, I did it, there's no doubt about that."

"No," he went on, "what do you think about it? Was it a crime or not?"

"Sure," I said. "I broke the law."

"Then, if you really think it was a crime, why are you unhappy about having to pay for it?"

Now I could see what he was aiming at. I had been afraid of this question all along, because I knew that for the Communists it was not just a question of breaking the law and accepting one's punishment. If a man had made a mistake he must be really repentant about it, since that was the only way of being certain he would never repeat it. At the time I certainly did not feel that what I had done was wrong. All during my time in prison this was the most difficult thing I had to contend with. The idea of being considered a criminal and being looked upon as such by everybody around was something I could not stand. In the United States, I felt, I had always been a most law-abiding citizen. I had never even been given a traffic ticket. And though I might have broken the Chinese law, I had clung to the belief that what I had done had been in the interests of my own country and of the Chinese, too. I refused to admit that I had ever wanted actually to harm anyone, and now it hurt to be thrown in with murderers, bank robbers, arsonists, rapists, thieves, and what have you, and to be considered as much a criminal as they.

Previously I had always managed to avoid the issue, but now Bao was putting me directly on the spot. I tried to hedge, claiming that I was not too unhappy about being in prison—that is, no more than was natural for any person cut off from his wife and faced with spending many years locked up in a cell. But there was no escaping Bao. He kept boring in, with the stubborn logic of a petty police official. Finally I was forced to admit my true feelings.

My hedging and self-justifications infuriated the other prisoners. Though they themselves were Nationalist counterrevolutionaries and American agents, the idea that a foreigner should try to justify his interference in China's affairs was more than they could stand.

Ma, whose sharp eyes missed nothing, also accused me of using our study to continue to collect espionage information.

"Look at his notebook," he said. "All he does is write down names of people, figures about production, and such. He doesn't care anything about their significance as far as China's progress is concerned."

This charge brought me almost to the verge of panic by its very truth. If the authorities learned that I was still collecting intelligence even in prison I would certainly be shot. Fortunately, Ma's charge was not pressed by the others, largely because just at that time something happened which occupied their attention even more.

On February 22, 1952, Chou En-lai, the Chinese Foreign Minister, charged the United States with using germ warfare in Korea.

When I first heard the news, though I was on the lookout for propaganda, it seemed to me that it might be possible. I knew that the United States had been developing bacteriological weapons for a number of years and, according to an article by Hanson Baldwin which I had read before leaving the United States, we would have used such weapons against the Japanese if World War II had not ended when it did.* Moreover, I had been taught that in war you used whatever weapon you had, and I could see no difference between napalm or atomic bombing and the use of germ warfare. My only question was, what were the Chinese kicking up such a fuss about? It seemed to me it was merely that we had it and they did not.

When this came out in the self-criticism meeting there was an angry explosion from all sides. Bao threatened to slug me and the commotion was such that Supervisor Shen swept into the room, his arms flying.

Bao, in an excited voice, told him what I had said, and asked that I be put in handcuffs and ankle chains.

Supervisor Shen listened quietly while all the prisoners spoke out their wrath against me, but after they had finished he waved them down with an awkward gesture, saying, "It's not strange that Li Ko should think as he does. After all, look at what he is. He's the product of a society which makes a virtue of total warfare, and can see nothing morally wrong in the wholesale slaughter of innocent women and children. Wiping out a whole city with one atomic bomb is, to people like him, a great scientific accomplishment. He's been filled with these ideas for almost thirty years. You can't expect him to get rid of them overnight. Reason with him. Ask him how he'd feel if an

---

* New York *Times* Magazine, June 30, 1946, p. 52.

atomic bomb or plague germs were dropped on his wife or mother and father back home."

With that he left, as abruptly as he had come. The furor in the cell subsided a little, but Bao told me ominously, "We've had enough of discussing your problems for the moment, but you're not going to get off easy. We know how to handle imperialists."

Thus ended my first major experience with self-criticism. Contrary to the cathartic effect this "soul-searching" was supposed to have on one's spiritual well-being, I was cast into the depths of despair. My six months had come and gone, and all chance of being released in the near future seemed to have vanished. My former bravado now gave way to utter confusion. For the first time I felt at a loss as to how to cope with the situation. Not even during the dark days of interrogation had I felt as desperately inse-cure as now.

My mental state was not helped by our new physical surroundings. Cell block A, as this building in the west compound was called, was in much worse condition than cell block B, where I had spent the first six months of my imprisonment. During World War I, when this compound had served as headquarters for a cavalry unit under the war lord Yuan Shih-kai, the building had been used to stable horses. The remains of a concrete slab which had been the base for an anvil still occupied one corner of the room. The rest of the floor was uneven packed earth, damp and musty the year round.

The whitewash had long since been rubbed or peeled off walls pock-marked with rat holes. The rats themselves scurried boldly about the cell, even during the day, dodg-ing our traps and blows with maddening nonchalance. At night they conducted raids on our soap, making off with an entire cake in one evening's revelry. A small window high in the wall afforded little light, but a cold wind con-stantly rattled through large rents in the paper which had been pasted over its glassless frames. I was told that the present Communist mayor of Peking had spent eight years in that very cell block. I often wondered how he had ever lived through it.

During that winter when Peking was suffering from a bad coal shortage the prison had only about six weeks' heat during January and February. Those of us who would have liked to complain could hardly do so, however, since not even the prison officials had a fire. And, too, every one of us knew that as bad as conditions were in the prison they were still better than those of the vast majority of China's peasantry.

However, it was not surprising that under these conditions I came down with a serious cough which set my whole body shaking for minutes at a time. Yet such was my rancor against my cell mates and the entire world that I refused to place myself in a position where I might suffer from some further indignity from Bao by asking to see the doctor. It was only after a couple of weeks that I swallowed my pride and asked him to report my condition. With the surliness of a petty monarch granting a favor to one of his slaves he complied, but by that time the damage was done and I was plagued by a cough the rest of my stay in prison.

I was not the only one to feel the demoralizing effect of Bao's assumption of power in the cell. Liao, crushed by the thought of no longer being cell leader and worried that this demotion might indicate a serious turn in his case, could offer no resistance to the dictatorial Bao. Ma several times attempted to stand up to him, but whenever he did he displayed such a violent temper that Bao could easily manipulate the others against him.

In order to secure forces against Liao and Ma, Bao cultivated the big promoter, Jin, by making a play of bowing to his superior knowledge and helping Jin to obtain permission to buy food from the outside. To further offset any threat to his power, he kept the cell in a constant uproar by attacking the rest of us. As the easiest mark I found myself the center of Bao's viciousness. I could do nothing that was right. My confused state of mind gave him ample opportunity to find fault with me, and the more I tried to avoid trouble the faster it seemed to arrive. In order to counter any accusation that I might be still trying to carry on espionage activities in prison, I gave up studying completely. During rest periods I walked up and down the cell in blind detachment, bumping into everything and stepping on everyone. Preoccupied as I was with hopeless self-pity, it never occurred to me I might be offending those very people who might have helped me.

My relationship with Bao reached a crisis one March night when I decided to take a sponge bath for the third time that week. I had just stripped to the waist and was bending over the small basin of water which served all seven of us when I heard Bao roar, *"Ta-ma-di!* Don't you think there's anyone else in this cell besides yourself who'd like to wash? Do you think you can monopolize all the water?"

At the same moment he kicked the basin out from under my hand with such force that it flew across the room, striking the opposite wall and scattering water all over the floor.

This was the last straw. Shaking with rage, I clenched my fists, and would have beaten him to a pulp in spite of my fear of repercussions if Liao had not stepped between us. The other prisoners managed to calm us both down, but the next day when Bao was out of the cell I told them that if Bao did not change his ways I was going to go to the authorities about it. I would not stand for it any longer.

"The government knows all about Bao," Liao replied. "He'll be taken care of very soon. But in the meantime, is there anything wrong with you?"

His even, reasoning tone made me reflect for a minute. I finally nodded, "I guess there is."

A few days later Ma was summoned for consultation with the supervisor. When he returned, Bao was called out. Something was obviously afoot and we sat eagerly waiting what Ma had to say.

"It's about Bao," he said, thrusting his long, wolfish face forward in a conspiratorial manner. "I talked with the assistant head himself. He wanted to know how things were going in the cell and when I told him it was a mess he said, 'Well, why don't you do something about it?' Then he read me off for five minutes for not accepting responsibility when I knew things were going wrong. I tried to explain, but he just waved me down and said, 'We know your good points as well as your bad ones. See what you can do to help Bao out and get yourself back into order again.'"

It crossed my mind that it was strange that Ma, who was still wearing ankle chains, should be called upon to try to straighten out the rottenness in the cell. He was notorious for his hot temper and was looked upon by everyone as one of the most obstinate reactionaries. He was only twenty-eight but he had been a lieutenant-colonel with the war lord Yen Hsi-shan in Shansi.

After liberation he had gone into business for a while, but that had been too much of a comedown from his rank as a lieutenant-colonel and affluence from black market racketeering in "the good old days." Therefore he had worked out a plan for organizing all his former Yen Hsi-shan army connections into a large espionage setup. Slipping off to Taipei, Formosa, he conferred with some of the top Nationalist intelligence people there, and after receiving considerable money together with instructions to set up a central communications organization for contact with various Nationalist underground groups he returned to China.

Ma had been very clever, but, as so often was the case, everything he had done had been known to the government and, after making all his contacts, he was suddenly picked up. The audacity of the man came out then when he tried to make a deal with the government to let him go in exchange for a list of all his contacts. The answer had been the ankle chains he was still wearing. But that did not keep the authorities from realizing that by virtue of this very audacity he was the one man in the cell capable of coming to grips with Bao.

When Bao returned we asked him about his interview,

but he refused to say more than that we must all think of ways to improve the conduct of our study. We all remained silent and, following Ma's lead, decided to wait for some specific issue on which to tackle Bao's problem.

A few days later Bao saw a fine linen handkerchief which belonged to "our capitalist," Jin, and promptly suggested a trade for the old piece of black cloth he was using. Jin, with his characteristic obsequiousness, was all smiles in his agreement.

"Just a minute," said Ma, in a strained voice, obviously determined to control his temper. "You know what the regulations are about using other people's things."

"I'm not using it," said Bao. "We're just making a trade."

"What kind of trade is that? A dirty, old rag for a nice handkerchief?"

"What business is it of yours?" asked Bao, sarcastically.

"It's all our business," put in Liao. "We're all here to reform and you had better not forget it."

"What did the People's Government tell you the other day?" asked Ma.

"Nothing."

"You're a liar. Weren't you told to think about your conduct here in the cell?"

"Yes, but—"

"Have you been doing it? I think it's about time you made a little self-criticism of your actions," said Liao quietly.

Bao was obviously disturbed and his weasel eyes, searching vainly for some support, darted uneasily from one to another of the impassive faces surrounding him.

But still he tried to bluster. "Cell leaders don't have to make self-criticisms except to the People's Government."

"Who told you that?" asked Ma. "Would you like us to call in the supervisor and find out?"

"Well," Bao began to hedge, "I'm not afraid to make an accounting if I've done anything wrong."

"Perhaps we can help you," put in Jin, turning on Bao for the first time as he saw the way the wind was blowing.

Thus began Bao's self-criticism. One by one the others brought out their accusations against him, but it was almost two weeks before he was willing to admit, even superficially, that he had tried to set himself up as a dictator in the cell. Even then it was clear he did not consider his actions wrong.

My victory came when my Chinese cell mates all reprimanded him for his violence in dealing with me and his sneering remarks about my nationality and foreign ways. They made it clear that my imperialist way of thinking and selfish, inconsiderate actions deserved criticism, but that in the new society all peoples were equal and their customs were to be respected. With this I started to feel less of an outcast, and the aching fear and confusion which had so gripped me during the preceding weeks slackened a little.

At the end of two weeks Bao was transferred to another cell, and after each of us had criticized himself for allowing Bao to develop into such a bully we all felt relieved of the tension under which we had been living and returned to study, this time under Liao as cell leader.

However, we had not heard the last of Bao. We learned from Liao that he had been transferred to a cell with some new prisoners, where he had assumed the role of a dictator again. Still smarting from his experience in our cell, he had tried to take out his resentment on the new men by striking a couple of them. One morning the cell leaders were called together and Bao was ordered to make an accounting of himself in front of them. When he refused to dig deep enough into the reason why he had not changed his ways, he was led away in handcuffs and allowed to think it over for several weeks.

Afterward he admitted that he had never taken seriously the self-criticism made in front of us because he had believed that as an ex-member of the People's Police he was above us and in no real need of reform. Seeing that he had at least come to some realization of himself the authorities then removed the handcuffs, but he never again was given charge of a cell.

With Bao gone a new feeling for reform began to emerge in the cell, a feeling which was given a considerable boost when we were moved back across the compound to cell block B. It was learned that cell block A was to be torn down and rebuilt as part of a general clean-up of the physical aspects of the prison. This activity coincided with the health movement launched throughout China in the spring of 1952.

A few days after our move, when Liao returned from a trip to the supervisor's office, he announced that we were to begin a health campaign, and from now on the cell was to be kept spotlessly clean. We were to be given time to whitewash the walls, and each Saturday was to be a day for general cleaning. Our quarters were to be inspected regularly, and those cells which did not come up to standard would be criticized. Liao's announcement came as welcome news to us. Up to this time even in the cleanest of the cell blocks bedbugs, fleas, and lice were extremely common; and since there had been no regulations about keeping one's clothes or body clean, some of the prisoners simply refused to wash at all. Dysentery and diarrhea were so common they were almost taken for granted, and in the winter colds and various rheumatic fevers ran rampant.

Why the authorities, who expressed such concern for our mental well-being, should have paid so little attention to our physical health has been asked by many people. Part of the answer no doubt lay in the notoriously bad sanitary conditions throughout China. For people used to the rigorous life of the countryside, as were most of the prison staff as well as many of the prisoners, disease and vermin were minor inconveniences, an inevitable part of the *"chih ku"* (eating misery) which made up the poor man's life. They, both the staff and many prisoners, looked with contempt on ideas of sanitation as being an expression of the softness of the city bourgeoisie, and they could see no reason why what was good enough for them was not good enough for us imperialists and former ruling class Chinese, too. Back in the winter of 1951, when I had suggested to the other prisoners that we wash our clothes and clean up the cell, they had accused me of still wanting to practice my high and mighty imperialist ways. It took the educational force of a nation-wide movement fired by the fear of bacteriological warfare to bring home a realization of the need for sanitation.

After Liao relayed the instructions we discussed plans for house cleaning, and everyone joined in a spirit of competition. Our cell could certainly outdo the others. But suddenly Ma injected a dark note into our cheerful conversation.

"What about Li Ko?" he asked.

"What about him?" queried Liao.

"He stinks something awful. We'll never be able to get that foreign smell out of the place."

"Maybe we could have him wash a little more," put in a new arrival, named Jiang.

"*Ta-ma-di!*" said Liao laughingly. "That's all he thinks of now. I'm afraid there's not much we can do about it. It's because these foreigners all eat butter and drink milk."

"No," I said, "I don't think it's that. I've been eating the same food as you now for almost a year and I still smell. I'm afraid it's just us."

"Well," said Liao, "I guess the People's Government will have to give us a handicap on this."

Everyone laughed and we went cheerfully on with our plans.

When we started whitewashing the walls, moving the *kang*, and doing other chores I found my size, which had always been such a source of discomfort in the crowded cell, was now a great asset, and I felt my depression further slipping away.

The changes wrought by the health movement were thorough. Under the onslaught of DDT and 666 there were times when I felt that I might be going the same way as the bedbugs. We were issued fly swatters, and woe betide any fly or mosquito that dared poke its head into the cell. As soon as one appeared some of us would grab the fly swatters and, with the others acting as ground observers, launch a devastating attack against the intruder.

In no time at all we would be able to chalk up the destruction of another enemy, and its remains were carefully deposited in a small covered jar to be counted later in a competition with the other cells.

The rats were just as summarily dealt with. All sorts of ingenious traps were invented by the prisoners and the rat holes were carefully plastered over.

By the time we had finished the complex series of inoculations I began to feel that the prison doctors were going to make us healthy if it killed us, but the changes did not stop at just these prophylactic measures.

The food was greatly improved from the spring of 1952 on and the diet became better balanced. We began to take regular baths and later a system of regular exercise was instituted. The palisades around the windows were removed, making the cells light and well ventilated. Gradually all the old buildings were torn down or renovated so that, as new cells were built and the number of prisoners decreased, by 1955 those cells which had formerly contained eight or nine men held only three or four, and there were many with only two. Moreover, from 1952 on, we had heat from early November until the middle of March. As a result of these measures disease in the prison dropped over 85 per cent and at least in its physical aspect life became much more comfortable.

10

Dell: I went to jail on the night of September 20, 1952. The car drove into a large courtyard, and, after I had checked my money and wedding ring with a young woman supervisor, I was led to a cell block in the adjoining compound. We walked down a corridor with solid wooden doors on either side to one that stood open, about halfway down the line.

Though I did not know it until some years later, this was the same cell block A where Rick had spent the previous winter plagued by rats, lice, and cold under the tyrannical rule of the cell leader Bao.

The appearance of the cells had changed considerably since then, however. As the door clanged shut I found myself alone in a narrow, deep room, about four by eleven, over half of whose floor was covered by a wooden *kang*. The walls were cleanly whitewashed and the floor was smooth concrete. A large arched window took up most of the wall at the back of the *kang*, on which was spread a clean, white quilt. I made a mattress of my own heavy quilt, folded a sheet envelope-style, and then put a couple of blankets over that, for September nights in Peking are chilly. Without undressing, I lay down to sleep, but, as might be expected, it did not come right away.

My thoughts were a curious mixture of fear and security. Having spent fourteen months under the watchful eyes of guards in the house, and having gone through an intense interrogation, I felt rather secure in the knowledge that I could expect fair treatment. But this confidence gave way at moments to a fear of the unknown. After all, though the guards might be from the same People's Army, how could I be certain that the discipline and routine in the prison would be on the same easygoing level I had known at home? There was one big difference already—I was now behind a locked door.

I drifted off to sleep and was awakened by the sound of a whistle. Although there was no one to tell me, I knew it was the signal to rise. I got up quickly, made my bed, and sat with my back against the wall. As I sat there I closed my eyes and thought about the night before.

Suddenly I heard a firm voice saying, "You are not allowed to sleep during the day unless you are ill or have permission from the supervisor. That is one of the regulations here."

It was the guard speaking to me through the small opening at eye level in the door. Murmuring something about not doing it again, I thought, with a slight feeling of resentment, "This is definitely not going to be as easy as it was at home."

At breakfast time the supervisor unlocked the door and told me to take my rice bowls out into the hall where the food was being served from big, steaming vats. I was curious as to what the prison fare would be, and it was to my surprise and delight that I was given a large bowlful of my favorite bean sprouts. I was told to take some *wo-tou* also. Though I had never eaten them on the outside I had always liked corn bread, and I went back to the cell feeling quite set up. If all the meals were as much to my taste as this one prison life would not be too bad after all. The *wo-tou* was too big for me to finish, and after eating about half I put the rest aside to nibble on during the day.

Later the guard noticed me eating and said worriedly, "If you can't eat it all, don't try to finish it. It might make you sick."

I took this as a way of telling me eating between meals was forbidden. But what should I do with the left-over *wo-tou*? I finally decided to throw it into the covered toilet bucket which was in the corner, out of sight from the little window in the door.

The evening meal was eggplant soup and *wo-tou*. Again

I took a whole one but could not finish it. Some time later the guard asked me how I had made out at mealtime and how much of the *wo-tou* I had eaten. When he learned that I had thrown the unfinished part away he gasped in astonishment and left hurriedly. A few moments later a man dressed in the blue uniform of a cadre threw open the door. As I later learned, it was Supervisor Shen.

"What did you do with the rest of the *wo-tou*?" he asked excitedly, in a rough, country accent I had difficulty understanding.

After I had told him, he explained more quietly that it was very bad to waste things. I gathered that if I could not eat a whole *wo-tou* I could break off what I wanted and put the rest back. He also talked in general about the prison regulations and the need for all prisoners to reform. Eventually he ended his monologue by saying, "You can have all the *wo-tou* you want, but you mustn't waste any."

I took Supervisor Shen at his word and before long I increased my capacity from half a *wo-tou* at each meal to a whole one, and by the second year I was eating at least one and a half, sometimes two. Though they are not as rich as our corn bread, I found the corn flavor sweetened by adding bean flour pleasant to taste. That and the millet which became the usual grain for the afternoon meal were both rich in nutriment. The old doctor asked me from time to time whether I would like to supplement this diet with extra food bought on the outside, but I refused. My continued good health on this *wo-tou*, millet, and vegetable diet soon eliminated from my mind the myth that a foreigner could not live on Chinese food.

Since I had understood little of Supervisor Shen's explanation of prison routine, I began to listen to the sounds around me in order to learn the ropes. When I realized that most prisoners were in group cells my reaction was mixed. I was uneasy in the thought that the government must have a special reason for confining just a handful of us to solitary cells. At the same time I felt quite satisfied at being left alone rather than having to make an adjustment to life with other women in a group cell.

It seemed merely a continuation of my situation at home, only more restricted. I had not brought my books and the first few weeks I had nothing to read. I made the time pass, however, by dividing the day into periods. Thinking that I might have been placed in the solitary cell because there were still points in my case that needed clarification, I spent the mornings going over our past activities to see if there were anything I had forgotten. In the afternoon I made up stories, sometimes fanciful, sometimes serious. After dinner I played mental alphabet or number games, and in the evening thought about Rick, home, and my family. I derived much enjoyment also from hearing the other prisoners sing, and learned a couple of songs that way.

About a month passed in this manner and then one day a supervisor came to my cell and asked, "Can you read Chinese?"

When I answered "Yes," he went on, "Here's the newspaper."

It was the *Peking Daily* and I read every word of it. From that time on I had a paper every day. I was not too interested in the content, but I looked on it as a way of passing time and of improving my Chinese. I read many articles aloud and every afternoon memorized passages and translated others into English in my mind.

Finally, in December, 1952, I asked the supervisor if there were any way of getting a few things from home. He said that they could send someone to pick up what I wanted if I would write out a slip listing the items. I made a long list and asked for a few extra pieces of clothing, my dictionaries, some Chinese books, pencils, note paper, and my thermos bottle. About ten days later they all arrived. Now I had everything I needed to keep me busy. I worked out a strict study schedule, allotting a certain number of hours each to the newspaper, books, note-taking, memorizing, and recreation. I estimated my sentence might run for another two years and was content in the thought that I could utilize this time to improve my Chinese. I worked hard as I thought how I was building up experience for an academic position at home.

To me those months in the single cell were not specially distressing. I was not given to feel that I had been put there as a special punishment and I found in myself a store of inner resources that enabled me to pass the time almost pleasantly. In fact, I somewhat resented the periodic visits of the woman supervisor, Fang. Each time she came into the cell she would stand embarrassedly for a moment, as if not quite sure how to talk with this foreigner. My answering silence reflected my mood: "I was getting along fine by myself. You don't need to come bothering me."

She would eventually ask me if I had any problems and, on receiving a negative reply, exhort me to study hard. During those months I always took pride in the fact that I had no problems to report, and kept hoping that Supervisor Fang would thus either become discouraged in trying to talk with me or become convinced that I was a model prisoner, in need of no extra attention.

Gradually I came to understand that there were certain times for doing things. Buying for all the prisoners was done about once every five weeks, so I kept a good supply of the three essentials—soap, toilet paper, and toothpaste.

The barber came once a month. I had started to let my hair grow when Rick was arrested and, as it grew longer, I conceived the romantic idea that I would not cut it again until we were reunited. By the fall of 1952 I could put it in braids on top of my head, but to wash it with cake soap was almost impossible. The soap, instead of washing the dirt out, simply glued it in. Every time I returned from the bath and sat trying to inch the comb through its tangled mess I sighed with vexation to hear one after another the teeth from the comb dropping to the floor. By November my comb had been reduced to a stub and I decided that cleanliness must take precedence over romantic vows. When the barber came I had him cut it off ear length. Perhaps it was not so romantic that way, but it certainly felt better.

The most disturbing factor in those first months was the din of excited, angry voices that surged up frequently around me from the group cells. I could not tell what they were shouting about but the noise was deafening and I sometimes held my head, wishing it would stop. With no idea of what was going on, I could only feel frightened by it. A glimmer of understanding came to me one day when I heard one of the prisoners say:

"We're only trying to help you. Can't you see it's for your own good?"

"They call that 'helping' someone!" I thought. "Thank goodness I'm in a solitary cell. I'd die if I were to be 'helped' that way."

The very fact that I was behind a locked door put me on the defensive. Even more than at home I avoided any situations which might give my wardens a chance to refuse a request. This attitude more than once worked to my disadvantage.

In early January, 1953, as I was cleaning the cell one day, I tore the cuticle on my right index finger. At first I paid no attention to it, but before long I realized that it had become infected. After a few days the finger had swelled up like an overgrown scallion and was extremely painful. I knew there were doctors because I had heard them visiting the other cells, but I kept hoping I could get along on my own. By the end of the week it was obvious I was going to have to give in, so that day I asked the supervisor if I could see the doctor.

He gave a cluck of sympathy at the sight of my finger and said, "Sure, you can see a doctor."

In the afternoon the door opened and a rather gaunt, stoop shouldered, grandfatherish-looking man in blue cadre uniform appeared to ask what my trouble was. When I showed him my finger, he peered over his spectacles with obvious concern and asked gruffly why I had not reported it earlier. I murmured something about not thinking it very important.

He shook his head. "Sickness is always important. Come along."

For the next two weeks I had a dressing every other day. The pain lessened almost immediately, but the bandage was awkward and it seemed always in the way when I washed or tried to clean the cell. This difficulty was suddenly resolved, however, on the afternoon of February 4, 1953, when one of the supervisors came in and told me to get ready to move to another cell.

Just why I had been kept in cell No. 7 for four and a half months was never explained to me, but my feelings on being told to move were a mixture of dismay and curiosity. I had thought many times how much better off I was in a cell by myself rather than being in with a group of women who would no doubt shout and harangue as the men did in the cells around me. On the other hand, I had seen only two women prisoners for a very short time in my cell block and I was curious as to just what sort of woman ended up in prison.

I carried my thermos bottle and one small bundle while a prison worker shouldered my big bundle of bedding and clothing and trailed along behind the supervisor and me as we walked out of compound A, across the drill field, and into what was called the East Compound. One-storied red brick buildings hemmed in a large, rectangular courtyard on four sides. A brilliant red-tiled roof sloped out over a verandah which ran along three sides of the buildings, facing the courtyard. Solid wooden doors and large barred windows of the cells opened directly onto this verandah. The side on which we entered was devoted to offices, with a large gateway in the middle.

I was told to wait near the gate and in a few minutes a short, stocky woman wearing glasses came up to help me carry my things to the cell. After the quiet of my former isolated state the room we entered seemed crowded, noisy, and utterly confusing. As I sat on the edge of the *kang* several women swarmed around to ask my name, how long I had been here, how I happened to have such a load of stuff, etc. Then one of them noticed my bandaged finger.

"What happened?" she asked sympathetically.

I explained about the infection, and then another one asked, "How do you wash?"

"That's been my trouble. I keep getting it wet."

"Well, we can help you until it gets better," said a third person.

I was struck by the interest and warmth displayed by all of them. True to their words, they washed my hair for me and did my laundry along with theirs for a couple of weeks, until the finger began to heal and I could take the bandage off.

After the first flurry of questions was over I looked around. I was in a long, deep room about nine by fifteen feet, with a *kang* running the length of one wall. Besides the window which faced on the verandah there was another fairly large one in the back wall. A basin of water was steaming on a small, flat-surfaced stove in the middle of the narrow aisle formed by the outer edge of the *kang* and the opposite wall. One of the women was washing her feet in a basin before the fire.

I turned to get a better view of the *kang* itself and was startled to see a foreigner sitting with her back against the neat pile of clothing and bedding. She sat aloof, a half-smile playing on her lips. With her hair curled and a little make-up she would have been stunning, but now she looked drab and wan, her bobbed, straight hair pinned back behind her ears, her figure clad in faded blue cotton padded jacket and trousers.

One of the others followed the direction of my glance and said, "Do you know her? She's a White Russian, named Sonya."

I shook my head. Sonya's half-smile widened a moment into a three-quarter one, but still she said nothing.

The girl who had given me the explanation then asked laughingly, "And what nationality do you think I am?"

I gazed at her a moment. She looked about twenty-five, but I later learned when we compared ages that she was over thirty. In the proper clothes and with a little grooming she would be exquisite, but I felt there was something just a bit different in her looks from the Chinese women around us.

"I'm Japanese," she laughed. "And my name's Maki-moto."

"She speaks Chinese as well as we do, doesn't she?" spoke up the woman who helped me carry in my things. "She's our cell leader. You're surprised, aren't you? But it doesn't make any difference what your nationality is here. It's your attitude that counts."

She went on, "You probably won't remember everyone's name at once but anyway mine's An Mei-ling, that's Wang Hsiao-yün and that's Liu I-nan washing her feet over there."

An Mei-ling was quite right. Chinese names had always been difficult for me to remember and now, faced with a whole string at once, I was lost. As the whistle blew to start evening class I was bewildered and apprehensive, and thought longingly of the little cell I had just left.

We sat around a small, short-legged table on the *kang* and some brought out notebooks and pencils. Makimoto, now very serious, explained to me that they were in the midst of a general self-criticism in which each woman reviewed her thoughts of the past few months.

"Let me give you a word of advice," she said, her dark eyes sparkling with eagerness under the delicately shaped brows. "Don't evade telling the truth. A lot of people try to make out that they have changed their old, selfish viewpoint and now want to 'work for the people.' They may fool their cell mates and even the People's Government for a time, but they can't keep it up very long. Living as we do in such close quarters, there isn't much that escapes the attention of one or the other of us. You might be able to pretend a changed outlook for a day, a week, even a month. But what you really think is bound to show up in your actions. As long as you are honest, you will be answered with patience and understanding. But a liar and a faker is not dealt with politely."

She paused to take a sip of water from her enamel cup. "You have just come to a group cell and don't know very much about the actual process of making a self-criticism, so we will let you wait until the end. The first step is to go back over your former way of thinking. It's not pleasant, I admit, to bare some of your innermost thoughts in front of other people, especially since few are things we can be proud of, but I think you will find that problems which have seemed of great magnitude will become ridiculously simple when spoken out. We have certainly found it to be so.

"When you have revealed everything, the next step is to analyze your thoughts—where did they come from, why should you think the way you do, and what are your motives. Sometimes this is difficult because you may not be aware of some of the external forces in your background which were instrumental in shaping your thought patterns. But we may be able to help you on that.

"The third step is then to *pi-pan* [criticize], that is, estimate whether these thoughts are right or wrong when measured against the common good. We must look at our thoughts and actions through the eyes of others. The most difficult thing of all is to *pi-pan* because most of us, having thought about nothing but our own interests and desires all our lives, find it almost impossible to criticize our own actions and thoughts in terms of what is best for everybody. This is the substance of a self-criticism. Last, of course, is to put our new-found set of ideals into positive action; in other words to live out the moral concept of thinking of one's fellow man. That is our reform."

I listened carefully to everything Makimoto said, but I understood only part. I felt vaguely that she was giving me some sort of formula to follow in order to get through this "course." If I could learn the steps she had outlined and perform each one successfully, I could graduate. Otherwise . . . But how did one get a 95 or 100 per cent in such a course? I decided my best bet was to study the techniques of the others, learn from their mistakes and, when it came my turn, try to keep from making a mistake myself.

The Japanese cell leader then asked, "Do you have any questions?"

I shook my head glumly. I did not know enough of what it was all about to have any questions. It turned out that three of them had already finished their self-criticisms, leaving only Liu I-nan and Sonya. If I had thought to learn anything from listening to Liu I-nan, I was sadly mistaken. This was a woman of forty or so who had had little or no schooling and had been buffeted around by life. Sold into concubinage at the age of eighteen, she had drifted from one man to another, spent some time in a high-class house of prostitution, and picked up the heroin habit along the way.

The others told me one day that when she came to prison she sat shaking on the edge of the *kang* for almost a day, desperately in need of the "white powder." Since then she had overcome her need for the narcotic, but her face would at times become bloated and her eyes dull. As a young girl she must have been beautiful—small aquiline nose, glossy blue-black hair, full lips, and a warm, almost pleading smile. I think it was through her fourth husband that she had become connected with a Nationalist agent, helped him obtain funds to escape to Formosa, and then covered for him.

It came out in her self-criticism that she thought she would probably be released any day now because she had "sat in prison" for a full two years and, in view of the lightness of her crime, two years was enough of a sentence.

"But, Liu I-nan," said Makimoto, in an exasperated tone of voice, "we're not here just to sit out a prison sentence. We're here to reform. Can you *pi-pan* your thoughts?"

The glazed look which I was to find was Liu I-nan's usual answer to any mention of analyzing or criticizing her thoughts exasperated Makimoto even more.

"Well, I tell you what," the vivacious Japanese said, finally. "We'll pass you over for the time being and give you a chance to think about it. It's about time, though, you began to realize you can't just muddle your way through. When you first came you could plead ignorance of the process of reform, but after two years—think of it—

the number of self-criticisms you've been through and you still can't *pi-pan!* How can you ever go back out into society if you can't tell right from wrong? If you're that confused, how do you know you won't be made a sucker of by another agent? You've traded on the fact that you're a woman without education and were never supposed to think for yourself before. Well, that age has passed in China forever. Chinese women have an equal position with men now and you've got to learn to take responsibility, the same as men. You've *got to wake up!*"

She uttered the last words loudly and firmly, emphasizing each syllable, and then stared hard at Liu I-nan for a few moments, but the older woman just looked at her blankly, her mouth slightly agape.

Sonya was about to start her self-criticism when the whistle blew for bed and we all scrambled up. About all I had gained from the evening session was the idea that somehow *pi-pan* was an important thing. If I could just learn to *pi-pan* . . . But again, the big question mark danced before my eyes—how?

The next morning we sat around the little table on the *kang* for a continuation of the self-criticism meeting. Sonya launched into a description of her changed thoughts. She said that she had come to a realization that China and the Soviet Union were really the peace camp; that in this camp people were truly working for the common good, and she wanted to become a part of this. She had been reading a lot of magazines, Russian, Chinese, and English, in the last six months, which had profoundly influenced her in coming around to this view and she was extremely grateful to the People's Government for giving her this opportunity. She now hoped that when she was released she could go out and "serve the people."

I was quite impressed by her little speech and thought she had made a very good showing. I was totally unprepared, therefore, when Makimoto, her lips trembling with anger and fire sparkling in her eyes, shouted, "Do you call that revealing your thoughts?"

As if they had all been waiting for the cell leader's re-action the others suddenly came to life and began shouting about how dishonest Sonya was. I stared at her in sympathy as she sat there, apparently unruffled by the pandemonium around her. For the rest of the day they alternately shouted, pounded the table, argued earnestly, or lectured, telling her to come clean with her real thoughts. She was not moved by any of this, and the session closed for dinner with a warning by Makimoto that she had better think things over during the rest period because her self-criticism meeting was far from over.

While the rest of us were eating I noticed that Sonya was writing on a little slip of paper. This, of course, did not escape the eyes of the others, but nothing was said. As we filed out for latrine call Sonya handed the slip to the supervisor and told him a problem had arisen in the cell.

When we had all returned, Makimoto spoke the thought which lay in all our minds. "You reported our afternoon session to the supervisor, didn't you?"

When Sonya made no reply, she went on, "You think you were unjustly treated, don't you? Well, you have the right to report anything you feel needs reporting, but let me tell you this. Instead of criticizing the cell for being too harsh, you'd better start thinking about your own self. After all, you know, you're only cheating yourself. It's no skin off our bones. We'll go ahead and reform and you can just stay right on here in jail. But don't you think you're fooling us or the government. We can see right through you."

As I have said, my sympathies were all for Sonya. I thought the others were persecuting her because she was a foreigner. I was amazed that she had the nerve to report to the supervisor and wondered what the government's reaction would be.

Shortly after the whistle blew for the evening class the door opened and a tall, angular-faced supervisor, named Deng, stepped in. He paced up and down the cell for a few minutes without speaking and then sat on the edge of the *kang*, near the door. First Makimoto and then Sonya told her version of the day's happenings.

After hearing them both through, he spoke in a restrained voice, so quiet I could barely distinguish his words.

"Sonya," he said, "you feel your cell mates treated you unfairly today—but were you fair with them? Did you honestly reveal what you have been thinking? Look at your record. All your life you've served anyone who could provide you with the luxuries you craved. The Japanese, the Nationalists, the Americans—it didn't matter. You know only one thing—money—and you'd sell your soul to get it. And yet now you talk about a selfless life of service. How did all this happen, Sonya? Just by reading a few magazines?

"You see, your cell mates are not so dumb. If you had really changed your way of thinking, it would begin to show in your actions right now. But has there been any change in your attitude here in the cell? Think about it, Sonya. You've been here a year and a half now; you know as well as anyone else that if you tell the truth no one will treat you harshly. But if you persist in lying—you know the answer to that, too. And I tell you right now, you're just one step from handcuffs. Straighten out, Sonya. Don't be foolish." Then, rising abruptly, he left as quietly as he had come.

I sat blushing with shame for Sonya, but when I stole a look at her face she showed little sign of emotion except for a slight tightness about her lips. Makimoto picked up where Supervisor Deng had left off and lectured for what seemed hours on the need to bare one's innermost thought as a preliminary step to changing one's outlook. The others then took up the theme in turn, but there was no more shouting that night.

Later, as I tried to sleep, one thought stood out clearly in my mind: In order to keep out of trouble, telling the truth was imperative. Yet, if one told one's true thoughts, would they not be held against one? I remembered my impressions when I had been in the single cell listening to the shouting going on around me. But if one didn't tell the truth handcuffs and leg irons might follow. I had been disdainful of the handcuffs while under house arrest, but here in the group cell I felt that chains would be a disgrace too miserable to bear.

In the house I had felt the aggrieved martyr and had bolstered my morale by thinking of the sympathy I would rate when I arrived in Hong Kong. But here, I could tell from the way in which the others talked about the few who did wear handcuffs, I could expect no sympathy. Only the most recalcitrant, obstinate, unprincipled liars wore them—and no one wants to be looked on as that sort of person. But even more discomforting than the thought of appearing before my cell mates in chains was the thought of having Rick see me in them. That would be more than I could stand.

I determined that night to tell my true thoughts in so far as I felt they would not bring too much recrimination upon me. If I could learn to *pi-pan*, of course, that would be even better, but after just two days in the group cell I had come to feel rather discouraged on that score. The mysteries of a *pi-pan* were as deep to me as they had been at the beginning.

The next day we all waited to hear what Sonya had to say. She made no reference to her remarks of the previous day but told simply and in straightforward fashion the thoughts which had really been in her mind the past six months. She said that after her case had been reviewed in July, 1952, she had expected to be released almost any day and so had sat through the fall in anticipation of the order telling her to go. She had paid attention to study only enough to keep the others from jumping on her and had made a show of reading the magazines provided her.

Ever since liberation she had planned to go to the United States, where she felt she could obtain the luxuries which were to her a necessity. Later she had felt that applying for an exit permit to go to the United States might raise some questions in the police department, since it was known that she had been a major in the Nationalist intelligence service and had been associated with Americans. Therefore she had applied for one to Australia.

She still wanted to go to one of those countries rather than stay in China or go to the Soviet Union. "If I were to return to the Soviet Union," she said, with a nonchalant shrug of the shoulders, "I'd have to work for a living, and I don't like to work. If I can't go to the United States or Australia, then I'd rather go back to my father's house in Harbin and live with my family."

I listened spellbound as she unfolded a train of thought completely different from the one we had heard yesterday. What would happen to her now?

But when she had finished, Makimoto merely nodded her head and said, "That sounds more like it. But you ought to start thinking, Sonya, about whether such a point of view is right or wrong. It doesn't do any good to mouth a lot of phrases like 'serving the people.' We all know you don't care a hang about the people. You care only about yourself. But you ought to wake up to the fact that life as your family enjoyed it in old China is gone forever. You look on the United States as a land of milk and honey where you can live off others. They work in the United States, too, you know, and if you go on depending on other people you're going to find some day that there won't be any other people willing to support you. You've got a lot of talent and education. If you don't like the idea of being confined to an office, there are a lot of other jobs you can do."

Sonya herself then made an analysis of her thoughts. She traced her luxury-loving habits to a childhood spent in a wealthy environment where doting parents, nursemaids, and servants had all sought to please her every wish. She had lived well all her life and even on first coming to prison had tried to demand special consideration for her pampered tastes. At the first meal she had asked the authorities to provide her with a bottle of wine, since, as she said, she was accustomed to having wine with her meals.

She ended by saying, "I realize that my environment was in large measure responsible for my becoming involved in criminal activities. Now I must find a way to get rid of this selfish outlook—but so far I don't know how to go about it."

Makimoto looked stern in an effort to hide her inability to provide a solution. "That is something you will have to work out yourself," she said finally. "We can help you analyze your thoughts, but the change will be up to you. The important thing is to be honest with us and yourself."

This seemed to be all that she and the others expected of Sonya and they then turned to me. I went very simply into my thoughts on being in the single cell, my fears about being "helped," superficial things which I felt would show a desire to tell the truth but which would not probe too deeply. They did not press me further and I came through my first experience with self-criticism rather proud of myself. I felt I had made a good impression. If I could just avoid making a slip that might show some of my deeper thoughts I could probably have an easy time of it.

But it is difficult to keep from telling one's thoughts when thought-revealing is a process related to everything one reads and does. I soon found that when we read the newspaper or sat around discussing international problems I would either have to reveal my thoughts or keep quiet. I certainly could not bluff my way through. I tried keeping quiet for a while, but one evening Makimoto said,

"You don't speak up much, Li Yu-an. You ought to join more in the discussion."

I made the excuse, "Well, my Chinese is so bad I can't think out the words fast enough and someone else always starts talking first."

"Nonsense!" said Wang Hsiao-yün, her beady little eyes staring at me sharply. She and An Mei-ling had both been commended for making thorough self-criticisms and there was a strong rivalry between the two to display their newly found "progressiveness." Wang Hsiao-yün had come from a well-to-do family, had gone to college, and had ended up in prison because she had shielded her husband, a Nationalist agent. She was selfish, spoiled, and petulant, and gave orders to the rest of us as if she were running a houseful of servants.

She spoke rapidly with a slight lisp. "You didn't have any trouble talking the other day when we were chatting about foreign films. You had more to say than the rest of us put together."

"Well," I went on lamely, "I just don't know how to speak very well. I've always been quiet—all through high school and college."

This elicited a whoop from the others. "You don't know how to speak?" queried An Mei-ling, peering at me near-sightedly through her glasses. She had a thick, country accent which was sometimes difficult to understand. "Huh, I bet you didn't have to learn how to speak when you gave all that information to the American Consulate."

"Excuses like that won't go, Li Yu-an," said Makimoto sternly. "You've got thoughts and you've got a tongue. You'll never make any progress if you don't speak out."

"But it *is* true that I never spoke out in class when I was in college," I thought stubbornly. "They just don't understand and they're not being fair." But a little voice inside me said, "That may be so, but is shyness your real reason for not talking now, or is it because you have something to cover up? If you were discussing these same questions with Rick would you be so reserved?"

I had to admit to myself that I had been worsted in that exchange, but then I reasoned, "Why should I be worrying about making any progress, anyway? What I'm concerned about is simply avoiding trouble until I get released."

The spring of 1953 went on in self-criticism, study periods, and further self-criticism. I was sometimes shouted at and sometimes I shouted at others, but the main point to which they kept returning was that I did not recognize the seriousness of my crime. I quite agreed with this but, preoccupied as I was with making an impression, I could not penetrate deeply into the rightness or wrongness of my past actions. During those four months in that group cell

I learned a lot about how to *pi-pan* from a theoretical standpoint, but I related none of this to my own thoughts and attitudes. I was learning techniques of thought-revealing and analysis which were interesting as a process but I remained detached from it all.

11

Rick: During the clean-up campaign that spring of 1952 we spent almost all of two weeks whitewashing, scouring, sweeping, taking apart our quilts and padded clothing to be washed, and so on, but after this we returned to the routine of study and self-criticism.

The study in our cell was greatly improved through the addition of the new man, Jiang. He had been connected with the revolution for many years and had held a high position in the Peking police until he had made the mistake of smuggling material from Hong Kong for his unit. He was approaching forty, a rather tall, gangly person with the air of one who makes haste slowly. This was extended even to his manner of speaking, which was the nearest approach to a drawl that one can achieve in the clipped, concise language of the Chinese.

Jiang, of course, had studied a great deal of Marxist philosophy and as a result the subject matter of our conversation changed. For several of the prisoners who had never known before that there was such a thing as theory a new world opened up. We spent days arguing about everything from the meaning of truth and reality and dialectics to concepts of class struggle and revolution.

The discussions were often crude and superficial but, unlike those of the previous winter, never lacked interest. In general, the men tended to adapt their conclusions to the standard Communist line. Partly this was so because of the old inclination to please the authorities, but at the same time there was an increasing feeling on the part of most that Communist theories must be correct; after all, the Communist-led revolution had succeeded. Moreover, as long as the discussions remained on a theoretical level, where the personal self-interests of the men were seldom involved, the acceptance of socialist ideals and the doctrine of the common good was relatively easy.

Armed with their newly discovered theories and taking the course of the Chinese revolution as a universal example, they maintained vehemently in arguments with me that the United States must also some day go through a socialist revolution. Furthermore, since this change would undoubtedly be violently resisted by the present American rulers, whom they always referred to as Wall Street, the American people would be compelled to use force just as the Chinese had, in order to establish their new society.

I was willing to agree that when a society advanced to a certain stage public ownership of the means of production became necessary, and some form of socialism in the United States was inevitable. But I refused to admit that we would have to go through a period of bloody upheaval similar to that which the Chinese had experienced. After all, I argued, unlike China, we had a democratic tradition which provided a means for peaceful progress.

One day the discussion became heated. Ma especially, with his innate love for violence, insisted that my views were only the expression of reactionary bourgeois sentiments.

Finally, lips trembling with rage, I exploded. "We Americans are not going to have our country turned into a slaughter house like China was. We don't need socialism that much."

Ma's eyes burned dangerously dark as he leaned forward to thrust his face close to mine, but before he could carry his attack further Jiang cut in, "Ma, I think you had better lay off Li Ko. You're forgetting that he is an American. He had no right to interfere in China's affairs and for that reason is in prison. But we Chinese also have no right to tell him how his country should be run."

As Jiang's soft, even tone had its calming effect on both Ma and myself he continued, "You're forgetting also that Marxism is not a dogma. We Chinese had to adapt its basic principles to fit our specific conditions and the Americans will have to do the same. I don't know anything about the United States, but it is quite possible Li Ko is right."

At this point Liao, who had originally supported Ma, said, "We are all forgetting something and that is, we are not here to settle the abstract problems of revolutionary theory. We are here to reform our own moral outlooks. The People's Government is not interested in making Li Ko into a Communist. With his self-centered outlook on life, that would be impossible to begin with. It does insist, however, that he realize that what he has done to our country has been wrong."

I listened to Liao, my mind crowded with doubts. Ever since the devastating experience of my first self-criticism under Bao, and the realization that my hopes of faking "reform" during the first six months had met with dismal failure, I had been tormented by one question in particular. What did the authorities really want of me before they would permit my release? Did they expect me to become a Communist and serve China and the Soviet Union against my own country? To me the one was synonymous with the other.

Several times that spring I had awakened from nightmares in a cold sweat. Each time the dream was the same. I was stretched out on a wooden platform surrounded by Roger, Kathy, and all my old friends, who pointed accusing fingers at me and shouted over and over again, "Traitor! Traitor!" Often I lay awake wondering what to do. I berated myself as a coward for not being able to stand up in open defiance, but the fear of being put in handcuffs and ankle chains and the realization that such open resistance was, after all, pointless always led me to compromise with myself. Each time I returned to the hope that, if I concealed my fears and played the game on their terms, eventually something would happen to deliver me from my quandary.

Liao's assertion seemed to render these fears groundless, but could I believe him? In the months following I often considered seeking affirmation of his words from the authorities, but here again the apprehension that they would only confirm my original fears or give me no answer at all held me back.

Some of the other arguments we had in the cell during that summer and fall of 1952 were no less intense, especially since I found myself, at the very mention of the United States, trying to defend things which I knew were indefensible. It was quite all right if I were to talk about the terrible treatment accorded Negroes in the United States, but if one of my cell mates were even so much as to mention the matter I was ready to do battle. I would assert that the oppression of the Negro was only in the south, and for most Negroes material conditions of life were better than those of the Chinese, etc. Gangsterism, political corruption, sharecropping, and the suppression of civil liberties were all dealt with in the same manner.

I was roused to fury one day when someone said all the workers in America lived in slums. My immediate retort was, "My father is a railroad worker and he doesn't live in any slum. In fact, our workers all have a much better standard of living than you Chinese. Just try to find a Chinese railroad worker with a refrigerator, radio, washing machine, and car."

And when the promoter, Jin, tried to insist that in my case my father must be a labor racketeer such as China used to have, the national insult became a personal one. It took Jiang and Liao some time to straighten that argument out. They conceded that not all workers in the United States lived in slums but pointed out that since the United States, with its 160 million population, was capable of producing over 100 million tons of steel per year while China, with 600 million people, could produce only about two million tons, there was no excuse for any person in the United States to live in slums and not enjoy many times the material comforts of the Chinese.

The most difficult question centered around the Korean war, which was still raging in spite of the protracted peace talks. I tried to be as careful as I could to avoid arguments on this explosive issue, but it was impossible to keep from revealing my point of view. For instance, there was the day that Liao, on seeing the newspaper headline, "200 Enemy Planes Shot Down, 300 Damaged," exclaimed, "Just look at that, we've wiped out five hundred American planes."

Hard though I tried to hold them back, the words slipped out, "Two hundred. The other three hundred got away."

As long as I held this concept of *our* side as Americans against *their* side as Chinese my reactions toward all the issues coming out of the war remained hostile. But as the year 1952 rolled on into winter my outlook toward war in general began to change.

One morning, after the daily paper had arrived and the general news had been read, Liao read to us one of the stories. It concerned the pilot of an American fighter plane which had been shot down after dropping napalm bombs on a North Korean village. The pilot had managed to parachute from the plane and had landed on a hill near the Chinese positions. Troops started off to capture him, when there appeared over the hill an American helicopter, sent to rescue the stranded American. Just as the Chinese were closing in he began to climb the ladder let down from the hovering plane.

As we all sat there intently living through the story, I felt sick inside. I knew what was going to happen. I wanted to shout out to warn the pilot but there was nothing I could do and, of course, the inevitable occurred. The American had almost reached the top of the ladder and the helicopter was beginning to move away when the Chinese opened fire, bringing down the rescuer and the rescued.

Looking at the rapt expressions on the faces of my cell mates, I suddenly realized how different our way of looking at those dying Americans was. To them they were an amorphous enemy with no faces, something merely to be destroyed. But to me they were people, kids too young to die, possibly from New York or Chicago or even my home town, Seattle. And then it came to me that in the United States right at that minute there must be millions of people reading a very similar story, the only difference being that in their stories those who were dying were amorphous, faceless Chinese.

I then remembered the violent arguments I had had with George Lee in the spring of 1951. My hatred against the Chinese at that time had been such that I could think of wiping out millions of innocent peasants, women and children, without the slightest qualms. Knowing the terrible devastation and loss of life caused by Chiang Kaishek's blowing gaps in the dike to let loose the raging waters of the Yellow River in 1938 in a futile attempt to impede the Japanese advance, I myself had advocated using atomic bombs to do the same thing again, even outdoing the Nazis in cold, calculated destruction of human life. In my hate I had forgotten that those who would die were people. To my mind they had been merely faceless creatures. But now I thought, "The dead all have faces."

My expression must have revealed some of my thoughts, for Liao suddenly spoke up, "Li Ko, what's the matter?"

"I hate war," I burst out.

There was a silence, and then Jiang, slowly shifting his lanky frame, said quietly, "Most people hate war—that is, except those who can get rich out of it. But what would you have us do? Let that pilot escape so he could bring back some more napalm bombs to drop on a defenseless village? Of course, since he's an American you feel badly about that pilot, but try looking at it from the point of view of those Korean peasants."

I shook my head and sighed inwardly. Once the cycle of killing had started, with retaliation upon retaliation, where would it end? One thing was clear in my mind then: This war must stop and never again could we allow another.

* * *

One evening a few weeks later, as we reluctantly broke away from our chess games and gathered on the *kang* for class, we heard the loud-speaker in the corridor being tested in preparation for a broadcast.

In a moment the voice of the warden resounded throughout the prison. His staccato accent rendered much of what he had to say unintelligible, and I had to rely on my cell mates for interpretation.

As usual, he began with a compliment. Most of the prisoners had been showing considerable interest in study and pride in the development of their country. Many had even reached a point where they could hear the word "socialism" without wincing. They readily agreed in principle, at least, that the socialist concept of living for the common good was right and that exploitation and oppression were wrong. But—

"For most of you," he continued, "this remains merely a matter of theory and you have failed to relate these ideas to yourself. Truth is never abstract. It is not enough simply to agree that men in their relation to society must be guided by what is best for the vast majority of the people. Real reform starts when you begin to carry these principles out in your daily living. Unfortunately, few of you are capable of doing that. This is because you are still unclear as to what is right and what is wrong in your own conduct. Therefore it would be a good idea if all of you were to begin examining your actions, past and present, in the light of these principles. It is only then that you will be able to know how to transfer your high-sounding words into deeds."

When the warden's speech ended we all leaned forward eagerly and vied in proclaiming our enthusiastic acceptance of the points he had made. But as we began our discussion the problem of how one was to carry out these principles in the confining atmosphere of the prison presented itself.

"After all," said a new arrival named Han, his round, boyish, cherublike face wrinkled in perplexity, "we haven't much chance to act like a landlord or a capitalist here."

"Well, there's more to thinking of others than just determining not to be an exploiter or oppressor. Look at all the selfish bickering and backbiting that go on in this cell. I think if we consider the matter carefully we can find a lot of things that need correcting. I have an idea. Why don't we follow the example of the workers on the outside and each draw up a list of resolutions for improving our conduct, just the way they do for increasing production? That would be a start in translating our words into deeds."

Liao had hardly finished his suggestion when Ma, oblivious to the noise of his ankle chains on the wooden *kang*, scrambled over to tear a piece of clean, white paper out of my notebook. There was confusion for a few moments while everyone went about searching for pen and paper. Gradually a silence descended. I gazed blankly at my sheet of paper and wondered what I should write. Casting a furtive glance to see what the others were doing, I found that they were showing no more signs of inspiration than I.

Finally Jiang broke the stillness. "Perhaps we had first better discuss what we are going to resolve. Then we can worry about writing it down."

The rest of the evening and all the following day were spent in discussion of each man's resolutions and it was not until the second day that we all began, in our best calligraphy, to write our lists. When they were finished we neatly pasted them with moistened soap on the white-washed wall. After considerable discussion it was agreed that Liao's calligraphy was the best, but the content of each one was about the same. As near as I can remember, Liao's resolutions read something as follows:

I, Liao Cheng-i, mindful of the many crimes I have committed and the lenient treatment I have received from the People's Government, in order to reform my evil character so that I may take my place in the new society and serve my country, do hereby resolve:
1. To root out all reactionary exploiter and oppressor thinking.
2. To reconsider constantly my crimes in order to report to the People's Government any new material I may have forgotten.

3. To refrain from all backbiting and vengeful attacks on others.
4. To use every effort to help others reform.
5. To listen humbly and open-mindedly to the criticism from the People's Government and my cell mates.
6. To overcome all my selfish habits and think of others before myself.

Several days later Liao was called out to give his periodic report on the happenings in the cell. We all waited eagerly to hear what the supervisor would have to say about our resolutions, but when Liao returned his handsome, boyish face was as crestfallen as it had been exuberant before.

"What's the matter? Didn't he like the idea?" asked Han in concern.

"Oh, he liked it, all right, only he said we could spend our time a lot more profitably if we were to ask why we had not been doing these things in the first place."

Ma broke in impatiently, "Well, what do they want? This is all we've been doing for the past year."

"That's what I thought, too," agreed Liao. "It seems to me now it's just a question of making up our minds what we want to do and then going ahead and doing it."

Jiang laughed. "Huh, do you think getting rid of the selfish thought patterns of a lifetime is that easy?"

The truth of Jiang's comment became apparent almost immediately. As one after another of us faced the tests of daily living, we found our resolutions negated by the force of habitual reactions.

During that period Liao's experience was perhaps the most striking. One day he was unexpectedly called out of the cell. When he returned we noticed that his face was drawn and his lips tight. We supposed that some question had arisen about his confession, but when we questioned him about it he said no, he merely had to write a letter. After finishing the letter, he tossed it to Jiang, who read it out loud.

Jing-an,
Your letter asking for a divorce has been received. My permission is granted. As for my personal belongings, please send them to me here. I'll let the court decide about the children.

Good health
Liao Cheng-i
11-27-52

The paper was fairly smoking with Liao's rage. When Jiang asked Liao how he felt about it, he answered stiffly, "If she wants a divorce, that's her business."

But we knew it was not. Liao had mentioned his wife and three children a number of times. He was the only person in the cell besides myself whose wife had attended high school and he had been very proud of that.

About a week later a supervisor brought him a bundle containing an old quilt, a couple of pieces of worn clothing, a pair of run-down leather shoes, and a few other odds and ends. As Liao began sorting out the things, he could hardly contain himself. "Where's this? What happened to that?" we could hear him muttering. "She must have sold every *ta-ma-di* thing that was any good."

This was a little too much for me. "What kind of an attitude is that?" I asked. "How did you expect her to support herself and those kids while you're in jail? Besides, what about your resolution No. 6?" Pointing to the wall I read aloud, "To overcome all my selfish habits and think of others before myself."

There was not much Liao could say, but it was obvious he was not happy. While we were discussing the matter the supervisor came in again and asked Liao what he thought about the divorce. Liao at first tried to deny he cared one way or the other, but when the supervisor said that was impossible he admitted that he was surprised and could not understand it. Theirs had always been such a happy marriage.

"Well," said the supervisor, "it has been the government's policy on these questions to discourage unnecessary divorces, especially where there are children. But when a woman feels that she has suffered too much, she has a right to ask for a divorce. You must remember that formerly the position of women in China was intolerable and now many of them are beginning to awaken to the situation. They feel they no longer want to go on with the old relationship.

"I think if you will look back on your marriage you will be able to understand why your wife has asked for a divorce. But if you still wish to object you may do so and the court will consider the matter. Why don't you talk it over with the others?" And with that he left.

That evening when we sat on the *kang* Liao again expressed his surprise at his wife's action. "I simply don't understand it," he said, shaking his head.

As he went on talking, however, we could see at least some justification for his wife's decision. Among other things there was that business with Jing-an's younger sister. Shortly after she had come to board with them while attending school in Mukden he had started sleeping with her. Jing-an had been unhappy. She had refused to speak to him for almost a month and nearly drove him to distraction with her crying. To put an end to the situation he had finally arranged a marriage for the girl to a fellow clerk in the bank where he was working. That seemed to have taken care of the matter. At least, Jing-an had never mentioned it again.

Perhaps she had also held a grudge against him for the loss of their youngest child. She had been particularly upset because they had already lost one boy through encephalitis and this little girl might have been saved had she been taken to a hospital and treated with penicillin in time. When she was first stricken, though, Liao had insisted it was only a bad cold. In spite of Jing-an's pleadings to call a doctor, he had brushed her aside and gone out to play poker with some friends.

Luck had been against him and when he returned two days later without a cent in his pocket the child was dead. He had been forced to pawn Jing-an's wedding ring to buy a coffin. When she would not stop her incessant crying he had become angry and slapped her a few times.

"But," he looked around at us almost pleadingly, "it wasn't my fault. How was I to know the child had encephalitis?"

"I don't suppose you think involving her in this mess is anything either," I said sarcastically. "She's supposed to sit around and wait for you for the next ten years so you can start slapping her around again. In the meantime she has three children to raise."

It took our combined powers and several days of talking to make Liao see that perhaps his wife had some justification for requesting a divorce and perhaps he was not the model husband he had always thought himself to be.

As I sat watching Liao take the first tortuous steps toward a recognition of himself I could not help being struck by the pathetic picture of this man who was so capable of seeing the weaknesses in others yet totally blind to his own shortcomings. He once told us that one of his earliest recollections was the impression he had gained on seeing a picture of the war lord Yuan Shih-kai, dressed in brilliant uniform and astride a white horse. On being told by his mother that this was China's first president, Liao had solemnly informed her that some day he too was going to have a uniform and a horse like that, and then he would be able to have all the candy in the world.

He had attended a Japanese school in Mukden and after graduation had become a teller in a Japanese bank. In order to marry Jing-an, who was a student in a missionary school, he had become a Christian. Handsome, charming, and clever, Liao had risen rapidly in the bank, but the humdrum life of a banker was far removed from the glamorous goal he had set himself as a child.

When the Japanese invaded China proper in 1937 Liao decided that history was calling him to save his motherland. Leaving his wife and job, he managed to work his way to Nanking, where he joined one of the many small groups of Nationalist guerrillas then fighting the Japanese. He soon learned that actual fighting held little of the romance he had envisioned, and when his group, under the pressure of Japanese attack, decided to turn puppet, he bowed to circumstance and gave up his short-lived patriotic mission in return for a vice commandership in the new organization.

This position also failed to satisfy him long and he ran away to Peking, where he became an interpreter of Japanese for a county magistrate. After the war he drifted from one thing to another, part of the time working in Chiang Kai-shek's secret police. Liberation found him out of a job, his money all gone through drinking and gambling. The new government offered him a job, but when Liao learned it was to be scooping the muck out of the North Lake in Peking he disdainfully turned it down.

Eventually he borrowed enough money to open a coalyard. For a while he did very well, but running a coalyard could hardly satisfy a man with Liao's heroic aspirations, and even though blackened stones were used to pad the baskets of coal it was no way to get rich quick. Therefore, when news of the Inchon landing arrived, he saw in the expected return of American-backed Nationalists a chance to realize his still unfulfilled dreams of wealth and power. He reestablished acquaintance with a few of his former cohorts in the Nationalist secret police and they decided to form their own little organization, with lavish plans for sabotage and taking over the city on the arrival of American and Nationalist troops.

Liao, as organizer, was to be commander-in-chief, and high-sounding titles were handed out to everyone. They knew an ex-bandit who had a few guns hidden away in sacks of rice in the back of a small shop. With a little blackmail and a promise of the rank of vice commander they persuaded him to contribute his arsenal. They also found out where they could obtain an old radio. In the meantime they heard it was easy for groups such as theirs to obtain money from the Nationalists and Americans. So they sent a man to Formosa to procure funds and establish the right connections.

At first everything went smoothly. Among other things,

they managed to set a small hotel on fire as proof of their invaluableness to their expected sponsors. But with the bad news of American defeats in Korea in the winter of 1950–51 Liao became discouraged, especially when no word came from the man they had sent to Formosa. He and his group then decided to call off their activities for a while and he went back to his coalyard. Only a few days later, as he was leaving his office, two young men in uniform with security police insignia on their sleeves appeared at the door. Without saying a word he raised his hands and was led away.

Through all the ups and downs of Liao's checkered career his magnificent conceit had never let him down. Even his arrest had failed to shake him. As he once boastingly told us, "My first day in prison I ate two *wo-tou*." Thus his wife's request for a divorce was a staggering blow to his self-confidence. The fact that this woman whom he had always taken for granted as so much property should be throwing *him* out was more than he could bear.

Several days later, when he had finally thought the matter through, he said in a subdued manner, "You know, it's funny. I don't know how many times I thought about sacking my wife and taking on a concubine, but when she wanted to leave me—and for a really good reason—I couldn't stand it." He smiled sheepishly. "I guess Li Ko was right. My reaction to Jing-an's decision hardly lived up to my fine resolutions."

Liao's experience set us all to thinking. We had all, in different ways, done things to our wives of which we were not proud. Ma, with his violent temper, had abandoned his first wife to marry a sing-song girl whom he subsequently mistreated to such a point that she was almost driven insane. One day, when she threatened to kill herself, he playfully handed her a knife and dared her to go ahead.

I was the only one in the cell who had never struck his wife, but even I had done many things I now regretted. Not the least of these was involving Dell in my espionage activities. Of course, what really bothered us most was the possibility that our wives might arrive at the same decision as Liao's.

While Liao had been wrestling with his problem I had been rather contemptuous of his inability to see himself, but he was no different from the rest of us. Prison life has a dramatic way of revealing a man's basic nature. The close confinement, with no chance of release, generates powerful tensions. Ridiculously petty differences readily become magnified out of all reason and give rise to the most intense personal hatreds. Under such circumstances the thin veneer of civilization is stripped away, leaving all the sordid ugliness of the individual exposed to the eyes of everyone but himself. By late 1952 this had become the case with the big promoter, Jin, and myself.

We had known each other casually on the outside, and what I had seen of him around the Peking Club had led me to regard him as a cultured, easy-going, altogether pleasant sort of fellow. But now as I saw him in the cell, devoid of his polished airs and with all his petty conceit and selfishness revealed, I could hardly stand the man. At the same time it was obvious that my know-it-all attitude irked him. Our mutual dislike had led to almost constant bickering, and it was clear that a serious explosion was in the making even in the autumn of 1952. One day when Jin was out of the cell Jiang brought up the matter.

"You ought to try to do something about your relations with Jin."

"What can I do?" I exclaimed. "The man is impossible."

"He's bad, all right. But I wouldn't say he was impossible. Every man has a certain amount of good in him. That's why the People's Government believes we are all capable of reform. Our task is to use this good to overcome the bad. Why don't you try to help him? At the same time, by helping him you will help yourself."

Jiang's argument seemed logical, and if that was what they wanted I would try to "help" Jin.

A couple of days later the weather had suddenly turned chilly and we all dug into our bundles of extra clothing for something heavier to put on. That is, everyone except

Jin. He had a bundle of clothes which he had worn on the outside. But he would never think of wearing that expensive British tweed jacket and cashmere sweater in the cell. They might become soiled. Then what would he do? It was no use arguing with him; he would rather freeze. Since the regulations against borrowing had never been strictly enforced in our cell, I had offered to lend him my padded vest until the prison authorities could issue winter clothing to those people who needed it.

Jin had accepted the vest with alacrity, but he no sooner put it on than he started to act very tired and during class took to leaning so hard against the whitewashed wall of the cell that my vest was soon covered with lime. As I sat there watching him trying to wriggle his fat hulk closer against the wall a small flame began burning inside me, but there was nothing I could do about it at the moment.

It was Jin himself who gave me the opportunity to retrieve my property without actually having to ask for it. Just at this time he was called to the interrogation office, for some reason. He returned, his face beaming with self-assurance, and whispered importantly to Liao while the rest of us tried to conceal our curiosity by talking among ourselves. The next time Liao was called out for his periodic report to the supervisor the subject of Jin must have been discussed, for when Liao returned he said straightforwardly, "Jin, I think we had better discuss your problem. Why do you want to hand all your property over to the government? Isn't that a rather rash step to take?"

Jin looked uncomfortably from one to another of us, as if unwilling to have his secret bared. "I, uh," he started. "Well, I have come to the conclusion that money is the root of all evil. As long as I have all that capital I can never become one with the people."

We shouted our disbelief almost in unison. "Are you sure that's your real motive?"

Jin looked even more uncomfortable, but denied vehemently that his motives were anything but the most altruistic.

It took several tempestuous sessions before Jin admitted his decision had been influenced by the thought that if he divested himself of his property and became a "true proletarian" it might cause the government to take a more lenient view of the theft of those documents which he had turned over to the American Consulate in Hong Kong.

"In other words," paraphrased Ma with his usual bluntness, "You thought you could bribe your way out of this mess, too."

As Jin remained silent Jiang took up the argument. "The government doesn't want your property. At the present stage there's nothing wrong with being a capitalist in China. Many of them are making great contributions to China's progress. The only thing the government wants of you is to see you reform. Just getting rid of a few stocks and a couple of houses isn't going to transform you into a proletarian—not as long as your thinking is still what it is.

"Look at the way you've been treating Li Ko's vest. I've never seen you rub up against the wall so hard with your own clothes. It's caked with white all across the back. It seems to me if you were altruistic about giving up all that property you couldn't be so miserly about wearing your own things here and being so inconsiderate of others."

Jin looked sulky, but mumbled a half-hearted apology as he took off the vest and disdainfully handed it back to me.

I almost tore it out of his hands and then made a great show of shaking it out.

My short-lived attempt to "help" Jin served only to fan the flame of antagonism between us, especially since I kept rubbing it in that selfishness was the most despicable of all human traits and how I had come to see the truth of Ostrovski's words that a man could never experience true happiness himself unless he was willing to work selflessly for the happiness of all mankind.

The situation came to a head in December, 1952, over an unimportant incident. Jin and I had the only soap in the cell, and, since we had continued to share daily necessities on a "voluntary" basis, the others made free use of it.

During the autumn, when we had both had plenty, Jin and I had vied in capitalizing on this situation to win the good will of our cell mates. But now I was down to my last cake and was beginning to worry. I still had no inkling of Dell's arrest but I was never sure from one time to the next that she would be able to send me more. Jin's supply was running low, too; but, not wanting to give the impression of stinginess, neither of us said anything.

However, one morning I noticed that as soon as he had finished washing Jin quickly hid his cake behind one of the legs of the *kang*, leaving mine alone at the mercy of the crowd. It was sheer agony to watch that precious bit of personal property vanishing onto the bodies of my cell mates. I gritted my teeth and swore under my breath, "That selfish so-and-so! Boy, does he need helping!"

Hot words rushed to my lips, but I managed to check them. It was better to wait for a more suitable occasion.

It was Monday and that night was our weekly self-criticism meeting to clear up daily problems which arose out of our life in the cell. Jin was the first to speak and I waited to see if he would say anything about the soap, but he made no mention of it. His self-criticism was simply a long discussion of a few innocuous generalities, and then it came time for the rest of us to give him our suggestions.

I could hardly contain myself, but when I began to speak it was with an air of pompous humility. Overcoming selfishness was indeed a very difficult task—something which faced us all. I myself had been carrying on a difficult struggle against it all week. I knew I shouldn't feel that way, but I was down to my last piece of soap and I didn't know whether Dell would be able to send me any more for *us* to use.

"But," and now my words came with a rush, "that character, Jin, really ought to examine his attitude. Of all the sneaky tricks—hiding his soap so people will all use mine."

My attack was too much for Jin. He reached over and picked up the green crockery spittoon, which was always placed on the floor next to the *kang*, and was about to heave it at me when Jiang, staying his arm, removed it from his grasp. Breaking into tears, Jin sat with his hands over his face, his fat shoulders shaking with rage. My charge was not true, he cried wildly. He had just accidentally forgotten to offer his soap to the others. All I did in the cell was try to find fault with him. These imperialists were all the same. Everything bad that had ever happened to him had been caused by his connections with them. On he raged, and it was quite some time before the others could calm him down enough to listen to reason.

Finally Jiang said, "Well, perhaps Li Ko was wrong in bringing up the question the way he did. He should have had more proof before making such a direct charge, especially when his own interest was involved. But this soap question is something we all ought to think about. The rest of us have known all along that we were using something which didn't belong to us, but we just went ahead anyway. I think from now on we had better stop this sort of thing completely."

After the others had all voiced their agreement, he went on, "As to whether Jin's putting his soap away this morning was as accidental as he says, let's let Jin worry about that."

With this I felt a little crushed. Jin was getting off too easily, but at least I no longer had to worry about my soap. With a slight feeling of triumph, I started my own self-criticism. I talked for some time about the general evils of selfishness, but firmly denied any such motive in my attack on Jin. I had only been trying to "help" him.

This cause Liao to explode. "Do you call *that* helping? Talk about dirty underhandedness—using the pretext of helping someone criticize himself as a cover for grinding your own ax!"

Now it was my turn to be offended, and it was only after being forced to go over the entire development of my thinking about Jin that I could admit the truth. There was no doubt about it, never during the entire pretense of helping him had I stepped outside the bounds of pure self-interest.

Finally Jiang spoke up. "The government has said over and over again that we will never be able to do anything right as long as our purpose is a selfish one. Maybe some day you'll believe it. In the meantime, we don't need any more of *that* kind of help."

12

Rick: A month after my clash with Jin over the soap he was moved to another compound. About the same time Jiang was transferred also. This left only four of us, Liao, Ma, Han, and myself. We missed the others, particularly on that day in mid-March, 1953, when a workman appeared to remove for the summer the stovepipe which had run through our cell, bringing heat from the pot-bellied coal stove in the corridor. The warmth which Jin's bulk had provided would have been welcome. As it was, the four of us sat close together, bracing ourselves against the sudden change in the room's temperature.

We looked up with more than ordinary interest when a new arrival was ushered into the cell, only to see at a glance that he would be a poor substitute for Jin as far as heat generating was concerned. He was so small and slightly built that I thought at first he could be no more than fifteen or sixteen years old. I was surprised to learn later that he was almost as old as I.

After introducing himself as Li Cheng-ming, he explained briefly in answer to Liao's questions that he had been arrested for providing information to Nationalist agents. He appeared to be a completely inoffensive little fellow, but from the first I felt there was something sly about his movements and the furtive way he avoided meeting one's gaze. During class he had little to say but would sit nervously working his long, feminine fingers, sometimes flexing the joints, sometimes rubbing the tips with his thumbs, sometimes bending them backward as if they were made of rubber. I took this as just an idiosyncrasy, although it did seem strange to me that he always picked things up between his middle and index fingers rather than with his thumb and index finger as people normally do. It did not take Liao, with his secret police training, long to spot it, however.

A couple of days after his arrival, while we were playing cards, Li picked up one of them in his peculiar manner. Leaning forward quickly Liao snatched it out of his hand. "What are you doing?" he roared. "So you're a dip. I knew there was something fishy about you from the start."

Li squirmed and looked around desperately as though trying to find escape, but as Liao pressed the point he admitted to being a professional pickpocket. From then on, every time any one of us noticed Li working his fingers or picking up things in an unnatural way we would immediately pounce on him, but all our shouting, arguing, and lecturing seemed to do little good. The crisis came one day when Li was caught with a silk handkerchief he had stolen from Han. We stopped our regular study immediately to concentrate on "helping" Li. It was a futile attempt, for his only reaction was a frightened silence.

The following day Liao took the matter up with Supervisor Shen. When he had heard the story through the supervisor nodded and said, "We know all about Li. He was trained that way as a child. These habits of his have become so ingrained they cannot be changed overnight. We'll put him in handcuffs to make him realize it's a serious matter, but when you help him, make him tell why he did it."

Shortly after Liao returned to the cell the supervisor came and took Li away to put handcuffs on him. While he was gone Liao told us what the supervisor had said. "Simply reprimanding him won't do any good," he explained. "We've got to dig deep into the reasons why he does these things."

When Li returned, hands pinned behind his back, Liao immediately began by asking, "Why did you steal that handkerchief?"

Li hung his head and replied in a weak voice, "I don't know."

"What do you mean you don't know? You took it, didn't you? You must have had a reason for it. Why did you take it?"

"Because I wanted it," was the hesitant reply.

"Wanted it!" everyone roared in unison. "Was it yours?"

"No."

"Why did you want it?"

Li was silent.

"Answer," shouted someone. "Why did you take that handkerchief?"

"Because I didn't have one."

"Is that any excuse for taking something that belongs to someone else?"

"No."

"Then why did you take it?"

On we went, trying to make Li think out himself why he was addicted to stealing, but we were able only to scratch the surface. We could go only so far and then Li would say he did not know. We still could not get him to think out why he had become a habitual criminal, how he looked upon stealing itself, or what his justifications for it were. Largely this was our fault, because at that time we knew too little about Li to be able to penetrate deep into his motivations.

After two days we gave up, on the promise from Li that he would never steal again. Then, after a long lecture by each cell member on the contemptibility of stealing, and warnings that if he kept on he was certain to be treated severely because in the new society there was no place for criminals, the matter was dropped and the handcuffs removed. A few days later Li was transferred to another cell.

It was a couple of years before I saw Li again, but in the meantime I heard that he had been caught stealing once more. This time he was put into handcuffs and ankle chains and, with help from prisoners who had come to know him better, he had been forced to make a thoroughgoing self-criticism. The question of why and the search for the chain of cause and effect had gone deep. Layer after layer of his motivations had gradually come to light, until the heart of the matter had been reached.

Li, as a child, had been abandoned by his parents and picked up by a gang of thieves. At first he was used as a beggar, and then, because of his slight build, to wiggle through small windows and openings in walls to rob houses. Later he had been taught the art of a pickpocket. Whatever he got was turned over to the gang. He was virtually their slave, and when he displeased them was beaten and starved.

He had lived in a realm of fear: fear of his masters, fear of the police, fear of everything around him. Even when he had grown up and become a full-fledged member of the gang his situation changed little. He had been caught several times and once imprisoned for many months by Nationalist police. They had let him loose only after he had paid the usual bribe and consented to work for them as a stool pigeon.

After liberation he had been arrested once as a pickpocket, but had been allowed to go after promising to reform. However, with no conception of how to work for a living, he had quickly drifted back to the only things he knew—stealing, informing, and running away. As his pathetic story had unfolded he had broken into tears and had begun to realize the hopelessness and sordidness of his former life. He realized that he had never looked upon stealing itself as something wrong. For him it was just a way of making a living. He had never really hurt anybody. Other people all had more than he had. If he could get away with it, why shouldn't he? Being a pickpocket was as much an art as that of a juggler, magician, or storyteller.

His cell mates then reasoned with him that there was nothing that did not come about through someone's labor, and that stealing the fruits of another man's work was criminal. How would he like it if he had been forced to work all day and then was given no reward for it at all?

They managed to break down Li's fear a little and helped him come to understand his relationship to society and the wrongness of what he had been doing. Other people had been able to live honestly, free of fear and contempt. Why hadn't he? Partly, they said, it was because of his own desire to get something for nothing, but for the most part it was the old society which was to blame.

Thus, while never being allowed to forget that he himself had been wrong, Li developed a passionate hatred for the old society which had produced not only himself but countless others like him. The dream of a world in which there would be no fear or want became almost an obsession with him.

The authorities then did what seemed a strange thing. This spineless pickpocket, the dregs of humanity, was made leader of a cell. For the first time in his life he was given some responsibility and a position of respect. In coming to a realization of his own background he found that he could help others and in so doing help himself. His fears gradually disappeared almost completely.

I hardly recognized Li the next time I saw him, almost two years later, when we were exercising in the same compound. He seemed inches taller and when he looked at you it was straight in the eye. There was not a shadow of his former cringing self. I heard he had joined the prison literacy classes and applied himself so well that he could now read and write. Just before I was released I read in the prison newspaper that he had been given an award for a proposal he had made for increasing production in the prison sock factory. I had no doubt that he was well on his way toward building a new life and would soon be released.

Although Li's problem was a special one in that he was a habitual criminal, the process of his reform was in many ways typical of what happened to most of the men in the prison. The American reader who is acquainted with modern psychiatric techniques has undoubtedly noted strong similarities between the methods used in helping Li and the rest of us to reform through criticism and self-criticism and those used in group therapy here in the United States. Yet it was clear from my experience with both the authorities and the prisoners themselves that none of these people had any systematic training in psychology.

Indeed, as far as I know, the Chinese have never tried to work out the techniques of thought reform in the sense of a textbook science. Rather, the entire process seems to have developed in a rule-of-thumb manner based on a common-sense insight into human character, something for which the Chinese have always been noted, a concept of self-criticism borrowed from general Marxian practice and techniques which grew out of the need to reform the troops and intellectuals in the early days of the revolution.

The nearest approach to an organized theoretical basis for thought reform is to be found in Mao Tse-tung's two philosophical treatises, "On Contradictions" and "On Practice," and his various essays dealing with the practical application of Marxist principles to human relations. In these works as well as those of Liu Shao-chi, who next to Mao Tse-tung is considered China's leading Marxist theoretician, the stress is placed on the necessity for using criticism and self-criticism as a means to foster personal honesty and social responsibility. These are supplemented by numerous articles in newspapers and magazines describing particular problems, such as selfishness, graft, male supremacy, conservatism, and the manner in which certain individuals overcome them.

Though this group activity of thought reform was going on all over China, it perhaps found its most systematic application in prison, where the process was concentrated to an intense degree. Where, on the outside, participation in thought reform was largely voluntary, with the only force that of social pressure, in prison it was a matter of compulsion. Therefore the actual process could be observed more clearly there. In our discussion and talks with the authorities certain basic concepts were emphasized again and again.

The point of departure in almost every one of our discussions on thought reform was the premise that the in-

dividual is a product of his environment, both from the
point of view of the historical period into which he is born
and the class to which he belongs. From birth he begins
to develop mental habits which reflect his material surroundings. The old, highly competitive class society presented the individual with a constant struggle for his own
survival and thus instilled in him a highly self-centered
set of mental habits and outlooks. At the same time
this society set up certain ideals of conduct which it considered necessary for the preservation of workable human relations.

The Judeo-Christian doctrines of the Ten Command-
ments and the Golden Rule found their counterpart in
China in the Six Confucian Standards of Behavior and
the saying, "Do not do unto others what you would not
have them do unto you."

It was only natural that the individual, then, would
be faced constantly with contradictions between what society presented to him as morally true and what experience
in daily life clearly demonstrated was pragmatically true.
Such contradictions existed for everyone, but they were
particularly sharp among members of the old ruling
classes who had to resolve the problem of preaching in-
dustriousness, thrift, and morality to others while living in
idle luxury themselves.

In order to resolve these contradictions the individual
would build up a set of rationalizations which he used to
justify his every action. The housewife who did not tell
the butcher when he had undercharged her, the clerk who
made personal use of office supplies, the politician who
embezzled millions of the taxpayers' money, and the general who ordered the annihilation of a defenseless population—all had their excuses.

It was no different for any of us in prison. Even though
we had been forced to confess our crimes, we too all had
our excuses. Thus the first step in our reform was to break
down our justifications and rationalizations and make us
face up to our true selves. To do this the attack was
launched on two fronts. Our study discussions provided us

with a yardstick to measure the rightness or wrongness of our actions. This yardstick was basic socialist morality. That is to say, what is best for the greatest number of people in a specific historical context determines right from wrong.

Under socialism—the goal of the Chinese revolution—with the elimination of man's exploitation of man, the individual is no longer compelled to engage in a life-and-death struggle against the rest of society. It then becomes possible in practice for men to live by the ideal of the Golden Rule and seek their own personal happiness within the common good. Self-criticism forced us to take this yardstick and compare our own actions and attitudes with it by criticizing them.

Merely being able to criticize, however, did not mean that one had reformed. Mental habits are not so easily changed. It requires a long and constant struggle and a sincere desire to change on the part of the individual himself. Many people in prison, after overcoming their initial distaste for revealing their shortcomings before others, became what we called chronic confessors. They would confess endlessly but never change. Most often this was because they were not interested in reforming but only in making a good impression on the authorities. Some would also resort to confession merely to gain emotional release from the stress and strain of prison life.

Most prisoners at some time or other went through a stage in which, though somewhat conscious of it, they had no genuine understanding of their guilt. Therefore they tended to indulge in highly emotional exaggerations of their crimes without trying to bring about any real change in their character. Their situation often resembled that of the alcoholic who may be sincerely alarmed about his condition and most vehement in his promises to swear off drinking, but still, because he lacks any real understanding of his problem, is never quite able to do so.

In line with this almost every prisoner met with the problem of having his original rationalization broken down only to find he had built up a new set to justify the old habit. This again was like the alcoholic who, having come to realize the fallacy in his former rationalization "I know how to handle my liquor," substitutes as a new rationalization, *"One* little drink won't hurt."

Therefore it was only when a prisoner ceased confessing for confession's sake or setting up false rationalizations and began to understand his true self and the harm his actions had caused others that he could develop a real desire to reform. At this point he could begin to struggle against his old, selfish, anti-social habits and outlooks and replace them with a new sense of social responsibility. In describing this process the analogy was sometimes made to teaching a person to throw a ball correctly after he had acquired the habit of throwing it incorrectly. Even though such a person may realize his mistake, his instinctive reaction is to continue to throw in the old way until an entirely new set of muscles and reflexes have been developed.

For the drifter elements who made up the vast majority of counterrevolutionaries in the detention quarters reform was particularly difficult because they had spent most of their lives trying to get something for nothing. Never having taken part in productive work, they not only had to be impressed with the necessity and desirability of becoming constructive members of society but had to be taught how to do so. This was the reason for the labor reform which most of the prisoners took part in after leaving Tsao-lan-tzu Hu-tung. The pickpocket Li was typical in the sense that his reform went through all these stages.

In contrast to men like Li, Ma, Liao, and Jin, who were all drifters in varying degrees, were a few prisoners who were anti-Communist more as a matter of principle than for lack of moral values. For these people the crux of their reform was different and their change in outlook often came about rather suddenly.

One afternoon in the spring of 1953 a tall, thin Chinese in padded clothes was ushered into our cell. His hands were cuffed behind his back and for a moment we watched him silently as he stood uncertainly just inside the door.

"Just arrived?" asked Liao finally.

"No, I've been here three days."

"When did you get those?" he asked, nodding toward the handcuffs.

"Just now," was the subdued answer.

"*Bu-lao-shr* [dishonest], eh?" sneered Ma.

The man was silent.

Finally Liao asked, "Why were you brought here?"

"Because I'm a Catholic."

"Nobody ever came here just because he was a Catholic. What are you charged with?"

"I can't tell you," was his answer.

"We know," replied Liao. "The new regulations do not permit us to discuss the details of our crimes with each other, but you can give us a general idea."

"They said it was sabotaging land reform and helping Nationalist agents."

"Did you?"

"Yes," was the reluctant answer.

"Then why those?"

The man hesitated.

"Come on."

"The interrogation officer and I had a difference of opinion. He said I was a traitor."

"Aren't you?" snapped Ma.

There was no reply.

"Aren't you?" pressed Liao, his face becoming tight, his eyes narrow.

The man still hesitated and then finally, after the others had told him to answer, said, "No. I was only fighting for God."

"Since when does fighting for God involve sabotaging land reform and giving information to your country's enemies? Isn't that being a traitor?"

"Well, it seems to me that the term traitor can have a broad or narrow interpretation."

"*Ta-ma-di*," swore Ma. "You're not a priest; you're a lawyer. What's your interpretation of a traitor?"

"Well, I'm not one," said the man, his eyes blazing. "The Communists want to destroy all religion."

"Listen," commanded Liao. Then during the brief silence which followed, we heard the bells of the big Catholic cathedral nearby tolling six o'clock. "We hear those bells every day."

Han spoke up, "Liao is a Christian but nobody has tried to interfere with his religion."

The man's eyes showed a flicker of interest. "Catholic?"

"No, Protestant. And don't get the idea you're here because you're a Catholic," answered Liao.

The new arrival's interest was replaced by a look of disdain.

"Let's get back to the point," resumed Ma, always eager for a fight. "Are you or are you not a traitor?"

"I'm a servant of God. I'm no traitor. May God punish you all for accusing me so." His eyes flashed as he strained at the handcuffs behind his back.

The others began shouting at him and the new man, Han, yelled, "Traitor! Traitor!"

Suddenly the commotion came to a halt when the door was thrown open to reveal the short, stocky figure of the warden himself. "What's going on here?" he demanded in his quick accent.

Liao hastened to explain that the man was trying to maintain he had been arrested because he was a Catholic and he was only fighting for Christianity.

The warden stared steadily at the man for a moment and then said in a contemptuous tone, "You're a fine Christian. I'm a Communist, but I have a great deal of respect for Christ. In His time He too fought for the people. He was the man who drove the moneylenders from the temple. But you? What have you been doing, huh? Not only helping the moneylenders, but lending out a little of your own on the side! Christ died for His people, betrayed by reactionaries and crucified by imperialists. But you? What have you been doing, huh? Betraying your people and working side by side with the reactionary Nationalists in order to serve the imperialists. And you call yourself a Christian, huh!"

His words came forth in staccato blasts punctuated by frequent "huh, huh." Then, more quietly, he went on, "We Communists are materialists and don't believe in a God. We believe that religion grew out of early man's superstitious fears of the natural phenomena around him which he could not explain and as soon as man can understand these things there will be no need for religion. Soon science will discover how to create life. Then the last hold that religion has on the minds of men will be gone and it will die its own death.

"We Communists know we are right, but we are no fools. Religion is a way of thinking and you can't use force to wipe out thought. The ancient Chinese emperors often tried to suppress certain sects and their beliefs. They killed a lot of people but they only succeeded in driving the beliefs underground. The laws of our land specifically guarantee religious freedom. However, that does not mean that you can use religion as a cloak for counterrevolutionary activities. There's no conflict between the teachings of Christ and socialism. If you want to be a real Christian, that's all right with us. But in the meantime just take a look at yourself. Compare what Christ stood for with what you have been doing." With that he left.

There was a silence for a few minutes as the man stood dejectedly, his head bowed.

"You sit down over there and think about what the warden said," was Liao's only comment. The rest of us turned back to our chess games and mending.

During the evening class we went on with the discussion. The new arrival, Pu, still clung to his contention that he was not a traitor. But he had obviously been shaken by the warden's words. That night I noticed that while the others slept Pu's eyes remained open.

The next day Liao continued the discussion, pointing out that now for the first time in China's history the people were being given the chance to lead a decent kind of life, the kind that Christ would have wanted His people

to enjoy. If Pu were a real Christian, why wasn't he supporting this instead of trying to tear it down? Pu now had
little to say for himself.

That afternoon he was called out and about an hour
later returned, this time without handcuffs. He had barely
sat down when a supervisor arrived with an order for him
to collect his things and move to another cell. We had
no opportunity, therefore, to learn the details of his interrogation, but a week later we noticed that Pu had been
transferred to the prison labor detail, the most coveted
position in the entire prison because of the chance it afforded one to move around freely outside.

No matter what our backgrounds and initial attitude,
for all of us in prison there was a big question—when could
one be considered reformed? Often it seemed as if we
were chasing a carrot on a stick, for, except for a nebulous
injunction to learn to serve the people and help others,
the government never gave us any specific indication of its
expectations with regard to us. However, as time went on,
though each man had his individual problems, those who
demonstrated a rejection of the old, selfish attitudes began to stand out. It was usually, however, a major crisis of
self-interest, such as Liao's divorce, which presented the
real test of progress.

By early 1953 most of the prisoners who had been there
any length of time were beginning to show some signs of
change. Their discussions showed little trace of their former
longing for the past and for the return of the Nationalists.
Partly this was due to the effectiveness of the Communist
arguments, but even more it was history itself which
brought this about. The progress of the war in Korea had
exploded the myth of American invincibility and the
dreams that a Nationalist–American landing might bring
about their release. The anticipated internal revolt and
economic collapse had failed to materialize. Instead the
country was united as it never had been before, and in
1952 over-all production stood 9 per cent above the record
levels in Chinese history.

But it was not just a matter of giving up hope; much

more it was a case of the prisoners no longer having any interest in these things. This was brought out with particular clarity one day in January, 1953, while the Korean war was still on. The announcement of China's first five-year plan came over the prison loud-speaker and when Mao Tse-tung was quoted as saying, "If the Americans want to talk, we'll talk; if they want to fight, we'll fight, but in the meantime we are going on with our economic reconstruction," a tremendous wave of applause and cheers resounded throughout the prison.

It perhaps seems unbelievable that these men, almost all Nationalists and American agents facing long prison terms under the Communists, should be applauding so enthusiastically the man they had looked upon a short time before as their worst enemy. But much of the answer lay in Liao's remark when he turned to me with shining eyes and said enthusiastically, "Nowadays it really feels good to know you have Chinese blood in your veins. Truly, as Chairman Mao says, we Chinese have stood up in the world."

The continuous progress of the revolution had a positive effect on the prisoners. Especially after 1953 the building of the new China absorbed the attention of almost all of them. Few could help but be infected with the spirit of challenge. While in the United States people grab their newspaper to find out the standing of their favorite ball team, in China interest was centered on the fulfillment of production goals. It was the same in our cell.

The announcement of a new invention, the building of a new factory, or the surpassing of a production target would bring forth excited exclamations, and the news of a drought or flood would throw the cell into deep gloom. The activities and accomplishments of model workers, such as the railroad engineer Yo Sheng-wu and the girl textile worker Ho Jien-hsiu, were followed with the same interest as those of a Mickey Mantle or Grace Kelly here at home.

The smallest incident affecting our lives in the cell could be related to China's industrial development. In early

1953 I had bought a pack of Chinese playing cards for 7,000 JMP (35¢). They were made of such poor grade cardboard they could not be shuffled without splitting. When a year later I bought another pack, this time for only half the former price but of much superior quality, they were passed around to be handled admiringly and acclaimed as proof of the improvements being made on the outside.

My cell mates were fired with the desire to be a part of the new China, and the feeling that they were criminals outside of it all weighed heavily on them. Thus there began to grow a new incentive to reform. No longer was it just a question of reforming simply to avoid punishment. Now there was the positive hope for a vital and fruitful future in helping to build their country.

The change was greatly assisted by the attitude of the authorities toward the prisoners. They were merciless in their contempt for the counterrevolutionary and spy, but they were careful never to let the prisoner feel this contempt was leveled at him as a person. We were told over and over again, "It is not you but your thinking which is bad." Although discipline was strict, we were at all times encouraged to be frank in our relations with all of the prison staff from the warden on down to the kitchen help. Any sign of obsequiousness was taken as either an indication of concealed hostility or a holdover from the "feudal" mannerisms of the past, and was sure to be met with a blast, "Speak out like a man!"

The prisoners were impressed by the fact that the staff applied the demand for reform to themselves as much as to us. This was especially brought home to us in the case of Supervisor Wang. He was a tall, good-looking man with a hot disposition which often got the better of him. Regulations strictly forbade striking a prisoner, but early in 1951 he had lost his temper and hit one of the inmates. Subsequently he had been given a year to think things over in a cell right along with the other prisoners. During this time he had come to a sincere realization of his mistake, and in the end returned to his old job of supervisor.

By 1953 the change which had taken place in him was clearly evident.

One day a new prisoner was placed alone in the cell opposite ours. The man was like a wild bull, shouting curses at everyone, and the cell door had no sooner been shut than he gave it a tremendous kick, knocking the bolt loose and sending parts of it flying across the corridor. My cell mates were furious at the man's unreasonable violence, but we could hear Supervisor Wang saying in a calm voice as he reopened the door, "Now what problem do you think that is going to solve?"

Then, after a pause, we could hear him just as calmly closing the door again. The man in the cell, who had been primed for a fight, must have been left speechless by the supervisor's tranquil air, for we heard no more from him for some time.

When it was over, Liao shook his head. "Two years ago Supervisor Wang would really have slapped that character down. And they say people can't change!"

Of extreme importance in the reform of every prisoner was the direct help given him by the prison staff. From the very beginning the authorities made a point of studying each individual's history to discover the dominant elements in his character and the roots of his thinking. But it seemed to me that during 1951–52 much of their effort was mechanical and negative. Undue stress was placed on class background and initial attitude displayed during the confession. They were more harsh toward landlords and professional agents, and in dealing with the prisoners as a whole the emphasis was definitely on suppression. Prisoners who showed signs of being particularly dishonest or obstinate were often simply put in handcuffs or leg irons without much attempt being made to learn the real reasons for their attitudes.

Partly, this impatience was due to the great bitterness engendered by the violence of the counterrevolutionaries at the time and the open defiance many of them displayed even in prison. There seemed to be a general feeling on the part of the authorities that only the constant threat of severe repression could keep these men, many of them hardened killers, in check. But also it was often a case of the prison staff being too busy or too inexperienced to deal in any other way with the situations which arose.

By 1953 the characters of the men in the detention quarters had changed considerably. Even the newcomers showed little rebelliousness, and the authorities acknowledged that their former overemphasis on suppression had been a mistake. From then on there was much more flexibility displayed in analyzing the problems of each prisoner and the means to help him overcome them.

Sometimes suppression was still required to make the individual realize the seriousness of his situation and maintain discipline. But sometimes extreme leniency was also required to help him overcome his fears and doubts. We were all espionage or counterrevolutionary cases and therefore regulations forbade any direct contact with the outside, but some prisoners were even allowed to see their families if it were thought this might help them toward reform.

Typical of the type of help administered by the authorities was that given to a man who came into our cell in late 1953. He had been a soldier under the war lord Yen Hsi-shan, and had been tattooed—as was often the case with Yen's troops to make them afraid to surrender —with a hideous anti-Communist slogan across his forehead. His crime was not serious, and he seemed not a bad fellow at heart. He had joined the Nationalist underground only because Chiang Kai-shek's agents had convinced him the Communists would certainly kill him for that slogan on his forehead.

After long arguments and citing many examples we managed to convince him he had nothing to fear from the People's Government, and he seemed to regret his past actions. But instead of reacting with enthusiasm to the prospect of a quick return to society, he would sit during class staring glumly into space, and no amount of prodding would move him to participate.

Finally, after several self-criticism discussions, we discovered what was troubling him. True, he was no longer afraid of dying, but how could he ever take part in the new society with such a slogan on his forehead? We tried to reassure him that no one would blame him for it, but to no avail.

One morning he was called out of the cell and was gone all day. When he returned, his forehead was bandaged but his eyes were shining. The government had taken him to the hospital where a specialist had removed the tattoo. The change which followed in the man's personality was almost miraculous. As he said, he felt he had been relieved of a "ten-thousand-ton burden."

I myself was particularly influenced by the high standard of conduct the staff set for themselves. It was probably Supervisor Shen who made the deepest impression on me. He was about my age, obviously of country background and little education. But his conscientious attitude toward work more than made up for any lack of schooling. He was on the run from early morning to late at night. Yet he always seemed to have time to listen to the troubles of one or another of the prisoners or to do countless little things which showed how serious he was in looking out for the welfare of his charges.

No matter how tired he might be, if there occurred a sudden change in the weather he was bound to make the rounds of the entire compound to see that everyone was well covered before turning in himself. "Hey, keep your stomach covered," we could hear him say as he checked each cell. "You don't want to catch cold."

At such times I had to repress a smile, for I was never able to take seriously the Chinese household science which regarded the stomach as particularly vulnerable to cold.

At first I was inclined to look upon this concern for our welfare as merely so much propaganda. It was a seemingly unimportant incident which caused my first thoughts that this suspicion might be unfounded.

One wintry Saturday the prisoners hung their wash out as usual on the line which stretched the length of the alleyway behind our cell block. That afternoon, in violation of the regulations, I looked through the crack in the palisade built around our cell window to obstruct the view. There was Supervisor Shen patiently going along the line turning every article of the prisoners' clothing to make certain they would be dry by the time we were to take them in after supper.

It came to me that the man could not be doing this to impress anyone. No one was supposed to be looking. Perhaps I had been misjudging these people after all, and I remembered my first impression of the Communists, received from the troops who had rescued my bicycle during the siege of Peking.

Though, along with my cell mates, I could admire the integrity and sincerity of such people as Shen, the other factors which were influencing the prisoners on the road to reform had little effect on me. The revolutionary spirit pervading China and the country's great economic and social transformation which they found so inspiring seemed far removed from me. I could envy my cell mates in their growing feeling of security and hope for the future, and understand their willingness to reform, but, as an American, I could see little use in any thoroughgoing change in myself.

My only desire was to gain my release somehow and return home, but even there the future looked anything but bright. I had already made up my mind that I could not recant my confession, as I had once so lavishly planned, and still live with myself. Yet, if I did tell the truth, and refused to cooperate with Naval Intelligence, I was certain that with McCarthyism still running rampant in the United States I was bound to be labeled subversive. Then all my high hopes for a teaching career would be gone. In fact, even making a living might prove difficult.

This contradiction in my longing for home and my fear of returning to an impossible situation dominated my thoughts to such an extent that any positive thinking toward reform was pushed aside. At the same time, my lack of any feeling of guilt in connection with my crime hindered progress in the direction of reform. I was willing to concede that what I had done had been a mistake from the point of view of my own self-interest, but this contained no sense of having harmed others nor a feeling of need to question the foundations of my own character.

Our self-criticism movements which occurred every few months demanded a deep searching into our thoughts and motivations, with a view to checking up on our progress toward reform. Since I knew that I had actually made little or no progress and was only desirous of escape from it all, I could look upon these movements only with dread. At the announcement by the authorities of a new self-criticism movement, my stomach would be gripped with fear and I would begin to wonder if this time the government's patience would be exhausted and I would end up in handcuffs and leg irons. Indicative of my state of mind was the care I took to put on clean clothes at the beginning of such sessions in expectation of a long period with hands fettered behind my back.

Each time when the discussions got under way I would wait until the others had all made their self-criticism, hoping to glean from the points they made something I could say myself. But this never seemed to help me. When it came my turn I would search desperately for something to say which might appease the demands of my cell mates for an honest accounting of myself without admitting completely that I had made no progress. Such tactics, of course, failed to satisfy anyone, and my cell mates would start hammering away with their endless "why, why, why" —why hadn't I changed?

Finally I would be driven to admitting the same things I had admitted time and time before—I had no feeling of guilt, all I wanted to do was go home, etc. Sometimes my cell mates would terminate my self-criticism after I had promised to try to reform. But the release thus gained was more than offset by the depression which engulfed me at the thought of the hopelessness of my situation. How was I ever going to get out of this place if I could not prove to them that I had become convinced of the wrongness of my actions? Often my soul would rebel within me. I would want to lash out and let them shoot me if they wished; at least that would settle the matter. But then I knew I would not be shot. I would only end up in handcuffs and leg irons, and that would solve nothing.

Since it was so obvious that my self-criticism had done no good, my cell mates would soon call for another "to help me solve my problem." The same cycle would then begin all over again. Once, I was reduced to such a state of despair that I said in exasperation, "If you will only tell me what you want—"

"If we did, you wouldn't understand," broke in Liao impatiently.

Then he went on, "Do you want to reform?"

"Ye-e-s," I replied, without much conviction.

"Why?"

"So I can leave here, of course."

"Well, if that is the only reason you have for wanting to reform, you haven't a chance." After staring coldly at me for a minute, he continued, "As long as you keep looking at things from your present self-centered point of view you never will understand anything. Why don't you stop thinking about leaving here for a few minutes—just long enough to take one half-way objective look at yourself? You know, we Chinese have a saying, 'In the search for truth the selfish are eternally blind.' That applies to all of us, but to you in particular."

Thus, although I was able from an academic standpoint to go through the mechanics of reviewing my past life and analyzing myself rather successfully, still, because it was done primarily from the point of view of pleasing others, it had little effect as far as changing my basic outlooks was concerned. It was this failure to face squarely the weakness and dishonesty in my own character and the refusal to admit to myself the need for reform that led me into the worst mistake of my stay in prison. And yet it was this very crisis which was finally to bring me to my senses.

13

Dell: In spite of the conflicts which arose at times in cell No. 12 during the spring of 1953, and the struggle that went on in trying to help each of us in turn, a feeling of warmth and comradeliness was clearly evident. Each time a new movement was announced we would assert solemnly to each other that *our* cell would lead the rest in efficiency and honesty. The feeling was expressed also in the give and take of our daily living. I felt particularly warm inside when one of the women asked me to help her make a pair of slacks out of a piece of cloth she had ordered from home. In turn, they took delight in teaching me Peking colloquial expressions and laughed at my clumsy accent.

It was with dismay, therefore, that we heard the woman supervisor, Fang, call through the little window in the door one Saturday morning in early June telling us to pack up our belongings. All the women in the compound were being reshuffled and I was told to move into cell No. 9, only three doors away.

I had to adjust to an entirely new situation. Though my new home was similar in size and shape to the one I had just left, the picture it presented was quite different. In the other room crowded conditions had made neatness mandatory and we had kept our bedding and belongings stacked in orderly fashion in a corner of the *kang* during the day. My two new cell mates had their things spread over a large portion of the *kang*. Each was sitting on her own mattress and leaning against her own fat clothing bundle. A little table piled high at one end with books and papers was placed between them. All in all, it looked quite casual and comfortable. They urged me to spread my mattress out in the remaining one-third of the *kang* toward the back wall and make myself at home.

The casualness was emphasized by the fact that the door was not locked at any time, nor were these women taking part in the organized study and criticism going on in the cells around them. They seemed a little world in themselves. Though I was elated at the thought that I was no longer behind a locked door, my feeling dampened when I learned that this freedom stemmed from the fact that my two cell mates were not political prisoners. Under such conditions I wondered how much of their privileges could be assumed by me.

The reason for my transfer became quickly apparent when I found that the women's cells in the compound had been reduced to only two and that Harriet was in the other. It was the government's policy to separate people involved in the same case.

I was accepted immediately into the pattern of life in the cell, and went out with them at all times of the day to the latrine and for water. Except for reading and discussing the newspaper together in the morning and evening, we kept on the whole to ourselves. Ordinarily I would have reveled in such an easygoing existence, but I could not relax completely, knowing the wide gulf that lay between us. Their every action showed that they considered themselves, as civil offenders, far superior to me, a counterrevolutionary.

My new cell mates, Jeng Ai-ling and Mei Chi-yün, were both in much better command of Marxist theory and practice than the women in cell No. 12. The very first day Jeng Ai-ling, who acted as cell leader, on learning that I was an American, praised to the skies the new American synthetic wool sweaters she had seen in Hong Kong the year before. I was slightly taken aback at this frankness, for in cell No. 12 no one would have dreamed of praising anything which came from the United States.

Jeng Ai-ling was a vivacious extrovert, with a dynamic, forceful character. Though thirty-five years old and the mother of five children, ranging from five to fifteen years old, she looked more like a college student, with her hair bobbed and dressed in plaid shirt and blue slacks. What she thought she said in straightforward terms, and in the eight months I spent in cell No. 9 I learned much from her.

She never talked much about her crimes, except for the fact that she had been involved in smuggling and the misuse of government funds. One day, however, she described part of her investigation, and said that in one instance there was a question about the placing of responsibility for some point in her crime. She maintained that the matter had not been her responsibility, but there were several witnesses who said it was. For eleven months the People's Government investigated this one point, and she was summoned to court sixteen or seventeen times to be confronted by witnesses. Each time she was asked to state her version of the story. A witness would then be brought in and asked to state his version. When he had finished, Jeng Ai-ling spoke again in her own defense, and in each case the witness backed down and admitted that he might have been wrong. Jeng Ai-ling remained steadfast during the questioning and in the end the People's Government told her they were satisfied that she was telling the truth. In telling us of her experience, she paced up and down the cell, her eyes sometimes crinkling at the sides with laughter, sometimes shining bright with excitement as she related the flustered shame of each witness as he admitted his mistake.

She then continued, "It does happen sometimes that mistakes occur and it takes a lot of stamina to see the thing through until truth is established."

Jeng Ai-ling told about a woman who had left the prison just a few months before. She had been arrested in connection with the Three Anti's movement on a question of bribery. Her crime was a minor one and, after making a full confession, she had expected to be released. It was a shock when her sentence was passed. She had been given two years.

When Jeng Ai-ling had looked at the statement of charges which the woman had brought back to the cell she was disturbed to find mistakes in it. The woman was prepared to let the matter go and work out her sentence, but Jeng Ai-ling urged her to appeal while there was still time. Just before the three-day limit was up, the woman finally gave in to Jeng Ai-ling's pressure and the appeal was sent in. The government then went back over the evidence and eventually found that one of the witnesses, an ambitious woman cadre who had hoped to gain position by ruining the defendant, an older, more experienced worker, had falsified evidence.

Jeng Ai-ling concluded, "The result was that my cell mate was cleared of that portion of the charges which was incorrect and granted immediate release. I don't know what happened to that other woman but I wager she had to make a pretty strict accounting of herself."

As long as Jeng Ai-ling's straightforwardness and fierce determination to uphold the truth were directed toward herself and others, I was very happy to listen to her talk, but in July, 1953, a few weeks after I had moved into the cell, she began to ask me for comments on the book I had been reading by myself during the day, a modern history of China.

When I gave her a few stock answers, she said in a musing tone, "You rather surprise me. Your understanding is so superficial. We'll have to talk at length about some of your viewpoints. Do you really believe that China has suffered at the hands of American imperialism?"

"Yes," I answered. "Rick and I never did like Chiang Kai-shek and we always felt that the United States was wrong in supporting him. Why, when we were still back home we used to—"

But I never had a chance to finish the sentence. Mei Chi-yün fixed me with a hostile glare and almost shouted, "You didn't like Chiang Kai-shek! Is that why you took that so-called scholarship money that he had squeezed out of the Chinese people?"

I looked at her in amazement. This mild-mannered,

fun-loving girl of twenty-two or twenty-three, who was always talking about wanting to learn how to drive a tractor when she was released was the last person I would have expected to be so belligerent.

"But we *didn't* like him," I insisted hotly, thinking back on the enthusiastic introduction Rick had given me to Edgar Snow's *Red Star over China.*

Jeng Ai-ling broke in, no less vehemently, "Yes, maybe you didn't like him, but from what point of view? You were fed up because he wasn't winning the war so you Americans could continue to dominate China. You weren't thinking much about the Chinese people. And you call yourself progressive! Why, you're a worse imperialist than MacArthur!"

"I am not! You just don't understand!"

As my attitude became even more obstinate, they lost all patience. Suddenly Mei Chi-yün shouted, "Stand down on the floor!"

I had been lulled into complacency during those first few weeks by the casual atmosphere of our cell, and her sharp command drew me up with a start. I was tempted at first not to take her seriously, but after seeing the determination in her cold, level gaze, I scrambled down and stood on the floor before them.

They both stared at me sternly for a moment and then Jeng Ai-ling said, "All right. You can stand there until you realize what's wrong with your attitude, even if it takes all night."

They each picked up a book and started to read, though from time to time I noticed Jeng Ai-ling stealing glances at me. She might have been checking to see that I was standing straight, but rather there seemed to be a look of concern on her face. I stood for about an hour, first on one foot and then on another, trying to figure out what they wanted of me. I was still angry at their accusation and felt very much the martyr. But when gruff, burly Supervisor Ming came by and told me I had better make an accounting of myself, I knew that I could expect no reprieve from the authorities.

As we heard the doors being locked in preparation for turning in Jeng Ai-ling suddenly asked, "What have you been thinking about the last couple of hours?"

Tears of self-pity welled in my eyes as I answered, "I've been thinking about all the terrible things the imperialists have done in China."

Jeng Ai-ling exploded, "Filthy spy! You really have all the tricks!" She turned to Mei Chi-yün, "Just look at her, trying to gain our sympathy. She's running true to form." Then back to me, "You don't have a human heart at all. You've got a dog's heart, haven't you?"

Afraid that a denial would bring on a further accusation of obstinacy, I remained silent, head drooping.

"Answer me! You've got a dog's heart, haven't you?"

I nodded and replied in a tiny voice, "Yes, I guess I have."

"Ha!" shouted Mei Chi-yün. "That's a fine thing. Defiling your parents like that. If you're a dog, what does that make them? Really you have the character of a filthy spy!"

Just then the whistle blew. The two women looked at each other hesitantly for a moment and then Jeng Ai-ling said, disgustedly, "Get to bed. And you'd better think about your attitude."

The next two or three days were spent in a struggle to make me face up to those elements in my character which made me one moment cringing and fawning, the next obstinate and defiant. Over and over they resorted to the method of having me stand on the floor two or three hours at a time, hoping that this would stir me to take a serious look at myself. It was obvious, however, that my continued standing weighed on Jeng Ai-ling's mind, for she used the flimsiest of pretexts to excuse me and let me sit down.

About the third day Supervisor Fang came by and saw me standing. She came in immediately, dripping water on the floor from the big poncho she had thrown over her shoulders to keep off the rain which was pouring outside. Her short, straight figure seemed weighted down by the heavy rubber cape.

Her eyes, wide set in a broad, square face, looked me up and down a moment in characteristic noncommittal fashion and then, turning to Jeng Ai-ling, she asked, "What's this all about?"

Jeng Ai-ling hastened to explain that my attitude had been very dishonest and they had been trying to make me realize my mistakes.

Supervisor Fang nodded at me curtly, "Get back up on the *kang*," and at the same time motioned Jeng Ai-ling to follow her outside to one of the compound offices.

When the cell leader returned a few moments later, she said in a rather subdued voice, "Supervisor Fang said we were wrong to make you stand, Li Yu-an. If you continue this way, though, and absolutely refuse to discuss your feelings honestly, you will probably be put in handcuffs. For your sake and ours, I hope you won't reach that point. Please reconsider and stop play-acting."

A few moments later the whistle blew for the mid-day two-hour nap. I lay down half fearful and half relieved. I knew I would no longer be made to stand, but might not the handcuffs which I had come to look on as the ultimate disgrace be much worse? I was so worried about how to make a favorable impression and avoid the handcuffs that I gave no thought to the question of the thorough self-criticism which still lay ahead of me.

The dreaded whistle blew all too soon and in no time we were seated on the *kang* again ready for class. I expected Jeng Ai-ling to begin with a tirade but she took an entirely different tack, with no mention of my previous attitude.

"Let's just talk a bit," she said mildly. "We've got our views on the United States, probably some of which are not quite accurate. You've got your views, some of which may be just a bit biased. If we're going to come to any understanding of the way you think, it might be a good idea for you to set before us what you like about America. Just why do you think it's such a wonderful place to live?"

I paused for a moment to assemble my thoughts. There was so much I could say about the land of my birth. First of all, it was my home and I felt at home there as I never had in China. My family, my friends, the familiar places where I had grown up and lived were all a part of me. I longed to be back in that pattern of life I knew so well.

I expressed this a bit haltingly and then went on, "I suppose, too, I love the tremendous sweep of the land from east to west. Every time I have crossed the country I have felt a wonderful pride in the beauty of the plains, the mountains, the lakes, and the seashore. Coming from New York, I have a special affection for that city with its endless variety of places to go and see. I love the terrific contrast of old and new which one meets on almost every street in New York. It never has failed to excite me. After I met Li Ko I discovered the beauty of the northwest, too. We used to go camping in the woods in the shadow of the snow-capped mountains up there.

"And then, too, I love the fact that there are schools and libraries to be found in every city. I used to be a librarian, and I have a certain sense of security, I guess, in knowing that wherever I might live I would be assured of a job because there are always openings in that field. But most of all, I guess what I like about America is the fact that I could shut myself off from the rest of the world and live with Li Ko completely free, with no feeling of responsibility toward anyone else. While we lived in Philadelphia no one bothered us and we bothered no one. We came and went as we pleased and had no obligations. The way of life is so carefree there."

I lapsed into silence and gazed at the two of them. Jeng Ai-ling finally said, "You talk about the length and breadth of America and I have no doubt there is beautiful scenery in many places, but did you ever stop to think how big the original United States was? Thirteen small states, am I right? The rest came about through expansion, and the wresting of land from the Indians. Suppose the Indians decided they wanted their land back, or suppose another minority group wanted to set up its own autonomous state, would you have anything to say?"

At the mention of the United States shrinking in size, or being altered in any way, I protested hotly. "You can't say that about my America! It's the United States the way it is, and it can't be changed!"

"*Your* America?" laughed Jeng Ai-ling. "You should have seen your face when you said that. Really! Nobody's saying anything about *your* America, but you ought to wake up to the fact that it wasn't always that way and that a lot of it was taken away from other people. But then, that's not our business."

She went off into laughter again. "You looked so funny."

I smiled, too, then. Somehow, talking about the United States had broken down my fear of bringing to light my feelings on a number of subjects, and for the next few days I revealed many of the thoughts I had kept locked inside me, thoughts I had not been actually conscious of.

It was about this time in late July that Supervisor Ming called me into the compound office one morning to ask how I was getting along. I told him what we had been discussing and he asked for my views on the People's Government, thought reform, and so on. We got onto the subject of war and the relationship of the individual to military conflict. I told him, "I have never felt much concern about war except when it threatened to separate Li Ko and me. I suppose that if a third world war were to bring us together again, I wouldn't care what happened."

He looked at me a moment, his eyes blazing, his lips compressed in a thin line. The freckles on his face stood out as if painted on. He was obviously trying to control himself. Finally he said in a strained, quiet voice, "How can you be so selfish?"

I stared at him in horror as I began to think what my words must sound like to another person. Thinking as usual only of my relationship with Rick, it had never occurred to me there might be something wrong with such a thought. But, voiced to another person who might very well be one of the dead in that war I was so blithely asking for, it revealed my self-centered blindness to the welfare of others.

I walked slowly back to the cell. After recounting the

interview to my cell mates I tried to minimize the significance of my statement by saying that I had not meant anyone any harm, I was just trying to express how great was my devotion to Li Ko. Jeng Ai-ling and Mei Chi-yün both refused to let this pass and I was forced then to think through for the first time the question of personal interest in relation to the common good. It was a shattering experience, those next few weeks of class. I revealed my thoughts on war, the working class, Negroes, work, religion, politics, status of women, and, again, Rick.

Quite unconsciously my former belligerent attitude had begun to disappear and thoughts which were ingrown and which I had never questioned as good or bad before were brought to light and examined by the three of us.

One day it was on race prejudice.

"Do you have any Negro friends, Li Yu-an?" asked Jeng Ai-ling, almost belligerently.

"Well, no, I haven't known many Negroes," I admitted reluctantly. Then, brightening a little, I continued, "But I don't think I have any prejudices at all. I've been concerned about the problem of race relations for years, and I think I've hit on the final solution—it lies in intermarriage. If white people and Negroes intermarry long enough, and Jews and Christians likewise, the prejudice in the United States will gradually disappear."

"I suppose you think it shows great tolerance to suggest that whites and Negroes intermarry?" asked Mei Chi-yün, her eyes curiously bright.

"Well, yes. After all, intermarriage is one of the difficulties in the United States today."

"But let me ask you, Li Yu-an," said Jeng Ai-ling, "what would happen? Would the whites become Negro or the Negroes white?"

I thought a moment. "I have always felt that the Negroes would gradually become lighter and then the basis for prejudice would disappear. The same with the Jews. They would probably all become Christians in the end."

Jeng Ai-ling snorted. "If that isn't the Anglo-Saxon race supremacy at its worst. You just want to wipe out whole races, whole religions. And suppose the Negroes said to you, 'You should all become dark-skinned'?"

"Oh, no," I said involuntarily. "I think the Negroes would rather be white."

"And did you ever *ask* a Negro?"

"No, of course not," I admitted. "It just never occurred to me that everyone wouldn't like to be like us. I guess that is race prejudice."

Our discussion that afternoon, painful as it was to admit that I was wrong, was actually an exhilarating experience in that it served to give me inspiration for going on to a fresh probing of my former outlooks. I felt grateful that the mistake in my point of view had been pointed out to me, for, when I considered the problem from another point of view, I could see my error.

We touched on religion only briefly. I told them my beliefs and they explained theirs. They expressed a tremendous respect for Christ as a champion of the oppressed and looked on Him as one of the great revolutionaries of the world, but they could not believe that He had divine attributes. Neither of us tried to convince the other on this, but left it as purely each person's own business.

Other times they would voice criticisms of me which I could not go along with. This was particularly true in their ideas about Rick and me. I told them one night about how Rick and I had met and married, how we had studied together, shopped together, violated etiquette at parties by sitting side by side at the dinner table, and how I had followed in Rick's shadow at parties rather than going off to chat with people on my own.

When I mentioned that I had written to him every night while we were separated during the war, they let out a hoot of derision. This was decadent, feudal, slavish. How could I talk about the emancipation of women in the United States if I were so dependent on Rick for my spiritual welfare? Maybe economically I could exist independently, but I leaned on him for decision making and outlook as much as the bound-footed ladies of ancient China did on their husbands.

Did I admit it? Well, no, I did not, but that night I tossed and turned as I went over the problem. Suddenly it was too much to bear. It seemed as if everything I had always taken for granted as right was being turned upside down. My whole attitude toward the working class in the United States, the foreign relations of the United States, who wanted war and who wanted peace, the justification for use of arms, who had really set up the Iron Curtain, and a host of other subjects had been discussed over and over. We had gone from one to the other and then back to the earlier ones again. And now we had come back to the question of my relationship with Rick. Decadent! This was too much. My pillow remained wet all through that long night.

The next day was Sunday and we played cards and sewed all day long. That night I again wrestled with the problem, trying to look at it from their point of view. Were they right or were they wrong? I finally decided they were carrying some of the questions too far and were deliberately trying to plague me. It was time for a showdown.

Monday morning, as soon as we sat down for class, I started with, "I've got to get something straight. I can't go on like this. It's not doing me any good and I'll never make any progress as long as I feel the way I do."

My voice trembled as I rushed to get the words out, and tears began swimming in my eyes.

Jeng Ai-ling sensed immediately the tenseness in my manner and said kindly, "Go ahead. What's on your mind?"

"I want to tell you what I think of you both. I think you're carrying things too far. You're persecuting me and I can't stand it any longer. There are so many things going on in my mind and so many different ideas to weigh and consider and you keep hammering away at them, never giving me time to collect my thoughts on any one question before we go to another. I feel as if my head were a soccer ball, being kicked hard from both sides at once."

The tears were streaming down my face now, brought

on both by the emotional strain I was under and, as I analyzed later, that defense mechanism which I seemed to revert to unconsciously in hopes of softening the expected blast from my listeners.

Jeng Ai-ling burst out laughing. "So you think we're persecuting you? Anything else?"

I went on, then, with a résumé of the points I could not accept in our discussions. We talked the matter over very quietly for the rest of the morning, with the result that the pace was reduced considerably. I continued to bring up points on which we disagreed, but our discussions never became heated. As soon as the pressure lessened I relaxed and began to work each problem over again. My head felt less like a soccer ball, but the questions were no less difficult to face. I had to admit that living in one's own little world was a selfish way of life and that others might suffer because of it. But it was so much easier that way. And always the same basic question: What did all this reform have to do with me in America, anyway?

In the midst of this strain an incident occurred which further helped me understand the significance of reform. In mid-August one evening the three of us went out to the latrine together. I had failed to shut the latrine door tight, although I did think no one could see. Supervisor Ming had passed by at just that moment. A few minutes after we returned to the cell he came to the window and asked who was responsible for the door being ajar. On learning it was I he turned to me and swore angrily, "Ta-ma-di. Don't you know there are men walking around this compound? What do you mean by leaving the door open? Where's your sense of modesty?"

I stood without saying a word as he delivered his tirade.

When he had left, I half-expected Jeng Ai-ling to echo his criticism, but she said, almost wonderingly, "I'm puzzled about Supervisor Ming's attitude. He had no business swearing like that. And there was nothing to get angry about. We closed the door as soon as we saw it still open. That was wrong of him."

She sat silent for a moment and then continued, "I think I'll send in a statement on it."

I did not take her seriously at first. How could a prisoner report the mistakes of a supervisor? The next morning, however, I noticed Jeng Ai-ling writing on a slip of paper and at breakfast time she handed it to Supervisor Wang. As she came back she said firmly, "There. Now we've done our duty. Supervisor Ming is an old revolutionary cadre and has contributed much toward the revolution, but he has never tried to correct that habit of swearing. He knows it's against regulations to swear at prisoners. Now he'll have to make a self-criticism before the other supervisors. Let's hope it will help him grow in character."

"That's fine," I thought, glumly. "If he has to do all that he's going to have some opinion of us. He thinks badly enough of me already for that remark I made about Rick and the war. Now he'll take all his humiliation over the self-criticism out on us. We'll really be in for a bad time."

At the same time I admired Jeng Ai-ling for pursuing the matter. Reform was not just something to "inflict" on the prisoners. This was apparently a process in which everyone was partaking.

In the next few weeks I realized that my estimate of Supervisor Ming had been wrong. He never swore at us again and he never seemed to hold it against us. Seven months later, in March, 1954, when I moved to the west compound, he shouldered one of my big, heavy bundles of bedding the whole long distance.

After my outburst about being "persecuted" there was a noticeable change in our life in the cell. Having revealed so much of my innermost thoughts, there was little room left for sham. The good impression which I had tried so hard to create in the previous cell had been wiped out and I had to start from scratch. But this time, though I had certainly not rid myself entirely of the desire to make a good impression, I began to feel the necessity for bringing my thoughts out in the open and obtaining the help of my two cell mates in criticizing them. There was nothing in my character that was not clear to them after the crisis of that struggle during the summer.

As I came to see myself for what I was, I found that the reading I was doing took on a new significance; I was able now to relate much of it to my own problems. One day I came across an unfamiliar four-word phrase, *ming je bao shen*. My dictionary translated it as "a wise man protects himself," but this explanation did not fit into the context of the passage. I asked Jeng Ai-ling what it meant.

"It refers to a person who never sticks his neck out," she said. "In the old society this was considered the attribute of a wise person. He kept out of trouble by never taking any responsibility. But in the new society this is a contemptible attitude. If everyone held back for fear of getting hurt, how would anything ever get done?"

Triumphant in the discovery of another facet of my own character, I exclaimed, "But that's just me. I've always shunned responsibility for fear of criticism. In fact, now that I think of it, that fear of criticism has been the root of my shyness, and even dependence on Rick. You know, I never will say, 'I such and such'; it's always 'we think this or that.' In that way the responsibility rests on him and I can avoid any blame."

We discussed this trait for some time, and in the same way I discovered many other points. The realization that I was selfish, arrogant, bigoted, and sly gave me cause to ponder, and I thought about my religion and my background as a Christian.

From childhood I had attended church, and at various times even taught Sunday School. I called myself a Christian. But now I wondered, had I ever really lived as a Christian? Did not Christ exhort men to think of their brothers first, to work selflessly for the good of mankind? In the new China people were urged to put the common good ahead of personal interests. This was the whole basis of our thought reform in prison. Here was a concept of Christianity being put into practice as I had never seen done at home.

I thought of the picture I had tried to give my cell mates of the United States—a beautiful land where everyone can do as he pleases. But was it so beautiful for everyone? I remembered the year I worked in the public library at home. The bus I took back and forth to work every day passed through the factory section, where coldwater flats were jammed up against each other. Instead of worrying about the conditions under which my fellow men were living, I thought only of the snug, comfortable home awaiting me as I rode by in winter, and the green lawn and shady trees that kept the house cool in summer. Poverty existed in the United States, too, but I had shut my eyes to it.

"Aren't there any beggars in America?" Mei Chi-yün asked one day.

"Nothing like there used to be in China," I answered. "You hardly ever see any around."

But then I thought of Market Street in Philadelphia where panhandlers walked up and down with tin cups and a poor attempt at a song; or the cripples with no legs who sat in the shelter of doorways, a few pencils displayed for sale. "The poor are always with us," say some. But why, I began to ponder. Is it not just because of people like myself? People who have always called themselves Christians and at the same time shut their eyes to the needs of their fellow men? Many times I thought back over Supervisor Ming's comment, "How can you be so selfish?" And each time I blushed with shame.

But other days I would become despondent about my growing new outlook on life. It put such demands on a person.

"It's all right for you Chinese," I said to my cell mates one day. "You're going back out into a society where the idea of working for the common good is the accepted outlook. But what about me? I'm going back to a society where the accepted rule is every man for himself, and starve if you don't. If I work for the interests of my fellow man I'll have to give up the carefree life I used to lead. No more ivory towers, no more aloof ignorance. I just don't think it's fair of the People's Government to expose me to these concepts and work on my conscience until I stop putting myself first."

The two of them laughed at the consternation on my face, and in a moment I laughed, too. No one was forcing me to put these principles into practice. The People's Government asked that I recognize the significance of my crime, it was true, but beyond that they could ask nothing. Everyone hoped that I would feel compelled to live up to the high moral standards we talked of so frequently, but whether I did or not was up to me.

Another problem which plagued me from the summer of 1953 on was my treatment on my return home. Up to that time I had always thought in terms of returning home as a long-suffering hero who had sweated out a prison sentence. I would be the center of attraction at parties from the time I reached Hong Kong until I arrived in Yonkers, and probably for some time after. But as I became more and more aware of the need for understanding and the creation of good will between nations, I realized that to repudiate my confession and try to act the hero over something which I had justly deserved would be doing both the American and Chinese people a disservice by furthering misunderstanding and animosity between them. To be honest with myself and fair to others, I would certainly have to tell the truth.

But what would happen to me? I had read of the threats and pressure which had been used at home against the G.I.'s who had supposedly been "brainwashed" while in prison camps in North Korea. If I were subjected to the same pressure would I be able to stand up against it? I told my cell mates of my fears. "I'm not very strong," I said. "It's easy to sit here and say I'd never retract my confession but if I actually were faced with the prospects of an insane asylum would I be able to stand firm?"

Naturally I could not answer the question, nor could they, but several times through 1954 I woke up from nightmares about being taken to an insane asylum.

The force of Jeng Ai-ling's character did much to determine me to stick to the truth under any circumstances.

For all my vacillation and discouragement, I knew deep
down in my heart that I had made some progress, for
now at least I had a real desire to become a better person.

14

Rick: During the summer of 1953, while Dell was going through her crisis in cell No. 9 with Jeng Ai-ling and Mei Chi-yün, I was rapidly approaching one of my own. Ever since my arrest I had clung to the hope that as soon as the war was over the Americans in the detention quarters would be released. With the signing of the agreement for the exchange of Korean war prisoners in June, 1953, it seemed as if the long-awaited day was at hand.

My hopes were given an added boost when I was asked to rewrite my confession on a special red-lined form. A few days later I was called out to have my picture taken. Surely the government was preparing to let me go home, but the days passed with interminable slowness all through the ups and downs of the final negotiations in Panmunjom.

My cell mates, knowing what I was thinking, tried to warn me that the Korean war had nothing to do with me. I was not a prisoner of war, but a criminal convicted of espionage. However, their words fell on deaf ears. July 25 would mark the end of two years in prison. Probably I would be allowed to go then, I thought. The 25th came and nothing happened. Maybe it would take another month. But when the end of August rolled around I seemed no closer to my goal.

I was now becoming desperate, especially since I had seen no other foreigners for several months. Perhaps they had all been allowed to leave, and only I remained—only I and Dell, that is. I had never been told officially, but I knew from the spring of 1953 that she had been arrested because in April the authorities had informed me our house was to be returned to the owners and the government would store our belongings for us. It seemed as if all I had achieved by confessing was to bring on her arrest, too. But why had they kept just the two of us? There could be only one answer, my connection with Naval Intelligence.

In the midst of this mental turmoil I chanced to read one day about supposedly brainwashed G.I.'s from North Korean prison camps being sent off to Valley Forge mental hospital, and my mind jumped immediately to my own case. Would not Naval Intelligence do the same to me if I held to my confession and implicated them on my return home? Since I was in the Reserves they could simply call me to active duty and then do as they pleased. It looked as if I might be leaving a prison in China merely to spend the rest of my life in an insane asylum in the United States.

I began to wish I had never mentioned that interview with Naval Intelligence in Seattle. After all, what difference did it make? I had had no direct contact with them after coming to China and my arrest had prevented me from sending them any reports. Perhaps I could rewrite my confession in such a way that my connection with Naval Intelligence would be rendered meaningless.

I tossed this around in my mind for several days and finally broached the subject to Liao.

"I made a mistake in writing my confession," I said. "I wonder if the government would let me correct it."

"Sure," replied Liao, "if you *really* made a mistake. The government only wants the truth. But you had better get things straight in your own mind before you start making any major revisions."

At a conference that night with one of the supervisors, Liao raised the question of my rewriting my confession. He returned with the order for me to go ahead. For the next week I spent my time alone in one corner of the cell writing a new statement. I sweated over the ignominious and knotty task of trying to admit the facts and yet deny them, but finally I had triumphantly succeeded in removing the significance of my connection with Naval Intelligence almost entirely from the picture. I claimed that after arriving in China I had never planned to carry out their instructions. After turning in this new confession, I settled down to wait.

October came and went but I heard no word from the interrogation office. A new idea began forming: If I could write Naval Intelligence out of my confession why could I not go one step further and claim I had never consciously intended to commit espionage but had merely drifted into it as a reaction to the deterioration of Sino-American relations? This would not only clear me with the Navy at home but, at the same time, by evading the stigma of criminal intent, it might reduce the seriousness of my crime in the eyes of the Chinese.

I therefore decided to bring up the matter of writing a third confession. Before I had an opportunity to do so, however, I was called, one day in late November, to the interrogation office. After the judge had finished questioning me about another matter, I decided that this was the time to raise my point.

"There is a question I would like to bring up," I said confidently. "It's about my confession. I don't think the one I have just written is quite right. I still did not bring out clearly why I started giving information to the Consulate. Could I rewrite it again?"

The investigating judge stared at me in cold hostility and for a minute I thought he was going to bite the bit off the end of his pipe. Then, "Go back to your cell!" came his curt reply. The loathing and disgust in his voice cut deeper than any whiplash. Shaken to the core, I walked blindly back to the cell.

Taking one look at my dazed expression, Liao asked, "What happened?"

"I guess I made a mistake," was my fumbling reply.

"Well, that's not surprising. We could all see you were heading for trouble, but there was no point in trying to talk to you. You wouldn't listen to anyone."

This time there was no need for the others to insist on my making a self-criticism. On the one hand, I was really frightened. Making a false confession was a serious matter. On the other, I was brutally struck by the realization of my own dishonesty. Gone was the former hollow, academic approach to the understanding of my character. The whole sordid rottenness of it was exposed in a flash of revulsion and fear.

For a while I wondered if I had any principles at all, and my whole body burned red hot with shame. I expected a fierce tongue lashing from my cell mates, but this time they were surprisingly gentle.

"You should have learned your lesson this time," said Liao. "A selfish mind will go to any lengths to fulfill its desires. Now maybe you can see just being an American doesn't lessen your need for reform. The kind of unprincipled thinking you've displayed here could get you into trouble anywhere."

This time I agreed with him. But this was only the beginning. In the following months I began for the first time to question the very foundations of my character, not as a matter of form because someone else insisted upon it but because I myself felt that unless I could determine the causes for my developing the way I had I would never have any confidence in myself again. On this basis I was able to speak freely about things in my past which I had never mentioned to anyone before. My childhood dreams, relations with my family, friends, and schoolmates, my attitude toward women, sex, and what I wanted out of life were all discussed in the most minute detail.

I remembered most vividly my early years in Spokane. As we were one of the poorer families in the neighborhood, my parents were seldom able to provide me with the luxuries the other children enjoyed. As a result, I always felt left out of their play. To my childish mind it seemed that if our family only had a car so that my father could take all of us fishing, or if I could only have lots of toys, I would be able to win the respect of my playmates. Since this was impossible, I had taken to boasting and making up stories about nonexistent rich and important relatives. Several times I stole toy cars from the 5-and-10¢ store so that I would have something which would make the other children want to come and play with me.

When, in the most bitter years of the depression, my father had resorted to making jigsaw puzzles to eke out our existence, I had tried to peddle them from door to door. I remembered the terrified feeling which engulfed me each time I approached a door as I anticipated how it would be slammed in my face.

The experience of those early years made a deep impression upon me, and as I grew up my greatest fear was that I might have to suffer as my mother and father had in those long years of unemployment. My father's often-repeated words, "A man who works only with his hands is nothing but a slave," stuck in my mind and I was determined to escape from that. Going to the university was my first big step. Then, when I became the only member of my family to hold a commission in the armed services during the war, I felt I was on the way up.

My decision to become a professor was a logical outgrowth of this background, for no other field seemed to provide the same combination of security and prestige. My hatred of the Communists after reaching China was partly inspired by the fact that as I watched the deterioration of Sino-American relations, and with it a dwindling in numbers of prospective students, missionaries, businessmen, and State Department people in the field of Chinese, I could see my chances of becoming a successful professor gradually disappearing. Thus my connections with the American Consulate had become even more important to me, for, though there might not be jobs open for a professor, if I could maintain an "in" with the State Department I still had nothing to fear.

As I continued my analysis I realized even more how my egotism had slowly developed to where I was incapable of seeing anything which was not to my advantage and where I was oblivious to the plights of others. I remembered how Dell and I had looked with revulsion on the poverty around us when we arrived in China. One morning in November, 1948, we had stepped out of the gate of a friend's house where we had spent the night, to find a man stretched out dead on the doorstep, obviously starved to death. It was a shock to both of us and had brought an ugly note into a bright morning. Reflecting on my attitude that day, I realized now that the little sympathy I had felt for the man had been more than overshadowed by annoyance over my day being spoiled in such a way. My attitude toward the Korean war had shown the same brutal disregard for the lives of others on a much larger scale.

In discussions with my cell mates I also began to reconsider the attitude I had previously displayed toward my own crime. I recalled a conversation I had had with the investigating judge in the spring of 1953, when I had been called in one day to clarify some of the points in my confession.

"How do you feel about all this?" he had asked.

I had told him quite frankly that I was sorry that I had broken the Chinese law, but that I had no feeling of having done anything criminal.

"Well," he had asked, "did you or did you not give information to the American Consulate with the idea that it would be used to harm the People's Government?"

"Yes," I had replied, "there's no question about that and never was."

"Then, how would you feel if someone were to go to your country and do the same things that you did here?"

"I wouldn't like it," I had answered, as I thought how angry I had been about the activities of Nazi and Japanese agents in the United States during the war.

"Well, how can you maintain that there is nothing wrong and criminal in what you have done?"

When I returned to the cell I had had to admit that what he said was right, but when I began to think about the ten years I might be spending in prison it still seemed to me a terrible price to pay. Preoccupied as I was only with a desire for release, my mind sought refuge in the excuse that I had only been trying to serve my country, with no desire to harm anyone.

The dishonesty of this rationalization was now clear to me. Not wanting to harm others was no excuse at all, since a person totally blinded by his own self-interest is incapable of thinking of others, to begin with. If I had not been so blind, I would have been able to see long ago the fallacy in my supposition that my espionage activities had been of service to my country. Actually, by contributing to the widening gulf between our people and the Chinese, I had been doing the United States a great disservice. I was now convinced that no country has the right to try to force its will and social system upon the people of another, as we had tried to do back in 1949–50. Such a course was immoral, and could lead only to resentment, hatred, and the threat of war.

Having one's innermost self brought out and dissected under the glaring light of self-criticism was a shattering experience, but the resulting recognition of myself made me determined to overcome the weaknesses in my character which had been the cause of those former mistakes. Thus began the struggle with myself which was to last throughout the rest of my stay in prison, and, indeed, goes on even today.

15

Dell: It is only through constant struggle and the inter-action of criticism and self-criticism that people can grad-ually build a new character. This we all realized, but often when two or three people live in one cell for an extended period the challenge seems to die away and the fight against bad habits is relaxed. Our cell No. 9 was typical.

Mei Chi-yün was released a few days before New Year's, 1954, and from then on Jeng Ai-ling and I settled down to a placid existence, broken only by occasional outbursts of temperament. We read and talked, argued and sang, sewed and played cards together.

Jeng Ai-ling taught me how to tend the stove, mend socks Chinese fashion, and how to make Chinese cloth shoes. Because of an acute stomach ailment she was given noodles every day instead of *wo-tou*. In violation of prison regulations, we saved some of the noodles and boiled them into paste on the stove. We tore up one of my ragged shirts, and, using the table on the *kang*, we stretched out a layer of rags, on top of that a layer of paste, then a layer of rags, and so on until we had about eight thicknesses. It took two days for the *go-bei*, as these sheets of cloth and paste were called, to dry stiff as boards. We then cut out as many soles as could be gotten out of the sheets. Several of these were placed on top of each other to the thickness of about three-quarters of an inch. I was about to learn how to sew these layers together with hemp thread to make a strong, durable sole when Supervisor Ming came in to tell me to pack up my belongings. It was March 5, 1954.

I sighed regretfully as I packed my half-made shoes.

Though Jeng Ai-ling had made my life miserable durin
the summer of 1953, and had been merciless in pointin
out my weaknesses, I was grateful for the help she ha
given me in learning to know myself. In view of our recen
laxity in observing regulations, however, it was not su
prising that we were being separated.

Supervisor Ming and I, each shouldering a bundle c
my belongings, walked toward the west compound, whe
I had spent the first four months of my life in priso
Was I going back to a single cell, I wondered, with a ce
tain amount of apprehension. And then I smiled to my
self as I thought how I had changed. A year ago I woul
have been happy to be by myself. Now I had come t
appreciate the advantage of group living. Not only wa
cooperation helpful in daily chores, but I felt utterly d
pendent on the help of others in the process of reformin
my outlook.

We passed by the cell block that I had formerly know
so well and went on to the far west compound. The *jia
yü-dwey* (Education Corps)! My cell mates had fr
quently talked enviously of those who had been luck
enough to be sent there, for much more freedom w
enjoyed. And now here I was. I waited at the entranc
while Supervisor Ming went to report my arrival. A fe
moments later a young woman appeared, dressed in fade
black padded trousers and dark red padded jacket. Sh
picked up one of my bundles and told me to follow he
We went down a short corridor and into a room abo
twenty feet square with *kangs* along two walls and a spa
about six feet wide down the center. After the cell I ha
just left it seemed enormous.

They were in the midst of class, so I scrambled up o
the *kang* next to Wang Hsiao-yün and An Mei-ling, tw
of the women I had known in my first group cell. I n
ticed Sonya, the White Russian, sitting in a corner ar
Harriet's friend, Little Yang, who had been under hou
arrest with me back in 1951. I counted eighteen wome
This was frightening. It was all right to talk about on

self in front of four or five people, but a whole roomful was a different matter.

When the whistle blew at noon for recreation, several of them crowded around me to wish me well and tell me something of the new discipline. The door was not locked during the day and we could go in and out to the latrine at will. Recreation time was always spent outdoors unless it rained.

It was time to go outside. The March wind was rather chilly for sitting around a chessboard, but the sun felt good. A volleyball game was being set up by some men prisoners with whom we shared the recreational facilities of the courtyard. One of the women asked me if I would like to play. When I nodded enthusiastically, the men assigned positions for the two of us. I was so intent on watching the ball soar back and forth that I did not at first notice who had taken the place beside me.

Suddenly I heard a voice shout, "Here it comes!"

There was something familiar about that voice. I turned to look. It was the warden himself! I was so flustered I completely missed the ball, which smacked to the ground beside me. Everyone laughed good-naturedly at my embarrassment, but I was unable to recover myself the rest of the game. I soon found that the supervisors and warden participated frequently in the recreation periods of the Education Corps. Ping-pong, volleyball, chess, bridge, and caroms were the most popular forms of play.

The next day was Saturday and I expected my cell mates to start cleaning the cell after breakfast as was the custom in the other compounds. We sat down for class again, however, and carried on as if it were any regular day of the week. I learned later that the schedule followed in the Education Corps was much closer to that of cadres on the outside, where the six-day week prevailed. All personal business was taken care of on Sunday. This was a program designed to give the prisoners an opportunity to train themselves in the rapid pace which they would find in their work after release.

There never seemed to be quite time enough to finish

all our chores on Sunday, and many of us would snatch five minutes after dinner and before recreation to wash out a handkerchief or write a letter. As a New Yorker, accustomed to a clock-watching existence, I found the pace exhilarating, but I often laughed as I found myself running instead of walking from one place to another.

Our level of study was much higher than that of my first group cell. They were quick to discover any trace of sham, and I was surprised to learn that An Mei-ling, who had been praised by our cell leader Makimoto a year before, was frequently criticized for the superficiality of her self-criticism. On the other hand, they were exceedingly patient with those who, though backward, were honest about it.

Rationing was one of the subjects of conversation shortly after I arrived in the large cell, and we all voiced our opinions about it. One of the older women heaved a long sigh and then said petulantly, "I think it's just a shame. My poor family. What are they going to do? They won't be able to buy enough flour to make *man-tou* [steamed wheat bread] every day."

"But, Wu Shr-min," explained someone kindly, "they can buy all the corn flour or millet they want. It isn't as if they weren't going to have enough to eat."

"And furthermore," said our cell leader, Meng Hsiao-mei, "think of what this means for the other people of China. In former years, while your family was eating *man tou* and rice every day those people were lucky to have a little sorghum or black beans. A lot of them had to exist on sweet potatoes and leaves from trees. But now these people have jobs and a steady income. They can afford to buy fine grains like wheat flour or rice several times a week. But if families like yours keep on eating so much of the flour, there won't be enough to go around. Our farmer can't increase their yield enough to meet this sudden demand.

"The only way to assure everyone of having some wheat flour at least a few days a week is to institute a system of rationing. I'm sure your family doesn't begrudge that flour when they know they are sharing it with people who have never been able to afford it before. I think you're worrying about them unnecessarily."

After several others had pointed out additional reasons for rationing, the old woman admitted the logic of their arguments and seemed willing to accept the idea. I thought back to the year before in that first group cell in the east compound. We had all known the theory of quiet reasoning, but sometimes impatient retorts would develop into heated arguments which solved nothing.

The fear I had felt at first about studying with eighteen other women soon vanished. They listened to what I said and gave me straightforward criticism.

Two weeks after I had moved to the new cell six of the women left, five to go to the prison factory and one to be released. The thirteen of us who remained felt drawn together by the very fact of having been left behind. I, as a foreigner, was particularly hit emotionally when Sonya, the White Russian, was told to pack up her things in early April. Since she was the only one leaving, we thought she probably was bound for home. Several voiced the opinion that a short period in a factory would do Sonya no harm. In the time she had been in prison she had never overcome a distaste for work, and in every self-criticism spoke of wanting to go back to her father's wealthy establishment in Harbin. At the end of each session she would express a determination to get rid of this desire to live off others, but if asked how she expected to do this she would shrug her shoulders helplessly and say, "I don't know."

Release, or sentencing to a prison factory or farm, was a frequent topic of conversation. Some of us felt that if we knew the length of our prison term we could settle down and study and work quite patiently. Others said that would be all right if one's sentence were only for two or three years, but supposing it were ten or fifteen? Would it not be better to remain in ignorance?

Our cell leader said, during one of these conversations, "My interrogation officer told me we ought to be glad that, having found us guilty, the court still deferred the actual passing of sentence. It is usually only those who refuse to confess who are sentenced right away. They get the maximum under the law and there is little chance of clemency.

"If the passing of sentence is held off, you have an opportunity to express your attitude. If you show a desire to reform and be honest your sentence may be greatly reduced when it is finally announced. In fact, you may eventually just be released right from the detention quarters without ever going to a factory or farm.

"And then, too, all the time you've been here since arrest counts. And think of the incentive. If you don't know what your term is, you can go along studying, improving yourself without any worries, because you know that you are constructively working toward a quicker release. If you knew what your sentence was you'd be inclined to sit here and mark off each day on the calendar—one day nearer release. You would be serving out your punishment, but you wouldn't be thinking about preparing yourself to become a better citizen."

We could admit that she had a point, but sometimes one or another of us would sigh, "If I only knew how long!"

Some of us could not get away from the idea that working to improve oneself was synonymous with giving the authorities a favorable impression. It seemed as if the only way to obtain release was to convince the supervisors that we had changed our viewpoint and could do constructive work in society. The distinction between really changing for the sake of being able to do good in the world and changing to impress others was, I think, the most difficult problem for most of us. We were constantly faced with this contradiction in ourselves and in others.

This came out in sharp relief in May, 1954, when our cell was assigned to *lao-dung* (work). We greeted the chance to work as a relief from the routine of study, but for some this enthusiasm went deeper. Those who were slow at books but fast with the needle felt that this was their long-awaited chance to "show their worth."

In the winter the People's Government issued padded jackets and trousers and padded quilts to all prisoners who had none of their own. These were used right through to warm weather. The clothing and bedding were then returned to the government, and it was our job to rip them apart, wash the pieces, fluff out the cotton, and then sew them all back together again.

I knew that *lao-dung* went on every summer but this was the first time I had participated in it and I was as excited as the others. I had always prided myself on my skill with the needle. Since high school I had made my own clothes and not a few for my sister and mother. I was confident I could hold my own. But before the sewing could begin we had to rip the garments apart and wash them. In the first batch we had over two hundred pieces. There were six large crockery wash basins and, of course, we all vied to do the scrubbing, since that was the most arduous task and gave the best opportunity to demonstrate one's mettle.

I maintained that I was stronger than many of the others and should take over one of the basins and scrub boards, but I had no sooner started to scrub than my cell mates suggested politely but firmly that my talents might be put to better use elsewhere. As I watched one of the older women rolling the cloth back and forth over the board in beautiful, rhythmic motion, never grasping too much or too little, never getting it bunched up, and then looked down at my own jerky movement which twisted the clothes into little knots I had to concede that perhaps washing clothes by hand was not one of my major accomplishments and I reluctantly gave my place to one of the women who had been standing impatiently by.

It was apparent that the former housewives, along with Jou Yu-jieh (Little Jou), a young girl who had had some schooling but had also worked long at home, had now come into their own and were going to make up for all those months of sitting on the *kang*, sweating over topics of study far beyond their grasp. They did not say in so many words, "You can take a back seat for a while and give us a chance to show off," but it was quite apparent in their attitude. When any of us "intellectuals" asked them to teach us how to scrub, they shunted us off with the excuse that it would waste time.

The washing took only a couple of days and during that time the rest of us kept busy pumping and carrying water, hanging the pieces on the line, stretching them out flat to get the wrinkles out, and putting the cotton padding out to air. We all swallowed our pride in anticipation of the sewing, where we felt we would surely be vindicated.

When some of the pieces had dried our cell leader took the lead in deciding who might have the privilege of sewing patches where needed. The rest of us were told to start fluffing the cotton padding. We would lay the quilt on the *kang* and fit the padding on top of it. New cotton padding is simple because it is thick and even all over. But the padding which we were working with was old. It fell apart at the touch and we had to go through the painstaking process of fluffing the matted pieces into a uniformly thick whole.

There is a trick to pulling the cotton apart and fusing the ends together again so that it comes out soft and fluffy. I didn't know the trick and though I succeeded in pulling quite a bit of cotton apart the ends were short and jagged and would not stay together. The assistant cell leader, Li Jing-yün, showed me how to pull the cotton so that the long fibers were not broken. I improved a bit, but I was still painfully slow.

At this point someone suggested we divide up into teams and have a competition. Everyone agreed, and we started to pair off. "Why don't you take Li Yu-an?" said Li Jing-yün to Little Jou, whose clever hands worked like lightning on the bits of cotton.

"Oh, she's impossible," replied Little Jou impatiently, "I don't want to be bothered with her."

My pride stung by her retort, I burst out hotly, "Well, I couldn't stand to work with her either. I tried to get her to teach me how to fix the cotton before but she wouldn't."

There was an uncomfortable silence, broken finally by Li Jing-yün, "You'll get the hang of it in no time, Li Yu-an. Come over here where I can guide you a bit."

A few hours later Meng Hsiao-mei came over from the cell across the corridor where the "patchers" were at work. "We need someone to help with the patching," she said, gazing at each of us speculatively.

"I'll go," said Wang Yü-lin, a tall, heavy-built young woman who had been through normal school.

"Better let Hsü Tsui do it," said Meng Hsiao-mei finally and, with no explanation as to why she had chosen Hsü Tsui, she turned and went back across the corridor, Hsü Tsui tagging along after her.

It seemed a strange choice, because Hsü was a young woman who was always being laughed at for her clumsiness. She had attended a Catholic university in Peking and, from what some said, she could speak English as well as I. She was the product of a completely Western education, out of tune with her own people, and in turn looked on with contempt by them. Her lack of knowledge of the simplest housekeeping tasks made her the butt of ridicule. I puzzled over this seeming harshness at first, for she was not the only one in the cell who had grown up with books rather than a scrubbing board, and it appeared to me she was trying as much as everyone else to do her share. It gradually came out that her reputation as a squeamish worker had been built up in previous years when she had backed away from any form of work which might make her dirty. The reputation had stuck and it was clear that she was going to have to work twice as hard as anyone else for a long time to bring about a change in her cell mates' opinion.

The two women had no sooner left than Wang Yü-lin flopped back up on the *kang* and exploded, "I'm so mad I could spit! Who does Meng Hsiao-mei think she is, playing favorites like that? I can sew much better than Hsü Tsui. For that matter, anyone can. She's the sloppiest, laziest—"

"Take it easy," soothed Li Jing-yün. "There's no point in getting yourself all worked up. Meng Hsiao-mei is just riding her position a little too high and it's about time she learned she can't boss the whole show. Just let her try one or two more little deals like that and she'll have something to reckon with. She's buttering Hsü Tsui up so she'll have her on her side when the blow-up comes."

There had always been a latent conflict between the cell leader, Meng Hsiao-mei, and the assistant cell leader, Li Jing-yün. The former had had little schooling and had been married off to one of Yen Hsi-shan's henchmen as a concubine while still a young girl. She had learned to write quite a few characters while in prison but still had difficulty taking many notes while we were studying. She was made cell leader mainly because of her ability to lead a group in discussion and because of her sincere expression of a desire to improve herself. The others told me one day that formerly she had often displayed a fiery temper and her shrill voice would rise to a shriek in criticizing the other women. But by the time I arrived in the cell she had gone a long way toward conquering this tendency and was able to maintain a patient attitude in almost any situation.

Li Jing-yün, as assistant cell leader, was in charge of our class discussions. She had been brought up in Shanghai and gone to college there. Having worked in a department of the government and taken part in study on the outside, she considered herself a bit different from the others. Even though she had ended up in prison through her connection with an American agent, she repeatedly maintained that after serving out her sentence she would be able to go back to her old job.

Her experience in Shanghai, her worldliness, education, and general command of study material should have made her an excellent balance for Meng Hsiao-mei in handling the large number of women in the cell, but there was bad feeling between them. Meng Hsiao-mei, insecure in her lack of education, was jealous of the assistant cell leader and felt that at any moment she would be pushed out of the number one position. Li Jing-yün, on the other hand, was contemptuous of Meng Hsiao-mei in that she felt the latter was an opportunist.

During my first two months in the cell the conflict had

been at a minimum, but now that our big project had started the issue had sharpened. Meng Hsiao-mei was determined to show that here she need take second place to no one, and aimed to consolidate her position as cell leader through taking the leadership of our work entirely into her hands. Li Jing-yün was on the defensive because she had little experience in sewing and washing and yet at the same time did not like being ordered around by Meng Hsiao-mei. Anything the latter said about lack of efficiency in the group she took as a personal affront.

The situation was further complicated by the fact that this was the first time the two of them had acted as cell leaders at the time of *lao-dung* and both were nervous about failing in their responsibilities.

There was a lot of patching to be done on the quilts and clothes, and before long everyone but Li Jing-yün, Little Yang, and Wang Yü-lin was busy stitching bits of material over holes and tears. I liked patching but labored over the stitches and soon found myself behind the others. When the pressure slackened I was the first to be sent back to the cotton padding detail. I found the three of them smoldering over being left out of the "important work."

This situation naturally could not exist very long without having some effect on our efficiency. With people pulling against each other or engrossed in showing off their own particular skills, we could not get through the work in the time it should normally take. About a week after we had started *lao-dung* Meng Hsiao-mei announcd at breakfast that we would not scatter to our jobs but would hold a self-criticism meeting to straighten out a few issues.

It lasted two days, as each woman in turn made an accounting of her attitude. The petty jealousies, uncooperativeness, factionalism, and backbiting all came out into the open and were criticized. Both of the cell leaders admitted their share in the deterioration of the atmosphere. The friction between them was brought to the surface and each promised to make a sincere attempt at cooperation.

In summing up Meng Hsiao-mei said, "After all, I think we have lost sight of the most important point—the purpose of this work. Why has the People's Government given it to us to do? They could send the whole load off to the laundry and have it back in no time at a very cheap price. But the government wants to give us an opportunity to learn how to work together, to cooperate in good spirit and efficiency. We have come from backgrounds where cooperation is almost unheard of—you had your work, I had mine, each in our own homes. But in the new society we may be going out to work in factories, on farms, in offices, schools, nurseries, hospitals—who knows where? In all those places people are working together and learning to cooperate. If we do not learn here we will be out of step when we return to society and no one will want us.

"We have been given this opportunity and what do we do? We're afraid to show anyone else how to do anything for fear they'll learn how to do it better than we do. Look at Little Jou. She's probably one of the best and fastest workers in the group, but when Li Yu-an asked her for help in learning how to fluff cotton she was impatient and refused. Suppose all the technicians in China took that attitude today. How would new technicians ever be trained and our country progress?

"In the old days that was the attitude of the master craftsmen, because they were afraid of losing their jobs if too many people learned their art. They would teach just so much, and then keep secret the crucial steps so that they would remain indispensable. Little Jou is not motivated by that fear, but she is afraid of losing what she considers an advantage over the rest of us so that she can make a good impression on the government. But I ask you all, does the government want to see a really good cotton fluffer or a woman who has the patience and bigness of heart to teach others and fit herself into a cooperative picture?"

Little Jou at first remained silent as the others criticized their shortcomings in turn. At the end she admitted that her attitude had been wrong and that she would share her knowledge with the rest of us. The meeting ended on a high note of enthusiasm as we went back to work. We had aired a lot of differences and were ready to start afresh.

In another week most of the patching was finished and our work was cotton fluffing and quilting. I was eager to try quilting and asked if I might do one or two. Two women worked on one quilt, which would take ten or eleven rows of wide-spaced stitches to hold the cotton in place. Here again, as in the patching, I found myself lagging far behind my partner. She gave me pointers to help increase my speed but I had difficulty making the needle go through the heavy padding with the ease that she did. I worked like mad, but the best I did was still one and a half rows behind her. It was a blow to my pride but I, too, had learned a lesson and when it became clear I could not keep up with the others I was content to go back to fluffing.

Our work moved along in this way through the summer. For a few days after a self-criticism we worked together beautifully, but the newly learned spirit of cooperation would soon begin to give at the seams and in a few weeks all work would stop so that another meeting could be held. Differences were again ironed out and we each examined our attitude toward work in general.

Little Yang voiced a point of view which, I think, was common to several of the "intellectuals."

"I think one reason I don't work better," she said, "is that I can't see any real point in becoming proficient at this kind of work. I don't expect to earn my living at cotton fluffing when I'm released. I was in an office before and I imagine I'll be going back to one in the future."

"That may be," agreed Meng Hsiao-mei, "but you ought not lose sight of the fact that you are not in an office now, and that the work at hand is important in its own way. Whatever the job to be done, one ought to do it to the best of one's ability. That is the attitude of the truly reconstructed member of society."

But no matter how many problems were solved new ones kept cropping up. A few days after one of our meetings during the summer Feng Hsiu-bin, a middle-aged housewife who had had little education, chanced to look across at the group fluffing cotton on the *kang* opposite us.

"Is that your second or third jacket this morning?" she asked.

"Second or third?" repeated Little Jou in surprise. "This is our fourth!"

Feng Hsiu-bin turned back to the jacket on which the three of us were working. It was our second. She was silent for a few moments but I could see her face grow dark and her lips working. Finally she leaned toward Meng Hsiao-mei and me and said in a hoarse whisper, "They may be on their fourth, but I'll bet they're doing a sloppy job. That Little Jou is quick but she's a careless worker. Just wait and see. Our padding will be inches thicker."

Meng Hsiao-mei and I smiled but said nothing. It would do no good at that moment to point out to Feng Hsiu-bin that her old enemy, jealousy, was still coloring her outlook on life. Later in the day when she was in a calmer mood, Meng Hsiao-mei brought the subject up again.

Feng Hsiu-bin sighed, "That's my *ssu-hsiang-ger* [root of all my thinking], that jealousy. It was what landed me here in the first place. Knowing that there is a root to one's thoughts is a wonderful thing. Just think, before I came here I didn't know there was such a thing as a 'root'!"

We laughed, but then Meng Hsiao-mei pressed the point home. "Yes, but, Feng Hsiu-bin, it's one thing to know you have a jealous streak in your nature and another to get rid of it. That's what you have to do now."

That summer of 1954 was to me one of the most profitable experiences of my life. Never before had I worked with others on such an extensive project. After college I had been employed in the New York Public Library, but in six months had decided that dealing with "the public" was unbearable. From there I had retreated to the quieter atmosphere of a publishing house. It was not until after Rick and I had become students at Penn and I had achieved the complete isolation of a seminar room in a corner of the library, however, that I felt really at home. There I was completely "free" and beholden to no one.

With this background it had been difficult for me at first to adjust myself to the group activity, but the satisfaction that came with the feeling of fellowship in working with others brought home to me the stuffy dryness of my former way of life.

During our *lao-dung* we made many mistakes in organization and were slowed down frequently by those internal conflicts. The animosity which had existed between Meng Hsiao-mei and Li Jing-yün and the resulting factions which were inevitable as each of us sided with one or the other continued right through to the fall and the situation was relieved only by the departure of Li Jing-yün. In spite of these conflicts, however, I did feel that we had made progress in learning to help each other and in developing ideas of work methods on a group level.

Our sewing continued through the third week in September, but about the end of August we received a shock to find that the Education Corps was being disbanded. Most of the men were moved to the east compound and the whole program stopped. Since we were still working, our door was not locked, but as soon as the project ended we returned to the routine of the locked door and regular times for recreation and latrine calls. All the compounds in the prison were uniform in discipline from then on.

We each had varying theories as to the reason for the change and displayed varying reactions. Those who had been in the Education Corps less than a year were not much disturbed by it, but to those who had been there over three years the locked door was not easy to take. The abolition of this program was only logical, however. The number of inmates in the prison had dwindled in the past year, and those who had derived the greatest benefit from the educational discipline of the corps had left for prison farms, factories, or had been released.

The reaction of most of the women was that a return to the regular cell routine was a punishment for not having lived up to the government's expectations. Even though, in the discussions which followed, we agreed that this was not true, we still watched eagerly for signs that the authorities were really not angry with us. One event which helped us regain our confidence occurred about a week before the October 1st celebration. The door opened one day to reveal one of the young cadres with an armful of bright-colored paper and coils of thin wire.

"This is for flowers," he said abruptly, as he dumped the armload on the *kang* and hurried out. A few moments later he returned with a spray of artificial flowers. "Here's a sample," he explained, and left just as quickly as before.

We all gathered around excitedly to poke at the different flowers, about ten in all, interspersed with shiny green leaves attached to a thick, three-pronged wire branch. Others turned over the packages of paper to see how many colors there were. We stopped studying immediately and began to discuss how we should organize the work. There were eleven of us, the assistant cell leader, Li Jing-yün, and one of the others having left a few weeks before.

Again it seemed as if the "intellectuals" were to take a back seat, as Little Jou and Meng Hsiao-mei explained how they had made paper flowers as children. But we began to use our imagination and before long we were producing zinnias, roses, camellias, gladioli, giant red cannas, and a few others that did not have a name but looked pretty and graceful just the same.

The housewife Feng Hsiu-bin had watched her daughter make a particularly beautiful type of chrysanthemum the year before and she sat off to the side experimenting for a while. She came up with a flower so real I wanted to touch it to make sure. We gave her a whole roll of paper and told her to go ahead.

I felt as I watched everyone working together that we had truly profited from the summer's experience. I had wondered at first if Little Jou would keep her skill to herself, but she started right out by explaining the different steps and then encouraged us to experiment. The spray the cadre had given us was made of several different flowers and we modeled our first sprays on this. As we progressed, we tried one of just pink roses and were so enchanted with the results that after a long conference we decided to take apart the ones we had already made and build each spray of a single kind. As we finished a spray we would hang it from the clothesline that stretched from the window to the opposite wall. When the paper was used up we took scraps of the pale pink and made a spray of early flowering plum, the kind that has myriads of tiny blossoms all over the leafless branches. It expressed to me the delicacy of Chinese art, and tears of appreciation for its beauty came to my eyes as I held it.

It was a dull-looking cell when all the flowers were taken away, to be used in decorating the prison offices. We cleaned up the cell and in the afternoon made a token gesture at study, although our hearts were not in it. It was September 30, 1954, and the next day, October 1, was a holiday, the fifth anniversary of the founding of the People's Republic.

There were no classes that day and we listened to broadcasts of festivities over the loud-speaker, played cards, and told stories. Little Yang suggested we try a few folk dances. The space between the two *kangs* was just big enough to do simple steps. One of the younger women showed us a west China folk dance, "The Sun has risen." Wang Yü-lin taught us a Sinkiang dance. Little Yang, with her Western education and long experience in the Chinese YWCA, insisted that we try a Virginia reel. With the two of us to teach the others, we were able to make it a lively one. She had been with us to a dance a few years before at the Peking Club and remembered the polka we had danced that evening. She asked me to show them all. There was room for only one pair at a time to skip up and down the room so we all took turns. I sat on the *kang* and clapped out the rhythm and ta-ti-ta'ed one or another of the polka tunes.

One of the older women, who had led an extremely sheltered life, sat on the *kang* and watched us dance. As we were doing the "Sun has risen" folk dance, she smiled happily, "Look at the foreigner doing our dances."

We tried to coax her into joining, and it was obvious that she wanted to very much, but she would only giggle and shake her head. She belonged to that generation which tradition had kept in seclusion and it would take some time to break down her reserve.

By evening we were worn out and sat around quietly talking. I looked at these women with whom I had worked and studied for several months. We had had our differences and they had become disgusted with my outlook on life more than once, but at the same time I felt closer to them than to any Chinese since I had been in China. I remembered the days in Yenching when I had seen students dancing together on the lawn. I had hovered in the background, wishing I could join them yet feeling miles apart. I had had to come to jail to learn a few things about myself in order to come closer to the Chinese among whom I was living.

I thought of the strides we had all made in our relations with each other. One day, a week before, we had been sitting around talking about China's new construction projects.

"Shanghai used to be the only city in China with tall buildings," said Little Yang, "but we're going to have a lot in Peking now."

"I was once in a building seven stories high," said one of the women proudly.

Little Yang laughed. "I guess that doesn't seem very high to Li Yu-an. They have real skyscrapers in New York, don't they?"

I nodded. "The tallest building of all has 102 stories."

There were gasps. "What keeps it from falling over?" "What does it look like?" "Did you ever go up to the top floor?"

I drew a rough outline of the Empire State Building and we talked about industrialization in the United States. When the subject returned to China's growing industrialization they commented confidently, "Well, the United States had a head start and the workmen there have built many wonderful things, but it won't take China long to catch up. You just take a look at *our* skyscrapers twenty years from now!"

The conversation showed how far we had progressed in our thinking. Only a year ago most of the women prisoners, with the exception of a few like Jeng Ai-ling, would have thought that listening to anything about the United States, unless it were a blast at U.S. foreign policy or the decadence of American life, would be considered "backward"; but now, secure in their understanding about the new society and the old, they could listen to things such as I was telling them with an analytical and at the same time appreciative mind.

It was exhilarating to talk with my cell mates about the United States. Those with schooling had studied about America, but the others had only a vague conception of that "foreign land." Their lack of understanding about our life here was brought home to me one day in August, 1954, when I was reading a letter from my mother. Meng Hsiao-mei asked, "Is that letter from home?"

When I told her it came from my mother, she asked, "Did someone write it for her?"

"No," I said. "My mother can write."

Meng Hsiao-mei looked at me wonderingly. To her, a woman in her thirties who had just learned to read and write, it was amazing to think of a woman a generation older able to use a pen. Little Yang explained kindly, "Meng Hsiao-mei, in the United States women have been emancipated for many years now and they have all gone to school. I suppose Li Yu-an's grandmother even went to school."

"Yes," I replied, "she did."

I was ashamed at having been surprised at Meng Hsiao-mei's question. Having lived all her life in Shansi with no access to books, how could she be expected to know much about how other people lived? This held true for so many millions in the old China.

After the celebration on October 1 we began to settle back to the regular routine again. Every afternoon we went out in the yard when the sun was warmest and walked around for half an hour or so. It was warm enough, when we exercised or walked fast around the compound, to take off our jackets. The others laughed at the patches on my blouse, an ancient light blue Wave shirt which I had had since the war. It had worn out on the sleeves and across the shoulders and I had patched it with many different colored bits of cloth.

It was while we were out taking our exercise on the afternoon of October 13, 1954, that a supervisor motioned me back to the cell and told me to get my things together. Meng Hsiao-mei went along to help me and we gathered my bedding, books, clothes, etc., into two big bundles. I felt I could not be leaving the prison on such short notice, but was I to be shifted to another cell in this compound or sent back to the east compound? My heart went ker-plunk, kerplunk as I thought of starting all over again with a new set of cell mates. Why could I not stay with these women with whom I had developed such a bond?

16

Rick: By the spring of 1954 the detention quarters seemed almost empty in comparison with former years. The occupants of our cell had been reduced to Liao, Han, and myself, Ma having been transferred a couple of months earlier. One day in June, Liao, too, was told to pack and prepare to move.

For a moment as I watched him excitedly collecting his few things I felt a little sad and envious, but at the same time I was glad to see him moving one step closer to release. When he had gone Han and I expected that we would either be put in another cell or someone else would come in with us. However, as the days rolled by and nothing happened we began to settle down to a new routine. Part of the day we studied by ourselves and the remaining time was spent either in working over our books together or discussing problems in the cell.

Han was a short, chunky man of exactly my age, but after our monthly haircut, with his head and face clipped clean, he looked more like a high school student. He came from a large, relatively well-to-do family of frugal, hardworking peasants, but his own character showed little trace of this. Born the last of a large brood, when his parents were approaching fifty, he had been a sickly child, doted on and spoiled by all the older members of the family.

At the age of fourteen he had been married to a girl five years his senior. This was not an uncommon occurrence in old China, where marriages were often arranged between families before the children were even born. As might be expected, the arrangement ended in bitterness for both Han and his wife. They had nothing in common, and while he was still out playing with other children she was either laboring out in the fields or in the house. To make matters worse, in Han's eyes her partly-bound feet made her old-fashioned and repulsive. From then on his ambition in life was to get away from her and acquire a "good-looking" concubine.

Because of his insistent demands to leave his wife, Han was finally apprenticed to a big silk merchant in Peking, where he soon acquired the city taste for flashy clothes and ready money. He remained in Peking all through the Japanese war, gradually working his way up to a small business of his own. After failing in several attempts at speculation, he had entered the Nationalist Youth Army in 1947 and eventually was drawn into their intelligence service.

In late 1948, as the Communists approached the area in which he was operating, he deserted and fled south to Nanking, Hangchow, and finally Canton. With no money to escape to Hong Kong or Formosa there was nothing left for him but to return to his home outside Peking. Terror-stricken at the thought that the Communists would certainly exact vengeance against him for the bloody suppression his unit had carried on against dissident peasants under the Nationalists, Han had remained in hiding on his family's farm for many months. But wearing peasant's clothes, eating coarse food, and not being able to attend a movie were more than he could stand for very long. Moreover, because of his unwillingness to take part in the work of the farm and clear himself with the new government, his welcome at home began to wear thin.

He finally returned to Peking to go back into business. But it was not long before he became involved with a gang of Nationalist agents and was eventually arrested.

From the time he arrived in prison in late 1952 Han was convinced that he would be executed. For months he went around in a semi-stupor, his mind turning to hypochondria as a mechanism for escape from the fear of death. By the time Liao left in June, 1954, much of this fear had been dispelled and along with it had disappeared most of his real and imagined illnesses. His actions were still those of a scared rabbit, however, and he avoided all possible contact with the authorities. He was never so happy as when the door was bolted and locked. To him it seemed to keep the government out as well as him in.

But with only two of us left in the cell a new problem arose to plague Han. We had no cell leader, and since my Americanized Chinese often proved unintelligible to the guards and supervisors, especially when I became excited, the burden of spokesman fell on him.

That summer I was told to rewrite my confession. In the midst of writing my pen point became so scratchy it tore holes in the thin paper. I asked Han to report the matter to the supervisor and ask for a new one. His face portrayed his reluctance, but that evening when we went out for latrine call he cautiously approached the supervisor, an older cadre named Hsi who had a rather abrupt manner, mumbled his request, and then dashed back to the cell again.

I waited all evening and the next day, but no pen point arrived. In answer to my impatient prodding to ask again, Han offered every kind of excuse imaginable, and it was only on the second day that he would consent to ask the supervisor once more. On our return to the cell from latrine call that afternoon, before the door had been closed, Han stuck his head out and asked timidly, as if expecting a blow, "Could Li Ko have a pen point, please?"

Supervisor Hsi's only answer was to slam the door so hard that Han barely withdrew his face in time.

"I guess they don't want to give us a pen point," he said, sulkily.

"That's nonsense," I snorted. "It's not the pen point. It's your attitude. You always go around acting as if someone were going to hit you. You may think you're being deferential, but all it does is reveal how antagonistic you are. How do you ever expect to get along in the new society if you spend all your time running away from the government?"

Just then, as if to prove my assertion, the pen point

arrived. I began writing while Han paced up and down the floor, lost in thought.

Suddenly he announced decisively, "I'm going to write a criticism of myself and hand it in. I can't keep going on this way—always afraid of even my own shadow."

For almost a week he labored over that document, writing and rewriting, until he had poured out his whole past outlook on life—his petty selfishness and determination to have his own way, his disdain for his wife and desire for a concubine, and his feeling that people, especially the government, were always "out to get him."

By the time he had finished and turned the statement in to the supervisor, he had come to realize that it was his own way of looking at life which had been his worst enemy. It was his own hostility which had been the root of his fear and which had created the barrier between himself and the new society.

Han's attitude toward the government improved steadily from then on and the supervisors responded with marked friendliness. They went out of their way to keep him supplied with toothpaste and soap, and even gave him a badly needed pair of shoes which he had formerly been afraid to ask for. However, it was some time before this new desire to reform was to bring about any real change in the rapidly degenerating state of our personal relations in the cell.

With Liao gone and no one to act as a balance between us, our widely differing temperaments began to clash almost at once. Being small of build and fastidious in nature, he was repelled by my lumbering clumsiness and general disorderliness. I never put things away neatly; I ate too much, too slowly, and too noisily; I washed my clothes just any old way, preferring to expend soap rather than muscle. Then when I showed my contempt for what I felt were his petty conceits, mincing ways, and lack of education, he was irked even more.

Under such circumstances blowups were unavoidable and sometimes we would stand red-faced glaring at each other over the most trivial matter. He would accuse me of being clumsy deliberately to annoy him, and I would take out my fury by calling him an "old woman."

Another bone of contention was my refusal to talk over with him problems which were obviously weighing on my mind. The lesson I had learned from my attempt to retract my confession had made me determined that come what might I would stick to the truth from then on, but still, all during 1954, I was plagued by momentary fits of depression. What was going to happen to me when I returned home? What would the Navy do? Would I be able to find a job? Perhaps I could slip through Hong Kong without attracting any notice.

At such times Han could tell immediately that something was troubling me and would insist on hearing about it. My reaction was usually one of impatience. "I know I'm wrong," I would think. "But there is no sense in talking about it. I'll just have to work it out myself. What's the use of listening to a long speech from you? You don't know anything about it, anyway."

I would deny that I was troubled and this would lead to further bitter arguments. By the fall of 1954 we were both disgusted with our attitudes. How could this be considered reform? We began then to hold a regular Monday evening self-criticism meeting to clear the air before starting the next week.

We soon became conscious of what we called the direction of our thinking. We found that almost invariably if a serious problem, either individual or collective, had arisen, it was because we were thinking inwardly and negatively instead of outwardly and positively. By making a conscious effort to set our minds working in the right direction, problems which had seemed insoluble simply ceased to exist. In our relations with each other, this change in direction usually involved an attempt to look at our differing points of view in the detached manner of solving a problem instead of each trying to force the other to accept his own ideas and win an argument.

I found, too, that by using the same technique of consciously trying to think outwardly and positively about my own personal problems I was able to shake off completely the fits of depression which had plagued me all during prison and, in fact, throughout most of my life.

In the ensuing months Han's progress was phenomenal. He put himself completely outside any disagreement which arose. Concentrating his energies on solving the problem, his entire attitude bespoke a desire to convince rather than batter me down. No matter how insulting I became he would not lose his temper. If I were not prepared to talk, he was willing to wait. When I ranted and raved he would ignore me. He kept plodding away with the determination of a small bulldog, only one thing in his mind, to help me reach the root of my trouble.

I, too, was learning a great deal. I could not help but respect Han's honest attempt to reform and I felt a desire to help him.

Han lacked education but he was by no means stupid, and as he saw the modernization of China progressing so rapidly he was fired by a desire to increase his knowledge about everything. Several times I offered to teach him mathematics, geography, history, or Chinese grammar, but he evinced little interest. I soon realized that it was my superior attitude which stung his pride and caused him to refuse my help.

One Sunday while we were resting between games of chess I hit on a plan. "Let's play something else," I said, "a problem game. If I wanted two and two-thirds *wo-tou* for dinner and you wanted one and one-quarter, how many would you bring back?"

He tried to figure it out in his head, but with no success.

"I could do it well enough if I had the *wo-tou* in my hands," he said, looking a little sheepish.

"But if you were out in a factory working with tons of cement, you wouldn't be able to pick that up in your hands. Write it down and figure it out that way."

The mere task of putting the sums down on paper in a workable form was a difficult problem for Han. Instead of using the simple Arabic numerals which the Chinese use the same as we in mathematics, he tried writing the fractions out in full Chinese characters—*san-fen-jr-erh* and *ssu-fen-jr-i*—and the common denominator was something he had never heard of.

It seemed strange that Han should be stuck by such a simple problem. For, though he had no schooling other than memorizing a few of the Confucian classics, when it came to juggling stock market quotations or figuring discounts on bolts of silk at black-market prices, nothing was too difficult for him. But now, faced with simple fourth-grade fractions, he was at a loss. At first I was afraid his pride might be offended again and he would refuse to go on, but by the time I had finished showing him how to work a common denominator he was so interested in the problem he had forgotten all about his pride and we spent the rest of the day working fractions.

The next evening, instead of bringing out the chess-board, he produced pencil and paper and we started to work again. In the weeks that followed, after going through addition, subtraction, multiplication, and division of fractions, we went on to decimals, and then to simple algebra. He was an eager student, and within a couple of months had exhausted my knowledge and was doing the problems in algebra and geometry much faster than I.

We also spent a great deal of time discussing agriculture, and I learned much about farming in China from him.

"Farming will be a lot better life when our new dams are built and we can start irrigating," he said seriously one day. "But now you never know how a crop will be. If Heaven is against you and there's no rain, you're finished."

"What about using wells to irrigate?" I asked.

"There are a lot of wells where I come from, especially since liberation, but they have to go down deep, and with no electricity, pumping the water by hand or animal power is killing work both for men and mules."

"The wind blows regularly here in north China. Why don't you use windmills?" I asked.

He looked puzzled and asked what a windmill was.

I sketched a rough picture of those I had seen in our own Midwest. The idea fascinated him and he wanted me to explain every detail down to the last shaft and gear. I soon found myself far over my depth, but we spent several days drafting plans for a windmill which he hoped to use on the wells in his village when he returned home.

We talked at great length about our dreams of the future. If the government did not give him a job in a factory, he wanted to return to his village. Perhaps the people there would let him join their new agricultural cooperative.

He smiled as he said, "It seems as if all my life has been spent in trying to get away from the farm and acquire an automobile and concubine. Now I feel that the most wonderful place of all would be back in the village at work with my family and neighbors. And if someday I could have a bicycle, I'd be more than satisfied. I can see it now—my friends and I cycling down the road—"

His eyes sparkled as he spoke.

"What about your wife?" I interposed.

He paused a moment, perplexed. "What about her?"

"Aren't you going to take her along? The best fun of all is being able to share your pleasures with your wife."

"Take her along?" he repeated. "I'd never thought of such a thing."

"That's probably been one of your troubles. You thought you had a bad deal being forced to marry a girl five years older than yourself. But how do you think she felt about it?"

For a while he sat silent. "She had a bad time, all right," he said at last. "My family arranged the marriage only because they wanted some extra cheap help around the farm. That's the way it was in the old days. My mother wasn't really harsh with her, but she never gave her a minute's peace. She had the old idea of mother–daughter-in-law relations. My wife was her slave. To make matters worse, it was seven years before we had a child. For a woman to be childless in old China was a terrible thing, you know, and she was the object of ridicule. I remember so well, often at night after all of us had gone to bed, she would sit there in the dark smoking her little pipe and the tears rolling down her face. I just ignored her, but she cried even worse whenever I went away. She was afraid I wouldn't come back, and then she would be left with nothing at all.

"Even after our son was born things didn't improve much. I could have helped her but I never did. One night after liberation we were sitting around with some of the neighbors learning a few of the new songs. We were to stop at the end of each stanza to see how we were making out, but my wife forgot to stop and in the silence her voice sounded loud and clear as she went on alone. Everyone turned to look at her, and I'm sure that if she could she would have died on the spot. One word of encouragement from me would have solved everything, but I just glared at her. She jumped up and ran back home in tears. I never heard her sing again. She's no dumb bunny, you know, and she's one of the best workers on the farm, but she never had a chance—" His voice trailed off.

Finally, he brightened, "I'm going to have a lot to make up for when I get back home."

17

Dell: When the supervisor told me to pack up my things that day in October, 1954, I had guessed that I was to be transferred to another group cell. I was astounded, therefore, when we turned into cell block A and I was told to go to No. 6, a single cell. It was next door to No. 7, where I had spent the first four months in prison. Now here I was, seemingly back where I had started.

By the first week of my transfer I had encountered several signs which indicated that this was the prelude to a major move. Among other things, I was told to sort out our belongings and put Rick's in one, mine in the other of the twin camphor wood chests in which our things were stored in the prison. I was also told to review my financial situation and list any debts still outstanding on the outside.

The money I owed the People's Government from the period when I was under house arrest was the only problem I had. In the spring of 1953 I had thought I would have an opportunity to clear off quite a bit of the debt when the People's Government offered to close out the house on Hsin Kai Lu and sell for us the furniture and odds and ends for which we no longer had any use. But instead of taking the money, 2,500,000 JMP (about $115), gained in this way to cancel out part of the debt the authorities had put that sum in Rick's account in the prison for us both to draw on. I brought the matter up now and asked what I should do about it. The answer was a simple "Forget it."

Perhaps I was to be released soon, perhaps sent to a prison farm or factory. Both possibilities crossed my mind but I pushed the former out of my thoughts. Without definite knowledge of when I might be able to go home, it could only be frustrating and unsettling to look forward from one day to the next for release. Furthermore, I shrank from facing that unknown which lay ahead. It was much more comfortable to limit my thoughts to daily living and spend the time reading the newspaper, playing solitaire, exercising, and mending socks.

As October passed into November and then December, however, I gradually came to grips with the problems of the future. The information which Rick and I had collected at the universities, from the deterioration in diet of the Chinese students to Chinese troop movements, had been used by the State Department in furthering its objective to interfere in China's internal affairs. The thought that such activities had been a factor in contributing to the animosity between the two countries even to the point of war was frightening, and I was determined never to be guilty of providing information which might be used for such ends again.

But how was I to avoid this? During this period I went to the extreme of thinking that the only possible course was to keep the subject of China completely out of my conversation with my family, friends, and business associates. But at other times I would consider this attitude childish and decide to tell the American people all I could about what was going on in China in an effort to help foster a real understanding between the two countries.

Such thoughts led me to speculate on my treatment when I returned home. If I stuck to the truth would I become the object of McCarthyite persecution? Would I be able to find a job? I remembered how glibly I had told Jeng Ai-ling about the security I felt in being a librarian. Perhaps I had better avoid the possibility of such problems arising by asking for asylum in China. The cowardice in this way of thinking made me ashamed and I came out of those months with this positive conclusion: Though I could not decide whether I should keep quiet or not, I must go back to the United States no matter what difficulties awaited me there. It was my home and that was where I belonged.

The woman supervisor Fang came often to talk with me. Ever since I had been arrested she had been solicitous of my emotional state concerning Rick. When I received a note from him asking for clothes, she had come back a few days later to make sure I had not been upset by the matter. She would ask me from time to time if I were worried about him, and then try to reassure me if she thought I was.

There were several couples in the prison and some were actually in the same compound, where they saw each other every day, though, of course, being espionage cases, they were not allowed to talk. But Rick and I never met. I am certain that the authorities deliberately kept us apart to relieve us, particularly me, of the emotional strain of seeing each other and, looking back on it now, I feel that it was better that way. An occasional few minutes' meeting with the subsequent parting would have been agonizing for both of us. Furthermore, I know that if I had been able to see him I would have thought of little else, and any ideas of reform would have been secondary.

On February 22, 1955, as I was walking up and down the cell after supper, the supervisor opened the door and ordered me out. I walked toward the interrogation office, but was told to walk on into a large courtyard instead of stopping at the usual corridor. On entering a long, rectangular room, I found seated at a table opposite the door a man dressed in khaki uniform. The little recorder-interpreter sat at his left.

I stood quietly just inside the door while the man in khaki began to read in a high, clear voice the document which he held in his hand. A military tribunal had found me guilty of assisting my husband carry on espionage for the United States Government. I was sentenced to three and a half years in prison and immediate deportation. When he had finished, the recorder read the same thing over in English. After signing the charges at a little table to my right, I was given a copy to take back to the cell.

But it was not until I returned to cell No. 6 and sat down on the *kang*, the sheet of paper in my hand, that I began to realize that sentence had actually been passed. What would happen now? Was I really going home? They had said "deported." Somehow the word had an unfinished sound, as if I were being eternally sentenced. As much as I longed to go home, the thought that I was being "kicked out" by a people whom I had come to feel very close to in the past three and a half years was almost too much to bear.

I did not have long to ponder the matter, however, for Supervisor Fang came hurrying in to say, "We've got to hurry, Li Yu-an. You don't have much time. What do you want to wear?"

"But, Supervisor Fang," I asked, still not quite daring to believe it all, "What does it mean? Am I going home, really?"

"*Ko-bu-shr-ma!* [Right you are!]" she replied, matter-of-factly. "Won't you be glad to see your father and mother?"

As I answered with a vigorous nod of the head, she looked at me speculatively. "Don't you want to wear something more presentable? Your trunks have been brought over from the storeroom. How about getting out a decent pair of slacks and jacket? And how about lipstick?"

I protested that lipstick was the furthest thing from my mind at that point, but I did go with her to find my wool slacks and tweed jacket. I also pulled out my fur coat. When we returned to the cell I made a pile of clothes and odds and ends which I no longer wanted and put the rest of my bedding and clothes in the duffle bag. As I was sorting out my belongings the warden came in to ask how I was getting along.

"I wonder if I might ask about Li Ko?" I asked hesitantly. "Has he been sentenced, too?"

"His case has not been settled yet," was the brief reply.

"Well, may I write to him?"

"Yes, in the future you may write whenever you want."

My heart soared at his words. It never occurred to me at that moment to ask for more. Under the circumstances and since I was being deported I knew I could not possibly see him, but I felt instinctively that he would understand when he received my first letter.

Suddenly Supervisor Fang hurried into the room. "Hurry up! Hurry up!" she said, breathlessly, "It's time to go. Have you got everything?"

I looked around at the little cell for the last time. Where I was going was not certain and as I heard the whistle blow in the corridor I wished fleetingly that I were getting ready for bed. But I could not linger, and in a moment I had walked out of the compound and climbed into the truck that was to take us to the station. There was another foreigner in the truck, an American whom I had heard some of the women refer to as Meng I, but whose American name I did not know. According to them he had been arrested for espionage the same day as Rick.

We boarded the train for Wuhan about 11 o'clock that night, a cadre, two guards, Meng I, and I. Although the train was crowded they found places for us in the open compartments of the second-class carriage. The berths were leather, sticking out at right angles from the narrow passageway which ran along one side of the car. Two tiers of three faced each other to make a compartment for six. I lay down without undressing and started to cover myself with my fur coat, but I soon found that in spite of the cold outside there was no need for it. As we rolled through the bleak February countryside with the wheels of the train giving off their rhythmic click, I could not help but revel in the feeling of being so warm and snug, and soon dozed off.

The next morning, after the upper berths had been fastened up, Meng I and I sat in the window seats while the guards and cadre played cards with some of the other passengers. I would gaze out the window at the flat, barren fields that stretched on and on across all north China, relieved only here and there by an occasional tree. And when

I tired of the brownness I would turn back to watch the card players and the passengers who kept walking through the aisle. I took in the earnest faces of the men, the serene smiles of the women, and the carefree air of the children.

For three and a half years I had been reading in the newspaper and magazines about the new character of the Chinese people, about the pride, security, and happiness with which they were meeting the problems of modernization and the building of a new society. In prison I had seen this character in action in the examples set by the supervisors and guards, but I had always looked on them as not being particularly typical. Somehow, living on the prison grounds as they did, they seemed apart from the average citizen to a certain extent. But, now, on the train I was viewing people from all walks of life, and the same eagerness and comradeliness were evident all around me.

A thirteen-year-old boy carried his baby sister down to our compartment to watch the guards play. He had her do the little stunts for them which are common to children the world over.

"Who's the best baby in the world?" the boy would say to his sister. And we all laughed heartily as she patted her chest with a fat little hand.

Meng I had brought with him several tins of food which his parents had sent him from home, and would not budge from his seat when mealtime came. The rest of us took turns going to the dining car. I was too worked up to have much of an appetite, although the cadre told me I could order whatever I wished. The cadre was quite at home with rice, but the guards, being from north China, had been raised on corn and wheat flour, and ordered noodles the first day. As one of them said, "Once we get south of the Yangtze, we might as well forget about eating noodles. They don't know how to cook them at all down there."

I will always remember the slight gasp of surprise that rose from the passengers at the next table when I ordered them, too. "Why, the foreigner eats noodles, too," I heard someone say. It was a trivial incident but it made me feel warm inside, for it was one of my first contacts with the world around me. I was no longer in a cell apart from other people.

As we moved farther south into the warmer area we began to see groups of people out in the fields getting ready to start the new cycle of planting. "Look!" cried one of the guards. "There's a mutual aid team out there in the field."

"And there's another over there," replied the cadre. "You don't see anyone out working by himself any more."

It seemed to me as we passed group after group of peasants working shoulder to shoulder that I was seeing again a manifestation of all those articles I had read in the seclusion of the cell. How many stories of agricultural cooperatives, their successes and problems, had I read in the past few years, and now here they were in action before my eyes.

Suddenly I cried out involuntarily, "Look, there's a group of nothing but women out in that field."

The others smiled at the pride which sounded in my voice. "Females will stick together the world over," their faces seemed to say.

"Lots of them are made up of women," added one of the guards. "You just watch."

As night fell I read a book for a while and then watched the others play cards, but I found it difficult to concentrate either on the printed page or the progress of the game. The time to decide how I would act was drawing close. Should I keep quiet or should I speak out about my arrest and prison experience? Each time I approached the question I would fall back on the vague conclusion that I could do only what seemed best as the situation presented itself.

I thought back to Peking—to Rick, the supervisors, my cell mates, the guards. Except for Rick, I would probably never see any of them again. They had helped me open my eyes to see China as I had never done in those three years at the universities and I was grateful to them. I felt as if I were leaving a very precious part of my past behind me and I was saddened by the thought.

But, in the midst of these mixed-up thoughts and emotions, I continued to derive tremendous uplift from the sights around me. In the early afternoon, while we were a couple of hours' ride from Canton, the little man who had come through the car every half hour or so to sweep the floor and empty the spittoons brought a notebook around to ask for our criticism of his work and his attitude. He had worked zealously to keep the car spotless and through it all his cheery smile and friendly exchange of conversation had been noticed by everyone. But he wanted to know whether we had any suggestions to offer which would help him improve his service to the people.

The guards could think of no criticism. Instead, they wrote a tribute to the man's efficiency and solicitude for the passengers.

I wondered, when we reached Canton, whether we would go on to Hong Kong the same day, but instead we were taken to a prison to spend the night. I was placed in a cell with one other woman and we laughed as we tried to understand each other. I could speak no Cantonese, and the little national dialect she knew was spoken with such a strange pronunciation that I could make very little out of it.

The routine was about the same as I had known in Peking but there were certain physical differences. We slept in individual wooden beds, and the food was brought to us rather than our going out into the corridor ourselves to get it. Instead of *wo-tou* they had rice every day, and the one day I was there we had a green leafy vegetable somewhat like spinach which I had seen only a few times in the north.

We had arrived in Canton late Friday afternoon. Sunday morning, February 27, as I was washing, I was told to get my things ready to leave. We were driven back to the station to catch the eight o'clock train for the border. My knowledge of the geography between Canton and Hong Kong was very hazy and I was surprised to find that we would not reach the border before one o'clock. I looked at the landscape, heavy with palms and bamboo groves, and thought of the brown, cold countryside to the north. China, like the United States, runs the gamut in climate and scenery.

The train arrived finally at the station on the Chinese side of the border, and we followed a long line of people into the customs shed. By the time we had gone through customs and said good-bye to the guards it must have been well after two o'clock in the afternoon.

Meng I and I moved slowly out of the shed, up a slight incline, and back onto the railroad tracks again. There were two rows of barbed-wire saw horses spaced about ten feet apart which had been set across the tracks to separate the Chinese side from the British. While under guard on the train we had carried over the habits of the prison in not speaking to each other, but now, as we stood in the small no man's-land waiting for some official word to set foot in the Crown Colony, we introduced ourselves and I learned that my companion was Malcolm Bersohn.

I still had my old expired passport, and I had sent it on ahead with one of the guards to give to the British while I was going through the Chinese customs. Malcolm had lost his passport some years ago and had no credentials.

In a few moments a young British officer came up on his side of the barbed wire and said, somewhat apologetically, "I say, I'm afraid we can't let you in. It's Sunday afternoon, and we can't get in touch with anyone at the American Consulate, and since you have no credentials— well, you see, we close up here at four o'clock, and—well, would you mind coming back around 9 or 9:30 tomorrow morning?"

Malcolm and I looked at the young man in amazement. Come back? But where would we go in the meantime? We had just been deported from China and were not welcome back there. The officer, seeing the consternation on our faces, murmured something about waiting a moment and hurried off again. We turned to tell the Chinese guards standing on their side of the barbed-wire saw horses what had happened. They were as puzzled as we were by the turn of events and began to hold a consultation among themselves.

About ten minutes later the officer came dashing back. "It's all right," he said brightly. "Will you come in now? We've located someone from the American Consulate, and they'll be at the station to meet you. Sorry for the delay."

Malcolm and I turned once more for one last look at China, and then followed the Britisher down the tracks and through the British customs office. The officer there waved us on through with a "Don't bother about your baggage." We came out near a little restaurant where the young officer insisted on treating us to something to eat and drink while we waited for the train.

"You weren't expected, you know," he laughed. "You rather took them by surprise."

We boarded the train about three o'clock and in an hour had arrived at the Kowloon Station opposite the city of Hong Kong. Not being quite sure where we were going, we sat waiting for the other passengers to get off. Suddenly, I heard a voice shouting "Dell!" and looked up to see an old Consulate friend, Ken, whom we had known in Peking, climbing through the train window. I stood up awkwardly and was engulfed in his strong embrace. In a moment the car was filled with men, some of whom called me by name. I blinked for a moment, trying to place them.

The reporters in the group were insistent on an interview immediately. Malcolm and I hesitated a few moments, and finally agreed. While Ken looked after our baggage, Malcolm and I sat in a corner of the deserted Kowloon Station tea room and talked with them. As Malcolm told about his activities as an agent I watched the faces of the twenty or so men and women around us. Lifted eyebrows, amazed stares, curled lips, and an unmistakably unsympathetic and unbelieving tone of voice as they plied their questions showed clearly the temper of the group. And, suddenly, all the doubts and fears with which my imagination had plagued me in prison vanished

They looked and acted just as we had four years before, and what was there to fear from those who were determined to be so blind?

When it came my turn to speak I told them that I had given information to the American Consulate and therefore had been quite justifiably arrested. I said I was sorry for what I had done and that I hoped to make up for my past errors by serving the people. These thoughts which had been so much a part of me for the past few years and which we had talked about incessantly in prison, coming out in English for the first time, sounded stilted even to my ears. The use of this, as the reporters put it, "Communist jargon" together with my rather unkempt appearance were seized on by them to picture me as a dazed, brainwashed wreck.

The first interview was soon over and they dashed off with their notebooks to get the hot news on the wires as quickly as possible.

Ken and I rode the ferry across to Hong Kong and he saw me safely settled in the YWCA. We talked mostly of old acquaintances—who had married, who had children, who was living where, etc., but there was a flatness about it all as we both realized that we were miles apart, years apart. To me he represented a way of thinking which I had once agreed with, but now could no longer sanction.

The next morning the onslaught of reporters began again. One of the first was an old friend I had known in Peking back in 1949. He started by saying, "Dell, what you had to say yesterday disturbed me very much. I'd like to ask you a few more questions."

I agreed and we spent a good part of the morning talking together. The report of his interview which I saw later in an American newspaper said "her mind has been twisted out of recognition."

Others were more frank in their sensation-hunting. One bright, red-headed woman reporter cooed, "Why, you don't look like a Communist at all!" and then went on to bait me with questions which she obviously hoped would provoke answers designed to make a further splash in the headlines.

Toward noon, another reporter brought me a copy of the cables which he had received of press releases in the United States. My mother was quoted as saying I must certainly be very sick and would have to be hospitalized when I returned home. The label "brainwashed" had already taken hold. I was not sure whether my mother had been misquoted or whether she had fallen for the line taken by the press.

The next step was not long in coming. My Consulate friend Ken came into the lounge at the YWCA the next morning with a tall, thin, bespectacled man who, he said, was very eager to meet Malcolm and me. This was a psychiatrist who "just happened to be in Hong Kong at the time" and he would like very much to talk with us about our thoughts and emotions. Ken had handled everything for us concerning passage, passports, money, and all with the good humor and generosity of spirit which had always been so characteristic of him, and for that I was immensely grateful, but having just been labeled "brainwashed" by the press and knowing that even my mother had been fooled by this I could only feel a little disgusted and angry. What right did these people have to look on anyone who did not fit into their own pattern of thinking as abnormal?

I refused to have an interview with the doctor, and after seeing that my attempts to create understanding about China were having only the opposite effect, decided to have nothing more to do with the reporters. It was with a feeling of at last being able to breathe some clean fresh air that on March 4 I boarded a freighter bound for home.

If I had thought, however, that leaving Hong Kong would end my encounters with the press, I was mistaken. Before crossing the Pacific our ship first went to Korea and Japan. During the week we spent in Pusan a reporter appeared who insisted most emphatically on having an interview. When I refused, he hung around the ship a day and finally that evening sent me a letter, which I quote in part:

Dear Mrs. Rickett:

Captain W— has told me of your desire not to be disturbed by newsmen during your trip home.

Quite honestly, I understand your wishes perfectly, but I am sure that you also must understand my position as a reporter.

I should explain that The Associated Press is the only agency which knows that you are aboard [this ship]. We would like to keep that knowledge to ourselves and I'm sure you would appreciate it. However, I should explain that without a suitable story I'm forced to write a story that you are aboard ship and refuse to see me. That means adding a lot of meaningless color which will identify your itinerary to the United States and probably mean that you will have a trail of reporters on your heels all the way.

I hope you will change your mind about seeing me. All things being relative, if you want to get back to the United States, I want to get back to Seoul and the sooner I make my mission a success, the faster I go and get out of your way.

> Sincerely,
> X— X—
> Associated Press Correspondent
> for Korea

I now knew what was meant by the "gentle art of blackmail"!

From Korea we went on to spend several days in Japan, where another passenger swelled our number of adults to seven. It seemed almost too coincidental that he was a psychiatrist from New York Hospital who had flown to Japan only a few days before.

The trip itself was a happy experience. The passengers and officers went out of their way to be kind and friendly. The enormous waves which tossed the ship from side to side or burst with a thunderous boom across the bow were a source of unending delight to me. Cold as the weather was I spent long hours sitting on the deck or walking from one end to the other. We came into San Francisco Bay in the dark. I was on deck to feast my eyes on the myriad twinkling lights of the city, and as we slipped slowly under the Golden Gate Bridge I reached up as if to touch it. The excitement of this moment of homecoming was unbelievably sweet and I shivered in the joy of it.

But I was not home, yet. At six o'clock in the morning, while we were still out at anchor in the Bay, the immigration officers came aboard. First each passenger was asked to fill out a long questionnaire. I took the sheet handed me and went into the stateroom. It was a Cornell Medical test. As I checked "yes" and "no" to the long list which included questions such as, "Do you ever feel that life is not worth living?" "Do you have any overt form of nervousness?" "Do you perspire freely when nervous?" etc., I wondered if this were a new requirement for entering the United States.

"This preoccupation with mental health must really have the country in its grip," I thought. "It doesn't seem possible that things have gone this far." It was only some time later, when I compared notes with other travelers from Europe and Australia, that I found that this was not the usual procedure for people entering the United States. It must have been especially directed at me, and the other passengers must have been asked to fill it out that morning, too, so that I would not become suspicious.

When I had finished, I was told that everyone would have to take a physical examination. My roommate went into our stateroom while I waited in the lounge. In a few minutes she reappeared and I went in. Two Naval officers there explained that they would like to know a little about my life in prison from the health angle, and in general the health conditions in China. Had I seen any epidemics while there? I told them briefly about my diet and the excellence of our living conditions from 1952 on, and that as far as I knew there were no epidemics in China.

It was not long before they moved on to the physical side of the examination. In obvious embarrassment they said they would wait outside while I undressed and lay down with a blanket over me. I was a bit perplexed as to how thorough this examination was to be, for I could see no signs of the instruments a doctor usually has at his side for a full examination. They returned in a moment, and using a small disc-like object with a pin point hole in the middle through which a tiny light shone they began their examination by peering into my eyes. Then they looked at my wrists and ankles and made me sit up so that they could look at my back.

"Are you looking for scars?" I asked politely.

"Yes," they murmured.

"I don't happen to have any, but in case you're disturbed by that mark on the side of my calf, perhaps I had better explain. Last week I was standing in the bathroom up on the next deck when the ship gave a lurch and I went smack up against the radiator. Before I could pull myself away, my leg had taken a perfect imprint of the number on the radiator. It looks just like a brand, doesn't it?"

"Yes, it does," said the solemn-faced individual wearing glasses who appeared to be in charge. "Just where did this happen?"

"I can show you, if you like."

"If you don't mind, when we finish here we'd like to take a look at it."

After thumping my chest a few times he called the "examination" completed, but before he and his younger companion went out to wait while I dressed he asked in a tight-lipped, expressionless voice, "You said in some of those statements in Hong Kong that you wanted to work for the people and do good in the world. How are you planning to carry this out? What organizations are you expecting to join?"

"I'm sorry I can't answer that," I replied. "I haven't thought that far ahead. I just know I want to lead a useful and decent life from now on."

He nodded slowly, and the two of them walked out.

I dressed hurriedly and then led them up to the bathroom where I had been burned. The older officer got down on his hands and knees, examined the number on the radiator and then the scar on my leg. When he saw that they matched perfectly even to the encircling design, he slowly rose and carefully brushed off his hands. His face remained as expressionless as ever, but he seemed satisfied and I was dismissed.

The bad taste left by the interview was soon dispelled as the ship slid up to the dock and my mother and cousin came aboard to greet me. As my mother wrapped me in her arms I felt I was really home at last.

18

Rick: By late spring of 1955 it had become clear that my long-awaited release was near at hand. In April I was informed that Dell had left and that my own case would soon be settled. Then one evening in late August, 1955, I was called out of the cell and directed toward a big room near the interrogation offices. As I entered, the guard remained on the outside and I found a man and woman waiting for me there.

The man stood up, bowed politely, and asked if I were Li Ko. When I replied in the affirmative, he motioned to a comfortable chair and said pleasantly, "We are from the Procurator-General's office. The Public Security Bureau has turned your case over to us and we would like you to tell us about your crime. You should speak freely and you may disregard any statements you have made before."

I told him that my last statement written in the summer of 1954 was correct to the best of my knowledge. I then proceeded to give him a rough outline of my relations with the Consulate and the British Negotiation Mission.

When I had finished he leaned back for a moment and asked, "Have you any complaints or requests which you would like to make?"

I faltered, "What do you mean? Requests or complaints about what?"

"About the way you were treated and the handling of your case."

I told him that I considered my treatment fair and my punishment just, but that I hoped that some day I would be able to return to the United States.

"Well," he said, standing up by way of dismissal, "we think your wish will probably come true."

September 11 was a Sunday. Han and I had a big project afoot. My Chinese-English dictionary had become so battered it was falling apart. Han, who had once lived next door to a bookbindery, had suggested that we try to rebind it ourselves. Saturday evening we had spent dismantling the volume and twisting cotton threads to sew the pages together again. We had just started arranging the guide strings Sunday morning when Supervisor Shen appeared at the door.

"Li Ko, put on some presentable clothes and come along," he said.

He stood waiting while I scrambled into a pair of clean slacks and shirt and then led me over to his office, where a blue-uniformed cadre presented me with a typewritten sheet bearing the stamp of the Superior Municipal Court of Peking.

"These are the charges against you," he said. "Read them over and see if they are correct."

I read them carefully. I had been charged with supplying information to the American Consulate and the British Negotiation Party, as well as carrying on activities intended to sabotage the revolution.

After assuring him that they were correct and signing the statement, I was led out to the courtyard where a jeep was waiting. We rode through the streets of Peking to the Municipal Court Building, where I was ordered into a small waiting room. In a few minutes the little interpreter who had accompanied us ushered in a man whom she introduced in English as Professor Wang of the Peking University Law School.

"He is to act as your lawyer," she said.

"I don't need a lawyer," I replied in Chinese. "I'm guilty of the charges against me."

"That's not the point," broke in the professor. "Let me explain. In the first place, since this is not a military court, the law entitles you to legal advice. If you are not satisfied with me, you can choose anyone you want to represent you.

Expenses will be taken care of by the government. Secondly, you may plead guilty or not guilty. But even if you plead guilty you still want to have your sentence reduced as much as possible. There are a number of points which can be argued in your favor."

"What?" I asked.

"The fact that you made a full confession and that your attitude since arrest has shown that you regret your past actions. And then, too, perhaps there were extenuating circumstances which forced you to commit your crime. All of these factors should be considered by the court."

We discussed my case for about half an hour and he then left with the interpreter, whose services had not been needed.

About twenty minutes later an attendant appeared to summon me to the courtroom. I walked down a broad corridor to a side door of a long, narrow room. To my left across the back of the room was a gallery of about twenty-odd people some of whom I seemed to recognize. They were probably witnesses called to testify against me if I should plead not guilty. Toward the front of the room on either side were long tables. I was motioned to take a chair at the foot of the table nearest me, where I noticed my lawyer sitting. The young woman on the other side of him turned out to be the court stenographer.

At the table opposite us sat the man from the Procurator-General's office who had interviewed me a few weeks before in prison. Next to him sat a clerk from his office and the interpreter.

I had hardly sat down when the court was called to order and three men filed in to take their places at the bench on the dais which filled the front of the room. The man in the middle, a heavy-set person of forty or so with a fierce-looking mustache, announced in a clear Peking accent that the court was about to consider my case and told me to stand up. He first asked me if I wished an interpreter, and when I declined, he introduced himself as the judge and the men on his right and left as people's assayers. From their appearance they might very well have been college professors. After he had ascertained that I was represented by counsel, the trial got under way.

The man from the Procurator-General's office read off the charges. I was asked whether I pleaded guilty or not guilty.

"I wish to plead guilty," I stated.

The judge then told me that I was free to make any statement in my defense.

I declined, but my lawyer stood up and made a plea for clemency. He cited the points which he had mentioned to me before. I was again asked if there were anything I wished to say and after I had declined for the second time the court record was read back to us and I was asked to sign it. The judges filed out and I was led back to the waiting room. The whole trial could not have taken more than half an hour.

I sat watching the clock as it ticked off the minutes. When twenty-five of them had gone by, the attendant appeared again to lead me back to the courtroom. This time I was ordered to stand in the center of the room.

The judge and two jurors returned to take their places again on the dais. After clearing his throat the judge began to read off the decision, a lengthy document. I was guilty on two counts but in view of my record since arrest, the plea for clemency was granted in part and my sentence was six years, dating from the time of arrest.

"Six years!" I thought, a little stunned. Perhaps I had not heard right. I had been so sure that I was already on my way home. But when I was asked to sign the decision and given a copy, I could see it clearly in black and white—six years.

Court was adjourned and I was led out. By the time I had reached the waiting room the initial shock had worn off.

"Six years is not so bad. I could have been given much more," I thought. "With only two more to go, I'll be home in no time."

While waiting for someone to take me back to prison, I began making plans as to how I would spend those next two years. The list of books I would ask Dell to send me was already taking shape in my mind. Much to my surprise, however, the court attendant reappeared to direct me to a small room opposite the courtroom. It seemed filled with people.

As I stood at attention, a man informed me that I was now before the Peking Lao-gai Wei-yüan Hwey (Labor Reform Committee, which acts as a sort of parole board). My case had been referred to the committee and in view of my record it was decided that my six years' sentence should be commuted to immediate release.

Mumbling some sort of thanks, I left the committee room in a state of joyous confusion and as I almost flew back to the waiting room my lawyer had a hard time catching up with me to explain that I had three years or three days (I was too excited to hear him clearly) to appeal my sentence. In any case I assured him that no appeal would be necessary.

The reader may be struck by the great difference between my trial and that of Dell, but it is understandable when one realizes that I was given a trial in a civil court while she was simply sentenced by a military tribunal. The difference in our treatment would seem to be in line with the general broadening of the jurisdiction of civil agencies after the implementation of China's new constitution in late 1954.

In a matter of minutes I was in the jeep again on my way back to the detention quarters. It was about noon. I was taken to a large room, where I found all my things had been assembled, including the scattered pages of my mutilated dictionary. For a moment I was at a loss. What was I supposed to do? Was I actually leaving? Seeing my watch lying in a box, I reached to put it on, but my hand stopped in mid-air as I thought, "Maybe I didn't hear right. Maybe I'm not really going home."

Supervisor Fang appeared to inform me that a jeep would be arriving in a few minutes to take me to a hotel.

I hastily threw my belongings into the chest and trunk which had been stored in the prison for me ever since our house on Hsin Kai Lu had been broken up in 1953. Then, just before I went out to enter the jeep, I remembered that the money which Dell had borrowed from the government during her stay in the house had never been repaid.

Turning to Supervisor Fang I said uncertainly, "I owe the People's Government some money and I'd like to make some arrangement to pay it back."

She looked me squarely in the eye and then said firmly, "You owe the People's Government a lot of things. Forget it."

The sharpness of her reply caused me to flush slightly with resentful embarrassment, but I realized there was no use in pressing the point. A few minutes later I was again in the jeep speeding through the streets of Peking. As we passed through the old, familiar thoroughfares I craned my neck to take in all the sights. New buildings seemed to be everywhere and some areas had changed so much in the past four years I could hardly recognize them.

We finally drew up in front of a large, Western-style hotel in the Chinese section of the city and I was taken to a neat, nicely furnished room.

"Anything you want you just go ahead and order," said the boyish-looking policeman who had accompanied me. "I'll be around to help you out. We'll try to get you on the train tonight if possible."

A bath, shave, and haircut were followed by a sumptuous dinner and a short time later the policeman poked his head in to say that I would not be able to leave that night because my baggage exceeded the regular limit and special arrangements would have to be made for it.

The luxurious, soft spring mattress and darkened room should have made sleep come easily that first night out of prison, but thoughts of home and anticipation of what was waiting for me in Hong Kong kept me tossing the whole night through.

The next morning at breakfast time I asked for a paper to be sent up, and when it arrived eagerly skimmed the lines looking for some mention of my trial. I had not far to look, for there was a short notice on the first page. What really caught my eye, however, were the bold headlines proclaiming the text of the agreement signed by the American and Chinese ambassadors at Geneva. It appeared that civilians of both countries were to be allowed to exercise their rights to return home. For a moment I felt a little perturbed. Had my trial and subsequent release by the parole board been nothing but a sham?

Then I remembered that settlement of my case had been under consideration at least since April, 1955, long before the Geneva talks and at a time when the United States and China were still on the "brink of war." Undoubtedly the agreement had affected the timing of my release but still it had come about only after going through the due process of Chinese law.

I spent the rest of the day sitting on the sun porch outside my room and drinking in the vivid coloring of the red walls and green and yellow tile roofs which so set Peking apart from any other city in the world. I felt a deep longing to pay one last visit to Tsinghua and Yenching. I had heard that they were both over twice their former size now. However, I did not quite dare ask. In spite of the solicitous treatment I was receiving I still was not certain just how free I had become.

That evening the policeman, whose name I later learned was Yang, informed me my baggage had all been arranged for and we would leave on the ten P.M. train for Hankow and Canton.

When we boarded the train that evening I found myself in a compartment with Yang and two other policemen who were to be my constant companions for the next four days. At first I was inclined to be a little on the defensive at the thought of having so many men watching over me, but later when I discovered I was allowed to move throughout the train at will and they seemed mostly interested in getting me and my baggage from one place to another on time I began to loosen up a little. Soon we were playing chess and chatting over endless cups of tea.

On the third day we reached Canton and put up at another hotel. It was neither as modern nor as comfortable as the one in Peking, but that evening, in celebration of my crossing the border on the next day, my escorts took me out for my last meal in China. It was a delicious one, but even better was the first real feeling of being free which came to me as we swung our way through the city streets, brushing up against the hurrying throngs and stopping now and again to view the well-stocked displays of the shops and fruit stands.

The next morning we were up early to catch the train to the border and as we rolled along through the green paddy fields and thickets of bamboo I became increasingly aware of the tension mounting within me.

It was about one o'clock when the train came to a halt. After having my baggage checked in one of the freight sheds and saying good-by to my escorts I was directed down a long arcade, through the now deserted customs station toward a row of barbed-wire covered saw horses which marked the border. Once I turned my head to look back. How many times I had dreamed of this moment! Yet now as I trudged along I felt that I was leaving a place of safety and understanding to plunge into an insecure and troubled unknown.

19

Dell: The telephone woke me out of a sound sleep around two o'clock on the morning of September 16. The clack clack of a teletype machine in the background told me even before I heard him speak that it was a reporter.

"Mrs. Rickett? I am calling for the United Press. We wanted to be the first to tell you that your husband has just crossed the border into Hong Kong."

When I had thanked him for telling me the news, he went on to ask me for a statement.

My simple reply, "I'm very glad," conveyed nothing of the excitement and turmoil within me. Sleep was impossible for the rest of the night and I sat next to the radio waiting to hear what Rick's first statement would be. Would he admit the truth? If he had been sincere in the long letters I had received from him during the months since I had been home his outlook had changed as mine had. But might he not possibly have been writing to make a good impression on the prison authorities? I could not be sure.

But even if he were sincere I knew, looking back on my own experience in Hong Kong, what pressure would be brought to bear on him as soon as he crossed that border. Might he not weaken? If he did, could we ever have a life together again?

The program of classical music which continued through those endless hours was frequently interrupted by maddeningly terse news flashes which stated only the fact that two Americans, Rickett and Rigney, had crossed the border. It was not until about 6:30 in the morning that my long wait was rewarded, when the announcer stated, "In reply to the question 'Why were you arrested?' Rickett replied, 'Because I was a spy.' "

Relief flooded my heart. No matter what trouble lay ahead, we would be facing it together.

Rick: As soon as I had crossed the border, I was greeted by the Superintendent of the Hong Kong Police and a representative of the American Red Cross, who drove me to the police barracks outside the customs area to await transportation into the city.

I had hardly stepped from the police car when I was surrounded by clicking cameras, outthrust microphones, and shouting men who bombarded me with questions. "Why were you arrested?" "Do you consider yourself a spy?" "Were you tortured?" on and on.

When I asserted that in fact I had been a spy and felt I had been treated very leniently under the circumstances, the expressions on the faces of the reporters quickly changed from enthusiastic welcome to disbelief and then to open hostility. Suddenly I heard the low but distinct voice of the Police Superintendent remarking to one of the reporters, "Hopelessly brainwashed."

I thought I had prepared myself long before for just such a reception but still, faced with the reality, I found myself on the defensive and at the same time my temper began to rise. Fortunately, this first encounter with the press did not last long.

An American Consulate car soon appeared to whisk me away to a room reserved by the Red Cross at the Gloucester Hotel in Hong Kong. There I found even more reporters waiting for me and, after being allowed a few minutes to wash up, I was asked to go through the whole story again for them. This time even the initial enthusiastic greeting was missing. Many of the questions fired from all sides were openly baiting.

Finally one reporter said in a cold voice, "Your wife said when she came out that she wasn't good enough to be a Communist. What do you think about that?"

I had been making an effort to control my temper for some time, but now, feeling my lips quiver, a physical quirk which the press was later to pick on as a manifestation of my brainwashed condition, I angrily turned on him, saying, "I'll stand by what my wife says. I just came from a country where it takes a damned good man to be a Communist." I also added a number of other things which might better have been left unsaid at that point.

When the interview finally came to an end a couple of hours later I sighed with relief. The sudden impact of an entirely different point of view hurled at me in the form of a hostile attack and the constant struggle to keep what I had to say from being misinterpreted and twisted into sensationalism left me exhausted. But I barely had time to gulp down a hasty dinner in my hotel room when the reporters began descending on me in small groups again.

Most of them were clearly interested in nothing but gathering material which could be used to create further hatred and suspicion in the United States against the mainland Chinese and justify Washington's policy of supporting Chiang Kai-shek on Formosa. A number of them were so rabid in their prejudice they did not even attempt to conceal their dislike for me.

One asked sneeringly, "If you like China so much, why didn't you stay there?"

"Because I'm an American," I replied. "I saw a lot of things I liked in China and some I didn't like, but America is my home and my place is there."

"Would you support your country if it were invaded?" asked another equally hostile reporter.

"If we were invaded, there's no question about it; I'd fight just as hard as I did before. But I feel we have no right to interfere in the affairs of another country. What I want is peace and I am convinced that friendly relations can be re-established between our two countries. This is to their advantage as well as ours. China is now developing at a tremendous pace, and the market she could provide for our trucks alone would be of considerable help to our auto industry. Believe me, I would much rather see American workers turning out trucks for peace than tanks for war."

Several tried to argue me into tempering my statements, by saying that I ought to look out for my own future. One of them informed me confidentially that I was being a sucker because I could get at least $800 for one interview if I were willing to tell "what was *really* going on in China."

Another went so far as to say, "Brother, you know what we think of Reds at home. If you don't change your tune, you won't even be able to get a job as a street cleaner when you get back."

As I sat listening to these men talk, as tired as I was I felt almost like laughing. I had no doubt that what they said was true about the dim prospects for my future, but I had just come from a society where the one argument a person could never use to justify an action was self-interest; yet this was the only one which appeared valid to them. The narrow blindness of these men whom I had at one time respected highly stood out in such sharp contrast to the attitudes I had become accustomed to in China that I found myself looking on them as so many children.

It was long after dawn when I finally lay down for a nap, but in less than an hour the telephone began to jangle again. While at breakfast, the waiter brought me a paper with the main headline "Peking Frees U. S. Priest, Pro-Red Scholar," and the subheading, "Father Rigney Says He Lived on Maize; Self-Confessed 'Spy' Reports He Ate Special Food." I gathered that the special food referred to the rice gruel I had been given during those first few weeks of interrogation. I did not know how many Americans would consider rice gruel as anything special, but the headline showed me one thing—to what extent the press would go to create the type of picture it wanted.

For a moment I wondered if I would be better off keeping my mouth shut and thus avoid any chance of their exploiting me, but I quickly realized that saying nothing could also be capitalized upon and that it was better to try to get at least some of the truth across. The price I paid for this decision was four days and nights of constant talking without ever touching the bed for more than a couple of hours at a time. What irony to read in an American magazine at the end of the week, "His voice wavers often as if he suffers from a deeper weariness than he knows."

It would be unfair to give the impression that all the reporters I met acted in the same way. There were a few who, while disagreeing with much I had to say, were willing to sit up all night with me in what seemed a sincere effort to understand why I felt as I did and what progress was being made in China.

What seemed to disturb them most was the problem of thought reform. Some objected to it as a matter of principle, saying that it was a violation of human rights. To that my answer was that it seemed to me a question of the ideas involved. Just at that time the Hong Kong papers were filled with the Emmett Till murder case. I expressed the opinion that the kind of thinking that would justify the bloody murder of a fourteen-year-old boy ought to be changed. In China reform was compulsory in prison, but the thoughts we were expected to reform were just such as those which led to the murder of Emmett Till. I then asked the reporters if they felt that reformatories in the United States were a violation of individual rights.

"The new government of China has made clear from the beginning that it is out to reform the entire Chinese society. But this is a question of education and not force. As for the Chinese people as a whole, the only force exerted on them is the pressure of general public opinion. In varying degrees this pressure exists in any society. Whether a person in China conforms or not is left up to him, as long as he does not break the law. As a matter of fact, I knew a number of professors who were much more outspoken in their criticism of the new government than I but they never ended up in prison because they had never carried on any actual counterrevolutionary activities."

Some of the reporters then conceded that in certain cases enforced re-education might be justifiable. What they objected to was "brainwashing," which they defined in a vague way as using various means to deprive a person of his normal rational processes so that he can be crammed full of ideas which he accepts mechanically without understanding what they mean.

I said that from a theoretical point of view it might be possible for a person to be deprived temporarily of his powers of reason by the use of shock treatments, sensory deprivation, drugs, hypnotism, or extreme mental or physical torture so that he could be forced to do and say things unnatural to him. But this would destroy the person as a functioning social being. Moreover, unless he had been reduced to a permanent state of idiocy, once the effect of these influences had worn off he would return to his normal state of reasoning and revert to his old way of thinking.

However, though I had lived seven years in China, I had never heard of such methods being used. In fact, they would be completely contrary to the very purpose of thought reform there. The objective of the Chinese was to bring about permanent reform in the individual's character itself and this could be done only by raising the level of his understanding through reasoning with him. My ideas in prison had undergone a change, but this was due to a perfectly rational process of examining my thoughts, testing them in the light of objective facts and moral principles, and arriving at new conclusions where I felt my former ones to be wrong. I had been placed in an environment where I had been forced to examine my thoughts, it is true, but whether I accepted any new conclusions was up to me.

Another reporter brought up the possibility of changing a person's thought by prolonged control of his sources of information, thus depriving him of a basis for forming an objective judgment. Here again I could agree in part, but I objected that it could only hold true concerning questions beyond the personal experience of the individual. It might be fairly easy to convince one man that another is his enemy if they are living in different countries and have no contact with each other, but to convince a hungry man that he is getting enough to eat would present considerable difficulties.

In China socialist propaganda has been effective in changing the ideas of the people because the government's promises of a higher standard of living have, to an increasing degree, been borne out by the experience of the majority of the people in their daily living.

I then spent some time discussing with the reporters the changes taking place in the life of the Chinese people and the resulting transformation in their social outlook. That I was unable to convince these reporters that this transformation was based on a higher concept of social morality surprised me little. After all, it had taken me four years in prison to understand that the personal happiness of the individual could be assured only when he was willing to identify himself with the happiness of society as a whole. How could they be expected to understand what it was all about in one night?

In the meantime our Consulate friend Ken proved as helpful to me as he had been to Dell in arranging for my passage by plane back to the United States. He tactfully avoided the term "brainwashed" in our conversations, but it was also obvious that he wished I would keep still and even suggested that I wait at least six months before making any more statements.

The Consulate itself was coldly polite and finally on the fourth day granted me a six-week one-way passport back to the United States. My experience in Hong Kong had left me slightly resentful and very much on the defensive, but a brief stopover in Tokyo where I met a number of old friends who went out of their way to wish me well helped dispel some of the unpleasantness of the previous five days.

I found, too, when I reached Honolulu that the press there seemed less interested in using me as a means of creating animosity against the mainland Chinese than had the "front line" in Hong Kong. As far as they were concerned, I was only another human interest story.

As I hurried out the airport gates in Honolulu, intending to duck the reporters, one of them, seeing my reluctance to answer any more questions, asked, "Well, just tell us how it feels to be home."

The simplicity of his question seemed to relieve the remaining tension. I was home, wasn't I?

"It feels wonderful," I replied.

"Well, that's all we wanted to know," he grinned good-naturedly. "Hell, nobody here likes Chiang Kai-shek either."

On the night of the 24th my plane reached Seattle, where my mother was waiting for me at the airport.

The time passed with tantalizing slowness as I waited for morning and Dell. We had both shrunk away from the idea of meeting, for the first time in four years, before a battery of clicking cameras, and had agreed that she would slip into Seattle quietly on a train arriving the next morning when no one would be expecting her. Then, as I caught my first glimpse of her coming through the door at home, it seemed as if we had never really been apart. Our long separation had at last come to an end.

A year and a half has passed since our reunion in Seattle in September, 1955, a year and a half of adjustment to and learning about a totally different society in our own country. Many people have asked whether during this time we have changed our views. A number of them seem to have expected that the influence of good living, warm companionship, and the old environment would wake us from the "hypnotic trance" they felt we were in and cause us to revert to our old selves.

With all that has transpired in the past year in terms of world events and our own experience it would be impossible for us not to have undergone some change and development in our ideas. Having spent seven years in a Chinese environment, cut off to a certain extent from the rest of the world, we came home with a tendency to oversimplify problems in the United States. While in prison, through our reading of Chinese newspapers and magazines, which frequently quoted Senators McCarthy and Jenner, we each independently arrived at a picture of a United States paralyzed by McCarthyite terrorism. This was one reason we both had such fears about our future if we returned home.

We were unprepared, therefore, for the complexity of the real situation. We found to our relief that America's democratic heritage had been rooted deeply enough to reject this development toward fascism and that McCarthy, as an individual, had been forced from the scene. In fact many people, some of them strangers who stopped us on the street, some old friends who disagreed with much of what we had to say, openly expressed their respect for the stand we had taken.

On the other hand, even though McCarthy himself no longer had any influence, we encountered everywhere the insecurity, fear, and shirking of social responsibility which had corroded the thinking of so many people during the height of his power. Shortly after we were reunited, Dell applied for a job in an institution which at first expressed great enthusiasm at the prospect of obtaining someone with her qualifications. However, while she was in the process of filling out the application form her name was recognized and someone whispered to the director, "She's the woman who made all those statements in Hong Kong."

This threw them into consternation and a week later they called Dell in and presented her with photostatic copies of newspaper reports of her Hong Kong interviews. Some passages had been underlined in red. They then told her that after lengthy consideration they had decided to run the risk of giving her the job if she would first sign a loyalty oath and write a statement recanting everything she had said in Hong Kong. When she stated that she could not possibly do such a thing, her interviewers were very much embarrassed and quite apologetic. They agreed that any true liberal in her situation would act in the same way but said that we must remember we were living in an era of political timidity and there was nothing they could do about it.

As for Rick, while the university went out of its way to welcome him back as a student any chance of his finding a teaching position in the foreseeable future remains highly dubious. Thus we learned that in the post-McCarthy era into which we were plunged, for the vast majority of the people, it was the economic threat rather than the political which forced them to conform.

We also had an erroneous view of the economic situation. During 1953–54 we often read in the Chinese newspapers reports based on material published by the U.S. Department of Commerce concerning the recession taking place in the United States at that time. However, we never heard that the recession had ended in late 1954 and prosperity was on the upsurge again. Thus we came home expecting to see the United States either in the midst of or on the brink of a major depression.

Our mistaken ideas were largely due to the incomplete and often one-sided view of the United States presented in the Chinese press. This has made us reconsider the place of the press in society. In China, though there is a special newspaper containing complete world coverage for limited circulation among people in responsible positions, the general press is primarily conceived of as an instrument for education rather than information. Publication of news is determined by its usefulness in increasing the people's social consciousness and morality and furthering the Communist Party's program for the development of the country. Therefore the content of the news is limited to what the authorities feel will serve these ends.

To our minds, no matter how sincere in their purpose the authorities may be, in violating the principle of the right to know they are taking a dangerous step. It was the very fact that a small group was given the right to determine what people may or may not know which contributed to the abuses of Stalinism in the Soviet Union. One of the most encouraging recent developments in China has been a liberalization of this concept of a controlled press. The slogan "Let the various schools of thought contend" has led the newspapers and magazines to a much freer discussion of the pros and cons on a number of issues. In other words, the free and open discussion which had from the beginning existed on local issues is gradually being extended to the broad problems of national and international scope.

Our experience in living in and reading the press of both countries has led us to the conclusion that the Chinese today are still receiving a clearer picture of what is happening here than the American people are of what is taking place in China. Moreover, in spite of the admitted dangers and weaknesses of the Chinese press, from both a theoretical and practical point of view we feel that it represents a much healthier influence than the press does here. In shirking its social responsibility and stressing sensationalism, the American press has contributed greatly to the alarming decline in social morality in the United States today.

These are only a few of the problems which have required a readjustment in our thinking since we have come home. But the basic conclusions at which we arrived in China concerning a moral outlook on life have not been negated by a year and a half back in the "old environment"; on the contrary, they have been strengthened as we have come to grips with the problems of our lives as Americans. To return to the ivory tower existence we prized so highly before would be to us now nothing short of contemptible. The Christian commandment "Love thy neighbor as thyself" and the concept that one must find his own happiness in that of the common good provide for us the only possible way to live.

It has been fifteen years since the above Epilogue was written and during that time many people have asked us whether we still felt the same about our experience, about China, and about the system of thought reform in general. Of course, over the years many of our ideas have been altered in accordance with the changes that have taken place in America and China, and particularly in our own personal lives. But on rereading *Prisoners of Liberation* for the first time since shortly after its publication, we were both struck by how much we are still in agreement with its contents. Perhaps our most acute emotion is one of embarrassment at having failed to live up to our idealistic expectations of the time.

By and large, we have managed to stay out of the ivory tower in spite of its continuing appeal, but our limited success has been due as much to external forces as to the strength of our own resolution. During the early years we gained some acceptance in this country's peace movement, particularly as the result of a country-wide speaking tour we made in the summer of 1957 after the publication of our book. Again and again we were informed by our hosts during the tour that this was the first meeting they had had since the McCarthy era of the early 1950s. After the tour we returned to Philadelphia and became further involved in peace and community activities while Dell worked for the American Friends Service Committee and Rick attended the University of Pennsylvania.

It should be said that in spite of our slight martyr complex and youthful bravado when we first returned home, we never really suffered for our actions. Open attacks were primarily limited to blasts in local newspapers usually delivered after we had left the scene of our talks. Most of the covert attacks we knew nothing about, and our friends, the university, and the Service Committee continued to support us even though they were much more vulnerable than we. We, after all, had very little to lose. Thus we escaped much of the fear and uncertainty of other activists of the time.

Furthermore, by the time Rick received his Ph.D. in 1960, the country had suddenly awakened to the fact that during the previous ten years of McCarthyism practically no one had been trained in Chinese except for interpreters and translators for military and intelligence organizations. Rick, who had originally despaired of ever finding a job in his field when he returned to academic studies in 1956, now found himself with a choice of jobs including an offer to stay at the University of Pennsylvania. He elected to stay and now teaches modern Chinese history and language there. Dell then returned to the university to take her Ph.D. in 1967, and now she also teaches at the university in the fields of Chinese language and literature. In the meantime we adopted two Chinese children from Hong Kong and gradually acquired all the accouterments of the American "good life."

In recent years, though we have continued to be somewhat active in community and peace activities, most of our energies have been devoted to the university and to speaking and writing about China. Explaining China to the American people has not been an easy task. Not only are the two countries worlds apart in terms of political and social systems, technical development, general way of life, and individual and national goals, but reliable information about what has been happening in China over the years has been extremely difficult to obtain. We found ourselves caught between the deadly dull propaganda of official Chinese publications such as the *Peking Review* on the one hand and the distortions of Hong Kong and other outside-based China watchers on the other. It was as though a door had slammed shut behind us when we crossed that border and we had become just two more outsiders attempting to peer through cracks in the wall. Our only justification for continuing to talk about China was the fact that we did have a certain experience which few other Americans could duplicate. Fortunately, we occasionally met non-Americans who had been in China more recently than we and who helped immeasurably in restoring our sense of reality. During the past year, of course, the flood gates have opened wide for information about China to enter the United States, and it is particularly refreshing now to have in our courses students who have been to China and have returned with the same enthusiasm we felt.

As a result, the picture of what has been happening in China is much more clear. Since 1955 China has gone through a number of movements aimed at pushing the revolution forward or rectifying problems which arose during its course. The campaign to "Let the Hundred Flowers Bloom" in 1956–57 was followed by an "Anti-Rightist Movement" in 1957–58, which in turn paved the way for the "Great Leap Forward" in 1958–59. The Great Leap, for all its remarkable achievements, including the rise of the communes and the beginnings of the technological revolution in the countryside, brought with it excesses and problems of adjustment that resulted in economic setbacks and the first major split in the Party's leadership. Mao Tsetung himself came under strong attack in 1959 and for a few years seems to have exerted less influence on the political scene.

The problems of the Great Leap, further compounded by three years of disastrous weather conditions and the abrupt termination of Soviet technical assistance as a result of the intensifying Sino-Soviet dispute, led to a severe economic crisis from which China required several years to recover. During these years, the Party leadership tended to be dominated by so-called pragmatists, technocrats, and bureaucratic administrators who looked upon the decentralization and mass mobilization of the Great Leap as sheer chaos. They opted for a return to conservative centralized planning and control over the economy with special emphasis on heavy industry, material incentives to workers, and strict profit-oriented cost accounting for management. In agriculture the communes were decentralized with much of their production turned over to individual households. The proportion of commune land allotted to private plots was greatly increased, and peasants were allowed to sell grain as well as other produce in free markets.

By 1965 China had recovered economically, but the growth rate was considerably lower than it had been during the 1950s. Furthermore, there was a feeling among many Party members that the revolution was in the process of being lost to bourgeois tendencies. In place of mass initiative and involvement had come bureaucratic fiat. In place of Yenan-type cadre leadership, there was beginning to appear a new elite made up of bureaucrats and technical personnel who were gradually taking unto themselves many of the special privileges of a ruling class. They dominated the Party apparatus and the middle and upper echelons in governmental and economic institutions, including the press and cultural organs. Their children filled the universities, thus providing the basis for a new semi-hereditary class of leaders. The ordinary workers and peasants were becoming increasingly alienated from the Party's leadership and turning their attention toward personal comfort and individual concerns rather than the building of a new society.

It was to counteract these developments more than anything else that Mao Tse-tung in 1966 launched the "Great Proletarian Cultural Revolution," the most profound movement in China since land reform and perhaps, in terms of the questions raised, one of the most significant movements for the rest of the world in modern times. Eric Fromm in his *The Sane Society* (p. 363) makes the point that "Man today is confronted with a most fundamental choice; not that between Capitalism or Communism, but that between *robotism* (of both the capitalist and the communist variety), or Humanistic Communitarian Socialism." Mao Tse-tung would hardly agree with Fromm's formulation, but from the very beginning of the revolution the Chinese have stressed the dangers of bureaucratization, and no other society has ever attempted to deal with the problem of bureaucracy so openly and forcefully as they have, especially during the three years of often violent struggle accompanying the Cultural Revolution.

No sooner had Mao Tse-tung launched his attack on the Party's bureaucratic leadership headed by Liu Shao-ch'i, the man who had replaced Mao as Chairman of the People's Republic in 1959 and one of the Party's leading figures for many years, than Liu's supporters commenced their countermoves. They did this not by questioning Mao openly—his position and prestige would not permit that—but by pretending to be even more Maoist than Mao; Red Flags were raised to beat down Red Flags, and for the first time since 1949 the ordinary Chinese citizen found himself without the clear leadership of the Party. Confusion reigned, and factionalism became rife. Student Red Guard units supporting Mao were formed in Peking to be followed by the formation of other Red Guard units throughout the country. Some of these were genuine supporters of Mao's line, while others were simply fronts created by the opposition to protect their interests. Shouting slogans and waving little red books, Red Guard units of both sides vied with each other as the true proponents of Mao Tse-tung's thought. As the struggle intensified, Leftist excess, often deliberately fulminated by the Right opposition, came to constitute a more serious threat than the Right itself. Some cultural monuments were destroyed, cultural figures were badly mistreated—so much so that a few of them are reported to have committed suicide—and a number of conscientious supporters of Mao were wrongly accused of bourgeois revisionism and held in confinement or otherwise unjustly punished. The complexity of the situation is revealed by one incident in August, 1967, when the Foreign Ministry was taken over by a Leftist group of students acting under the leadership of two members of Mao's Cultural Revolution Committee. They attacked the British Embassy in Peking and created incidents around the world under the pretext of exporting the Cultural Revolution abroad. Later these two Committee members, Wang Li and Yao Teng-shan, were accused of having connections with Liu Shao-ch'i and were ousted from power, but not before tremendous damage had been done.

The violence, which reached its peak in 1967, fortunately tended to be sporadic and local in scope, but for a time large-scale civil war threatened. In July of that year serious trouble erupted in Wuhan with numbers of local troops and workers supporting right-wing commanders. It was not until Chou En-lai personally made a very risky trip to the area that the situation was brought under control. Fortunately again, the People's Liberation Army, which had gone through something of its own Cultural Revolution under Lin Piao before the major movement began, remained loyal to Mao Tse-tung and his objectives. However, it was not until 1969 that the political situation began to stabilize and various factional disputes were sufficiently resolved to make possible the remarkable advances in economic construction and foreign relations of the past two or three years. Even now, however, intense discussion continues around many of the issues raised during the Cultural Revolution. Such Leftist slogans as "everything for the public interest; nothing for oneself" have given way to "public interest first; personal interest second." Many forms of literature, scholarship, and other cultural activity, which had ceased to exist during the Cultural Revolution, are now being eagerly pursued. The political awareness of the ordinary person, especially the peasants, has been raised tremendously. Such rural communes as Ta-chai have provided a new inspiration and leadership for the country as a whole, while "barefoot doctors" have imparted new meaning to the slogan "serve the people."

But this does not mean that all the problems of China have been solved or, for that matter, ever can be. Visitors returning from China report that the Chinese still regard bureaucracy as one of their major problems along with the fact that women, for all their tremendous rise in position since 1949, still do not enjoy universal equality with men. The need to relate education to practical life and to prevent it from becoming a steppingstone to a new social elite is accepted without question, but how to accomplish this while at the same time providing the society with the well-trained scientists, technicians, and cultural workers it needs is still a matter requiring great thought and experimentation. Indeed, the entire question of how to maintain an essentially equalitarian society in the technological age is far from resolved. But given the level of their awareness and the stage of development of their society, if anyone can cope with this problem, it is undoubtedly the Chinese.

One might well ask, if the system of thought reform we experienced really worked, why was it necessary to have a Cultural Revolution, and why was it still necessary in the 1960s and even today to keep reiterating such slogans as "serve the people" and "public interest first; personal interest second"? It would be a gross mistake to imply it did not work, but it must be kept in mind, as Lenin said, "The force of habit of millions and tens of millions is a most terrible force." Change does not come easily, and furthermore, as we indicated in the book, there is no such thing as complete and final reform. It is an ongoing process, and particularly as a person's life style and position change, he is liable to develop bureaucratic or corrupt tendencies without being really aware of what is happening to him unless he himself remains on constant guard and the system works to keep him honest. As a person's position becomes more responsible, it is very easy to convince himself that his importance justifies certain little privileges such as not having to stand in line or not having to participate in routine work or meetings. He gradually assumes for himself the right to such advantages as first choice of theater or sporting event tickets allotted to his unit, a better place to live, the use of a car, or special education for his children. Since he is very busy, he assumes he should not be expected to sit around waiting for seemingly endless discussions to resolve matters and takes to making decisions on his own. When these are later questioned, it is only natural that he should become annoyed and even attempt to quash his critics.

All of this is consciously or unconsciously rationalized as

consistent with the new society, and if he were subjected to frequent sincere criticism and self-criticism sessions the problem would most likely never develop. Unfortunately, for many of these people criticism and self-criticism sessions are among the first meetings they are too busy to attend.

This situation was abetted by changes in the society itself. As China's society began to stabilize, particularly after the end of the Korean war, there seems to have developed a general tendency toward formalism in thought reform. During the early years, revolutionary ideology was still very fresh, the memories of the old society were still vivid, the enthusiasm for building a new society abounded, and in general the Yenan spirit of self-sacrifice was exceedingly strong, especially among the young. Later, as the period of crisis passed, the newness of the revolution began to fade, and people began to find their individual niches in society, revolutionary idealism tended to give way to careerism and the amount of sincere attention paid to reform and criticism and self-criticism diminished.

This tendency was further augmented by the complexity of many of the issues associated with the heightened demands of each new stage of the revolution. Discussions were inclined to become more issue- than attitude-centered, more about what we should do and less about why we are doing it. Therefore, during the major movements, extremists would sometimes dominate the show and people who were unable to stand up to their revolutionary rhetoric and personal attacks would back away from real participation.

Thus, even though there was constant criticism of bureaucratism and frequent minor movements to curb bureaucratic practices, their success was limited. Minor excesses could be corrected and the petty kingdoms established by individual bureaucrats toppled, but the central core of bureaucracy in the Party and in government was hardly touched.

During the Cultural Revolution, the struggle was so intense and the leadership so confusing that criticism frequently became a weapon of attack rather than reform.

"K'ai-men cheng-feng" (open the door to accept reform) often gave way to "tsa-men cheng-feng" (beat down the door to reform others), leading Mao Tse-tung himself to proclaim in 1968: "Let the two sides do more of self-criticism; the mistakes of others should be left to them to discuss." The essential element of successful criticism is the application of Mao Tse-tung's formula of "unity—struggle—unity." That is to say that out of the struggle should come a resolution of contradictions and a new unity on a higher level. Unfortunately, in the heat of the struggle this principle is too often forgotten, and the motivation becomes one of winning the personal struggle rather than resolving contradictions. Naturally, in some cases the contradictions are so antagonistic that suppression is the only answer, but when this approach is applied indiscriminately throughout the population it amounts to civil war. It was not until the People's Liberation Army entered the factories to serve as mediators in the disputes there, and later both army personnel and workers together entered the universities, that most of the violent struggles were resolved.

Clearly the lesson of the Cultural Revolution was that for thought reform to be successful on a national scale, genuine, not sham, criticism and self-criticism must be applied constantly, especially among persons in positions of authority. Furthermore, it must be carried out under a strong, united, and dedicated leadership armed with a theory inspirational in terms of goals, realistic in terms of current social conditions, and flexible enough to meet changing situations. On the individual level, it must never be forgotten that the purpose of criticism and self-criticism is to solve problems, not win arguments; to achieve the common good, not personal gratification.

However, in spite of all these problems, thought reform, which lies at the very heart of the revolution, has been instrumental in producing an entirely new Chinese society and a new Chinese man. When one considers the complexity of China, its size, population, its former backwardness, and the strength of its traditional institution, the extent and nature of this achievement becomes even more remarkable. It is equally remarkable that the revolution should still be alive after a quarter of a century. Nothing is so debilitating for the spirit of revolution as success, and most revolutions, including that of the Soviet Union, quickly lose sight of their goals after their initial victory. In China, however, people on a mass scale are still willing to struggle, not just for immediate material benefits, though these are important too, but also for continuing progress toward a social ideal. While in the Soviet Union and the West crime is on the upswing and the alienation of individuals from society has led to a general social malaise, in China one finds an optimism, enthusiasm, and sense of social responsibility that has confounded most foreign visitors.

Perhaps one of the most amusing spectacles of the TV coverage of the Nixon trip was the confusion of American commentators when they attempted to explain how hundreds of thousands of Chinese could cheerfully take to the streets to clean away the snow after a sudden storm. The commentators were obviously beset by feelings of both envy and suspicion. Envy because with all our technology and wealth we in the United States have found it impossible to clean our streets of trash, not to mention a sudden snow. Suspicion because, notwithstanding their inability to find any evidence of coercion, they could not believe people capable of such a volunteer effort. Therefore they insisted on describing the event as an appalling example of regimentation. There undoubtedly was organization, but not the forced regimentation the commentators implied. The problem is really not that difficult. It was merely the act of a people with a high sense of social responsibility who understood that if they wanted their city cleaned, it was up to them to do it and that by everyone assuming his share of the load, the task would be easily accomplished.

The sad thing is that Americans should understand this perhaps better than any other people. So many of our past accomplishments were based on volunteer efforts, from barn-raising to social services performed by church and club groups. This is not to mention the tremendous outpouring of volunteer effort which accompanies any disaster. But all too often as we have grown rich and soft we have switched to letting the government or "George" do what we used to do ourselves.

People have frequently asked us about the applicability of Chinese thought reform, criticism, and self-criticism to the United States. This is not a simple question to answer because, though the techniques of criticism and self-criticism, in theory, can be applied anywhere, the whole process of thought reform cannot be separated from the total revolutionary experience of a society. Since returning home we have encountered many groups practicing variations of criticism and self-criticism. They have ranged from such basically religious groups as the Sharmanites, who attempt to reform themselves by comparing their actions with the words of Jesus, to political consciousness-raising groups of various persuasions and to formal group therapy as applied in institutions or under formal supervision. In general, our reaction to these American experiments has been mixed. The basic problems are motivation and follow-up. Where the problem is clear and motivation is thus relatively high, as in criminal reform or alcoholism or drug therapy, the initial results seem to be quite successful. Our experience with ordinary groups, particularly so-called political consciousness-raising sessions, has usually been negative. All too often we have found such sessions motivated by unrealistic idealism or by a simple desire to release one's own frustrations rather than any solidly based desire for personal reform. The failures of well-based programs more often than not may be blamed on the general social situation rather than the method itself. Where experiments have failed in connection with criminal, drug, and alcoholism reform, it has often been due to the fact that such treatment occurred in a very restricted environment, and those involved returned to a society that not only failed to provide ongoing support but in fact presented him with constant temptations to return to his old ways. Where the therapy has continued to work, it is primarily because of continuing support from concerned organizations.

In our own personal lives we have found that the experience in China has been of tremendous value. The knowledge that criticism, even though often painful and sometimes not one hundred per cent correct, is bound to be helpful has made our marital relations and relations with other people much smoother. Though we have admittedly fallen far short of the goals we once set for ourselves, nevertheless we are both convinced that what we learned during our prison experience has made us far happier and more active people than we otherwise would have been.

Allyn and Adele Rickett
Philadelphia, 1972